Feminist Nationalism

Feminist Nationalism

Lois A. West, Editor

ROUTLEDGE
New York   London

Published in 1997

Routledge
29 West 35th Street
New York, NY 10001

Published in Great Britain by

Routledge
11 New Fetter Lane
London EC4P 4EE

Library of Congress Cataloging-in-Publication Data

Feminist nationalism / Lois A. West, editor.
      p.   cm.
  Includes bibliographical references.
  ISBN 0-415-91617-8 (cloth : alk. paper). — ISBN 0-415-91618-6
(pbk. : alk. paper)
    1. Women in politics. 2. Feminism. 3. Nationalism. I. West.
Lois A.
HQ1236.F4463   1986
305.42—dc20   96-2928
    CIP

To my husband, Jack Brodsky,
and to the future
for a united nations
for our children.

Acknowledgments

I am most grateful to international studies professor Elisabeth Prügl, and to the editors at Routledge, Cecilia Cancellero and Claudia Gorelick, who had faith in this project. I am grateful for the support of my husband, Jack Brodsky, who helped me during the six years it took to get this to press, to our wonderful children, John and Beth, and to my mother, Alice Johnson West, who supported my three trips to the United Nations' conferences on women (1980–1995), and who went with me to two of them. Many thanks to the contributors for their hard work, and to Michelle LaMarre.

I am grateful as well to the following sources for permission to print updated versions or reprints of articles for this collection:

Carmel Roulston, "Women on the Margin" is an updated version of the article first published as "Women on the Margin: The Women"s Movement in Northern Ireland, 1973-1988," *Science & Society* 53, no. 2 (Summer 1989): 219–236. Reprinted with permission of *Science & Society Quarterly Inc.*

Haunani-Kay Trask, "Feminism and Indigenous Hawaiian Nationalism," was first published in *Signs* 21, no. 4 (Summer 1996): 906–916, copyright © 1996 by The University of Chicago Press, #0097-9740/96/2104-0004. Reprinted with permission of The University of Chicago.

Acknowledgments

Alma M. Garcia, "The Development of Chicana Feminist Discourse," was first published as Alma M. Garcia, "The Development of Chicana Feminist Discourse, 1970-1980," *Gender and Society* 3, no. 2 (June 1988): 217–238, copyright © 1989 (Sociologists for Women in Society). Reprinted by permission of Sage Publications, Inc.

Contents

Contents

Introduction:
Feminism Constructs Nationalism

Lois A. West

On the brink of World War II in Europe, Virginia Woolf was asked how she would prevent war. She answered in *Three Guineas* that women had historically been excluded from war-making decisions, which would lead a woman to ponder:

> "What does 'our country' mean to me, an outsider?" To decide this she will analyse the meaning of patriotism in her own case. She will inform herself of the position of her sex and her class in the past. She will inform herself of the amount of land, wealth and property in the possession of her own sex and class in the present—how much of "England" in fact belongs to her. . . . "Our country," she will say, "throughout the greater part of history has treated me as a slave; it has denied me education or any share of its possessions. . . . in fact, as a woman, I have no country. As a woman I want no country. As a woman my country is the whole world." And if, when reason has its say, still some obstinate emotion remains, some love of England dropped into a child's ears by the cawing of rooks in an elm tree, by the splash of waves on a beach, or by English voices murmuring nursery rhymes, this drop of pure, if irrational emotion she will make serve her to give to England first what she desires of peace and freedom for the whole world.[1]

Woolf presented the dilemma of women who had not yet achieved full citizenship rights yet were asked to support the nationalist cause in time of war. How could women be nationalists when they did not have equal rights? How could women not be nationalists when they loved their country, people, and home?

Fifty years ago Woolf explicated the dilemma modern women face today. We struggle as outsiders with the decision-making powers of the state, still overwhelmingly in male hands, while we view ourselves as an integral part of our country or national group. As a U.S. citizen, I have the obligation to pay taxes to the state, but I am not guaranteed equal rights under the U.S. Constitution, which has no Equal Rights Amendment. I have the right to vote as men do, but I have no obligation to fight in combat to defend the nation-state. In the United States as elsewhere in the world today, women are constituted as citizens *differently* than men.

The United Nations Decade on Women (1975–1985), with its ten-year assessment in Beijing in 1995, demonstrated that women have come to a global consensus on (re)constructing both feminism and nationalism with the concerns and interests of women at the center of discourse and action. The Mission Statement recognizes "that the status of women has advanced in some important respects in the past decade but that progress has been uneven, inequalities between women and men have persisted and major obstacles remain."[2] It sets out specific goals for governments to work toward the equality of women with men worldwide—as citizens in nation-states. Where women share with men in their ethnic group territorial occupation or armed conflict, the document asserts that

> an environment that maintains world peace and promotes and protects human rights, democracy and the peaceful settlement of disputes, in accordance with the principles of non-threat or use of force against territorial integrity or political independence and of respect for sovereignty as set forth in the Charter of the United Nations, is an important factor for the advancement of women. Peace is inextricably linked with equality between women and men and development. (p. 59)

This statement linking feminism (women's equal rights) with nationalism (territorial integrity, political independence, sovereignty) has a significant history. For the past several decades activist women all over the world have been organizing around women's and nationalist issues— sometimes quietly advocating nonviolence and working for women's citizenship rights, other times working in consort with armed guerrilla movements under situations of occupation. Although there has been contention over how much these activities count as "feminist" or "nationalist," evidence presented in this anthology will demonstrate that women have been creating social movement organizations and working in international "solidarity" networks in activities and efforts that are varied and diverse. One effect of these efforts is to reconstruct old words—*feminism* and *nationalism*—in new contexts.

This book presents case studies of feminist nationalist movements in Europe, the Middle East, Africa, Central and East Asia, the Pacific Islands, and the Americas. Various types of feminist and nationalist movement activists on both a grassroots and elite level work today for the identification with their national group—be it based on shared history, culture (language, religion, ethnicity, styles, fashions, tastes), sense of place (the region), or kinship—while simultaneously fighting for what they define as the rights of women within their cultural contexts.

What makes these movements and the analysis of them different is that women are (re)constructing the meanings of both nationalism and feminism from a women-centered viewpoint, what some feminists call women's or feminist "standpoint theory."[3] This theory begins with women's viewpoints where we reside in our everyday lives. Whereas women like Virginia Woolf saw females as outsiders and victims of states, today's women in every region are viewing women as definers of nationalism and feminism. Women are undeniably still being victimized by individual men, states, nationalist conflicts, and wars, and women's interests continue to be actively marginalized in the development of political economies and states. But women are taking control—not only by defining this victimization as Woolf did by organizing against it.

Women in feminist nationalist movements are struggling to define and reconceptualize their relationships to states, nations, and social movements as activists central to the debate, not as passive recipients. By using the women's standpoint theory, the viewpoints of both men and women are neither unitary nor dualistic but eclectic. Like working women in all countries who juggle the demands of household, children, family, and workplace, feminist nationalists juggle the competing activists' demands of women's rights with civil rights and national struggles. While one demand surfaces at one time as prescient and the other demands get held in the background, none are mutually exclusive or binary. They may continue to be resolved one demand at a time or with one in foreground, others in background, but social change is being created and re-created by women activists.

Academia has not caught up with women in current political struggles. In much of the academic discourse on nationalism, women remain invisible, subsumed under the "fraternity" of nation; constitute another "variable" to be studied, like ethnicity;[4] or get ghettoized under cultural nationalism. Gender is too often absent from discussions of political or economic nationalism, although there are recent feminist attempts to remedy this exclusion.[5]

Not only must we begin with the women's standpoint on nationalism and feminism, we must move to an understanding of the construction of nationalism as an inherently "gendered" phenomenon. Men have presented the construction of nations and states as centered on struggles over power between men, such as in wars. But these struggles have not been analyzed for how they are gendered—created through processes of the construction of male status hierarchies, male bonding, homosociality/homosexuality, and so on. Except for very rare instances of gender isolation, nationalism and feminism get constructed in the *processes* of ongoing enterprises and of daily social interactions between women and men. They are not fixed, given, immutable, or binary. They are (and always have been) created and re-created in daily interactions between the genders. Academic research has not really demonstrated how complex gendered social contexts and qualities are being created and analyzed at the point of their production. By analyzing *how* they are created and produced, we can begin to understand how they are being re-created and reproduced as *gendered* phenomena between and among women and men. Where feminism has traditionally focused on how women have been victimized, newer methodologies of process offer the potential to re-create the dynamics of how nationalism gets created as a phenomenon of interaction between and within genders.

This anthology seeks to demonstrate the ways feminism is constructing nationalism as inherently gendered and processual. Feminist nationalist movements differ by culture, level of economic development, and political context but share characteristics of women's lives everywhere that make us gendered beings based on the facts that we are primary caretakers and economically and politically marginalized.

In dealing with comparative cases, questions of cultural relativism and moral universalism become important. The United Nations' documents on women demonstrate there is an ongoing global consensus among the world's governments on women's rights. This is seen in the mainstreaming of feminism as "women's rights are human rights."[6] But it is also important to recognize that women are reconstructing meanings of both nationalism and feminism within culturally specific contexts.

I have argued elsewhere for the necessity of using a method of a "gendered cultural relativism"[7] seeing the world through women's eyes (to use the theme of the Beijing conference)—but understanding how the nature of seeing is culturally relative. By beginning with the way *women* define feminism and nationalism within their cultural context (gendered cultural relativism), feminist nationalism is born in varying historically specific cultures. The tenets or aspects that are shared cross-culturally should be regarded within a framework of moral universalism, a way of moving toward a more universal feminist discourse but realizing that it may always be circumscribed by cultural differences. Because cross-national versions can differ in some fundamental ways, this creates its own kind of twenty-first-century eclecticism. Despite political attempts to dismiss the outcome of the United Nations' Decade on Women as "Western" or "elitist," feminist social movement activists have been demonstrating on a daily level through their organizing over the past twenty years that there can be a global phenomenon of feminist nationalism. Through the globalization of information and technology, this possibility is rapidly increasing. The rest of this chapter will examine how academic discourse constructs nationalism as a male enterprise, frequently unconsciously gendered, and how feminists are struggling to put women at the center of analysis.

The Academic Discourse on Women and Nationalism

An ongoing debate in women's studies is whether women are sufficiently "mainstreamed" in the academy to transform "women's" studies into gender studies or to simply eliminate it altogether. Much of the academic discourse on nationalism provides sobering examples of how women and gender still get ignored or marginalized. The 1994 Oxford University anthology *Nationalism* contains excerpts from some "leading" theoreticians and historians on the subject. In it, women are in a section in "Beyond Nationalism?" with "ethnic nationalism" and "Europeanness." In their introduction to the collection editors John Hutchinson and Anthony D. Smith, define their subject matter:

Nationalism was, first of all, a doctrine of popular freedom and sovereignty. The people must be liberated—that is, free from any external constraint;

they must determine their own destiny and be **masters in their own house**; they must control their own resources; they must obey only their own "inner" voice. But that entailed **fraternity**.[8]

For them, gender is one "concept" of collective identity (like class, region, race, religion). But "what is often conceded is the power, even primacy of national loyalties and identities over those of even class, gender, and race" (p. 4). Making "gender" one variable with ethnicity or religion under a broader category of "nationalism" while maintaining that nationalism is a "fraternity" perpetuates a male-centered construct that is surprisingly unreflective about the centrality of gender, given the developed level of feminist theory in the late twentieth century. The "nation" in this discourse is viewed as "*la patrie*" (p. 9). But how the nation gets constructed and perpetuated as discourses and struggles between men as "fraternity" is left unanalyzed. The editors' own choice of words suggests the centrality of gender to the construction of nationalism, but they emphasize it as just another "concept" and variable.

The symbolic construction of "nation" as gendered needs to be better understood for the connections between symbols, beliefs, actions and state policies. In some European traditions, the construction of nation is viewed as having patriarchal origins. Where nationalism connoted tribalism—one's family, one's tribe, writ into a larger context of the nation—it was assumed that one placed one's blood and family ties above all others. The family was patriarchal in that it was headed by a "master" of the house in the historical accounts—individuals began to assert "allegiance to the nation, to *la patrie*, to the homeland, to the Fatherland."[9]

In one example, an 1882 lecture at the Sorbonne, Ernest Renan viewed the rise of nationalism as the move from patriarchal tribalism to the construction of the nation-state.[10] In his account, before the rise of nationalism, there were pre-national patriarchal tribes, "agglomerations of men," where women were the booty of the male conquerors. The nation was *la patrie*—the male-headed tribe or family writ large—a patriarchal construct. Symbols get turned into actions in policies where states constructed rights and obligations based on the concepts of male-headed households. The Roman legal system of *patria potesta*, for example, gave fathers absolute power of life and death over their children. Where nations developed using Roman traditions, women as wives and mothers had their rights subsumed under patriarchal family law, as did slaves, captives and others.

Patriarchal nationalism was disseminated through colonialism, and is not only found in the West. Partha Chatterjee has written at length about the social construction of Indian nationalism historically, and he has gone further than other authors in demonstrating how struggles over views of nationalism are inherently gendered. In many anticolonial contexts, nationalism has been defined as oppositional to Western colonialism. Yet even in these traditions, women are limited to the context of the family, although the centrality of family relations is reinterpreted and emphasized.[11] The discourse over nationalism in India situated "the 'women's question' in an inner domain of sovereignty, far removed from the arena of political contest with the colonial state" (p. 117). The condition of Indian women that manifested itself in cultural practices like "*satidaha* (immolation of widows)" was used by colonialists as an example of the "unworthiness" of Indian customs and traditions, which necessitated embracing the "modernization" of colonialism. Indian (male) nationalists reacted to this by situating women in the spiritual realm of the home, which was superior to the material realm of the world being constructed and represented by colonial interests.

Chatterjee argues that women's association with the home came to represent the very essence of Indian nationalism—as the spiritual, private world of Indian tradition and customs untainted by colonialism: "The subjugated must learn the modern sciences and arts of the material world from the West in order to match their strengths and ultimately overthrow the colonizer. But in the entire phase of the national struggle, the crucial need was to protect, preserve, and strengthen the inner core of the national culture, its spiritual essence" (p. 121). Although women are still not viewed as actors in the construction of the public world, the strength of Chatterjee's account is that at least in the arena of the family, the construction of nationalism is a dynamic—a gendered creation in reaction to colonialism, and the construction of "a *new* patriarchy." (p. 127)

Both early Indian nationalists and British colonialists exercised a "hegemonic form of exercising dominance" (p. 130), combining overt coercion with subtle persuasion, but in a dynamic in which men were defining the terms. Chatterjee goes on to explain that if researchers wish to find women's voices in the construction of Indian nationalism, they must look in the middle-class home, in autobiographies of educated women (p. 137). By looking there, Chatterjee finds the origins of the cultural politics of Indian nationalism (p. 147): "Women from the new middle class in nineteenth-century India thus became active agents in the nationalist project—complicit in the framing of its hegemonic strategies as much as they were resistant to them because of their subordination under the new forms of patriarchy" (p. 148).

While nation in some contexts is fatherland, in others it is motherland. Russians, for example, speak of "Mother Russia." Chinese speak of the "Chinese socialist motherland." Peterson argues that conceptions of nature as female make it easy to conceive of nation as "the Motherland as spatial, embodied femaleness: The land's fecundity, upon which the people depend, must be protected by defending the body/nation's boundaries against invasion and violation by foreign males."[12] Rape which is used by men as a tool of war against a nation's women is both the rape of women and the rape of the nation as woman. For nationalists, women serve as "the symbolic markers of the group's cultural identity" (p. 7). However, in these symbolic constructions, women are still viewed as caught in the struggles between men, not as powerful symbols in their own right. There are no real differences in reconstructing views of nation and nationalism in this interpretation.

The construction of both nations and states is gendered phenomena and needs to be analyzed as such. Still, in contemporary Western academic analysis, the ways in which nations and states are created as gendered is missing. Women too often continue to be invisible in definitions of nationalism[13] and in discussions of the state and nationalism.[14] Even when treated as a variable, women are often missing in quantitative survey research.[15] By circumscribing the meanings of nationalism to its relation to ethnicity, many authors ignore gender.[16] In their analysis of the limitations of the discussion of ethnonationalism to women in the work of a number of prominent writers on nationalism, Linda Racioppi and Katherine O'Sullivan See argue that kinship arises as an important component—but with women missing.[17] To define women as one category of oppressed group equivalent to racial and ethnic groups has been useful for affirmative action arguments.[18] However, these definitions in themselves can reproduce status hierarchies and miss the dynamic of construction between groups.

Feminist Critiques

Feminist scholars have analyzed how gender gets circumscribed. Sylvia Walby argues that the literature on women and nation "has engaged but little with the differential integration of women and men into the national project."[19] She contends that literature on gender and citizenship/ethnic/national/"race" relations (she lumps them together) has shown that gender does not effect citizenship, citizenship does not effect gender, women suffer from combined forms of the list of oppressions and thus white women's oppression is not relevant to other women, and citizenship/ethnic/national/"race" relations affect one another and are dynamic, which involves analyzing casual connections.

Walby argues for analyzing patriarchal constructions in the household and public spheres as states get differently "restructured" (her term) across time and within "boundaries," such as the "typically more local" political activities and greater pacifism of women (p. 93). Although she argues that "patterns of gender relations sometimes take the same spatial units as those of class and ethnicity, nation and 'race,' but often they do not," she concludes that "women have less often than men been engaged at the level of the nation" (p. 97). Walby uses the definitional terms linking nation and ethnicity, and her conceptualization of the discourse of women and nation is not unlike those laid out by such earlier writers as Woolf.

Nira Yuval-Davis and Floya Anthias focus on links among nation, gender, and ethnicity, as women get constituted in relation to the nation in terms of the functions they fill as reproducers of ethnicities, cultural transmitters, and participants in nationalist struggles.[20] They note that as women get constructed by both states and customs, "the sphere of 'civil society' and the sphere of the 'state' can link hands in the construction of women in some ways although in others they may be in conflict" (p. 10). Women, when they are "markers of collective boundaries and differences" may find themselves involved in contradictions as participants in antistate struggles or when "difference" from men gets pitted against struggles for equality with men. Yuval-Davis and Anthias's functionalist account linking ethnicity to gender and nationalism pointed the way for this area of research into the relationship between gender and ethnonationalism. Many recent accounts focus on this relationship among ethnicity, gender, and nationalism wherein "ethnicity is mobilized to generate nationalism."[21]

For Cynthia Enloe, "nationalism typically has sprung from masculinized memory, masculinized humiliation and masculinized hope."[22] Enloe appears to argue that women are more than victims or functionaries of the state, but she makes her own kind of assumptions about women and men in varying cultural contexts. For example, she concludes that women pictured in colonial postcards were "abused" by foreigners (a Zulu and Maori woman are shown) without presenting evidence about how these specific women were actually abused. The possession of these postcards by a male Algerian nationalist must mean, according to Enloe, that he "and other male nationalists seem remarkably *un*curious about the abused women's own thoughts—about the meaning they might have assigned to foreign conquest" (p. 44). The women in the photographs do not speak for themselves, nor do the male nationalists get to defend themselves. Similarly, when Walby concludes that women are somehow more pacifist than men (pp. 92–93), she ignores the cultural contexts in which women have been revolutionary, armed guerillas. Theory construction is one thing, cultural assumptions about gender without data are something else.

Kumari Jayawardena makes the links between feminism and nationalism in the late nineteenth century and early twentieth in Turkey, Egypt, India, Sri Lanka, Indonesia, China, Vietnam, and Korea. She says that "feminism was not imposed on the Third World by the West, but rather that historical circumstances produced important material and ideological changes that affected women."[23] She argues the important role of women but concludes that women's role was only "contributive" to nationalist movements. "Men were the main movers of history" because they organized and set the parameters for nationalist movements.[24]

V. Spike Peterson and R. W. Connell argue respectively for a processual analysis of gendered nationalism and for state construction. Peterson links the process of gender hierarchy (male over female) with nationalism (insider over outsider). She argues for "mapping" the ways in which nationalism gets gendered: "Gender is a structural feature of social reality . . . and as such must be 'put on the map,' systematically studied, and its symbolic and material effects incorporated in our production of contextual, relational accounts."[25] According to her account, international relations and foreign policy studies in particular have neglected the private sphere, wherein reproductive processes (individual and group identity formation, cultural socialization and social reproduction) and "group compliance, cooperation, and conflict" get contextualized: "We must understand . . . how group identities are formed, how cultural loyalties are reproduced, and how nationalist movements in support of those identities and loyalties affect the foreign policy making of existing states." A "gender-sensitive analysis" does this by helping us understand the production of collective identities and their political effects, and domination dynamics (p. 183). Peterson's idea of "mapping" the gendered processes of nationalism is a good methodological start.

Not only is the construction of nationalism gendered, so is state-building—particularly as the public-private dichotomy and limitation of women to the cultural sphere get institutionalized into states and regulated by them. R. W. Connell schematizes how gender comes to structure state apparatuses and argues that "each empirical state has a definable 'gender regime' that is the precipitate of social struggles and is linked to—though not a simple reflection of—the wider gender order of the society."[26] Gender regimes are "the historically produced state of play in gender relations within an institution, which can be analyzed by taking a structural inventory" through gendered divisions of labor and structures of power, such as bureaucracies, and "structures of cathexis, the gender patterning of emotional attachments" (p. 526). Connell speculates that the rise of nationalism may be an emotional response to the growing impersonality of the state (and its bureaucracy?). What he sees, though, is that the psychological attachment to political authority may be "a discourse about masculinity and the ways men can be attached to political leaders" (p. 526).

In one such masculine "gender regime," gender was pivotal to the construction of a primordial nationalism in Nazi Germany. George Mosse argues, "The homoeroticism always latent in nationalist symbols and the ideal of masculinity now faced the danger of coming into conflict with respectability" because women were to maintain that respectability in the home. In his account, Nazi Germany was inherently a male state, a *männerstaat* based on the comradeship of men. "The *Männerstaat* symbolized an aggressive nationalism based upon the ideal of masculinity. It would crush all those who threatened respectability and the nation."[27] The state got constructed from an inherently gendered masculinity in which women (along with minorities and almost everyone, for that matter) get circumscribed to rigid hierarchies of superiority and inferiority. In this account, nationalism and state building are fundamentally gendered—but from a certain kind of primordial masculinity.

Although some analysts of nationalism ignore women, theories of gender place relations between women and men at the center of analysis. Given that women and men are constituted as citizens differently, analysts here understand gendered nationalism as processes of construction contexualized to specific cultures, localities, and even emotional relationships. Feminists who have a political agenda go a step further. We seek to undermine the public-private dichotomies that undermine women, to end inequalities between people, and even to end war and male militarism. Feminist theory is necessary to understanding the construction of gender, nations, and states by placing women at the center.

This Anthology

This book is a beginning attempt to reconceptualize feminist nationalism toward an eclectic twenty-first-century view of a feminist theory of nations and states. The contributed chapters focus on contemporary feminist nationalist struggles in the past several decades, understanding that women's current rights struggles had previous histories that acted as precedents to current movements.

The first three articles focus on Europe. In the first essay, sociology professor Gisela Kaplan, who has written in depth elsewhere on the development of feminism in Western Europe,[28] casts a critical eye on the relationship between feminism and nationalism in Europe. Kaplan presents a dualism that grows within European nationalism from its beginning as a struggle for civil rights and liberal traditions to what it became under German fascism as a legitimation of subjugation, exploitation, and genocide. She argues that European feminist nationalism must be viewed within these historical traditions, and that the development of movements that attempt to meld feminism with nationalism have been precarious because of these histories.

Kaplan believes there are feminist nationalist movements that have been able to avoid the minefields of European traditions. She describes historical movements in nineteenth-century Italy and Finland (the first European country to give women the vote), and women's efforts in local and regional areas, such as women in the Catalan movements. Although it does not attempt to be exhaustive of all European women's efforts, Kaplan's article is an excellent introduction to the construction of feminist nationalism within the European context, pointing the way for further historical and sociological study.[29]

University of Ulster professor Carmel Roulston demonstrates how feminism grew out of women's everyday lives in Northern Ireland during the mid-1970s. Feminists' relationships to the nationalist struggle developed over time, with feminists becoming ever more present in Sinn Fein, the Irish organization dedicated to national sovereignty. Various groups fragmented over political issues and over whether to prioritize anti-imperialism or women's rights during the 1970s and 1980s, but a form of feminist nationalist activism emerged that incorporated cross-religious coalitions. More recently, loyalist groups have expressed interest in "women's issues." However, Roulston argues that women and feminist issues remain "on the margin" in terms of women's involvement in the political powers that be: "Northern Irish women will have to be 'qualified' feminists, fighting for space within and against their communities and hoping to be ready for the new political order."

Jill Benderly begins by stating that because nationalism has brought war to the former Yugoslavia, feminists would most likely be antinationalist. She goes on to show, however, that contemporary Balkan feminists include both nationalist and non-nationalist camps. Feminist nationalism in this context has meant "the patriotism of the victimized."

Where the Yugoslav socialist federation failed to deliver on its promises of gender equality, feminists were organizing into women's groups before Yugoslavia's dissolution; "Feminism posed a strong challenge to rising nationalism in Yugoslavia, by linking women's groups across republic lines, and by critiquing the manipulation of reproductive rights for nationalistic demographic purposes."

With war among the Yugoslav successor states, war crimes took on a particularly gendered character; rape became a weapon of war against women.[30] Women's groups that had organized to help battered women and provide support to women before the war, continued to maintain themselves through silent vigils against the war (the Belgrade Women in Black), the dissemination of information about war crimes against women, and the organization of women's centers for refugees and female survivors of the war, including rape survivors.

Although war crimes put women in the role of victims, Benderly says that the very debates over nationalism divided the feminists. Nationalist Croation feminists saw rape as part of a distinctly Serbian-generated plan of genocide and blamed Serbian women (and women arguing for dialogue with anti-war Serbs) for perpetuating genocide; nonnationalist Croation feminists maintained communication and joint antiwar activity with their "former sisters" from Serbia. Women debated whether one *could* be antiwar, nationalist, and feminist. Importantly, a form of feminist internationalism developed whereby an international set of organizations show solidarity with Balkan women, and a strong Balkan feminist presence was felt at the 1995 UN women's conference. The UN report stated the need "to integrate a gender perspective in the resolution of armed or other conflicts and foreign occupation" and "promote non-violent forms of conflict resolution."[31]

The three cases here from the Middle East, Africa, and Central Asia provide an interesting set of contrasts. Afghanistan was unable to move toward reform, falling back on religious orthodoxy, as did Iran, but Palestine and South Africa are currently state-building, with South Africa the more promising in terms of feminist nationalism, and Palestine as yet unresolved

Valentine Moghadam has written elsewhere on the relationship among nationalism, national identity, feminism, and Islamization. In another work on gender and national identity,[32] Moghadam argued that in some cases women are linked to modernization and to gender equality in socialist terms of discourse; in others, to cultural rejuvenation through religious orthodoxy or conservatism. Among Iranians and Algerians, feminists became disenchanted with their revolutions' (and the aftermaths') failure to incorporate women's rights.

These issues were played out in Afghanistan, the case presented here, where Marxist modernizers fought Islamic traditionalists over the "woman question." Moghadam situates contemporary Afghanistan in the "patriarchal belt" stretching from northern Africa across the Middle East to the northern plains of the Indian subcontinent to parts of rural China. In this belt, authority and control in the extended family derives from age and gender; senior males have ultimate authority over all family relations, females are segregated. Because of the strength of patriarchal customs, social change for women's rights has frequently developed through government reforms by modernizing elites, and struggles over women's rights have been particularly contentious.

Moghadam argues that the role and relationship of the state to civil society is crucial to understanding how gender dynamics get played out. The historically weak state in Afghanistan is correlated with a fragmented society resistant to attempts at modernization, a society in which primordial loyalties are paramount, although Islam has been a key organizer of national identity. Yet in both the 1920s and the 1980s, there were challenges to the gendered order in struggles among ruling men over autonomy for women and changes in family law. In the 1970s and 1980s, the Marxist People's Democratic Party of Afghanistan with its Democratic Organization of Afghan Women (later All-Afghan Women's Council) developed an impressive feminist platform, which they made compulsory and tried to implement coercively. This led to resistance at the local levels and became part of the motivation of the mujahideen armed uprising. The country became embroiled in a civil war; the Soviet Union supported the Marxists, and the United States, China, Iran, Pakistan, and Saudi Arabia supported the mujahideen—the element most opposed to feminist reforms. With the withdrawal of Soviet assistance, the government fell to the mujahideen and the feminist agenda disappeared.

Moghadam's article emphasizes the importance of the conjunctures among state, civil society, and the international community in the success of feminist nationalism.

In contrast to the negative outcome in Afghanistan in the 1990s for feminist nationalism, Palestine and South Africa are state-building and it is still unclear where state-building is headed because negotiations continue. Sherna Berger Gluck has been following the women's movements in Palestine.[33] She repeats a theme heard in similar grassroots movements: the mobilization of women activists and the emergence of a class of women intellectuals helped to pave the way for a new feminist nationalism that did not submerge feminism into nationalism. Quite interestingly, although discourse among feminist groups seems contentious and at times seems to submerge feminism, Gluck notes that the actual activities of these organizations in terms of grassroots organizing was really quite "subversive" and helped to promote feminist consciousness. The political involvement of women during the *intifada* helped to break down the segregation of spheres, allowed women more freedom of movement, and impacted men's attitudes. What distinguishes feminist nationalism in the Palestinian case from the previous Algerian struggles is that there is now an organized women's movement underlying the ideological shifts.

With the processes of state formation under way, however, the outlook for feminism is not so positive. At the same time that some women are engaging in what they have called a "foot in/foot out strategy,"—not wholeheartedly supporting the transitional government, but trying to work with it—others have distanced themselves. Yet, all these forces came together to develop the Women's Bill of Rights, which they hope will be placed into the future constitution of a Palestinian state. It is unclear how much women will gain with the transition.

South Africa, in contrast, appears to be making great strides under the new government in incorporating the progressive positions of the African National Congress and other nationalists into its state-building. As Zengie Mangaliso emphasizes, the new constitution promises the creation of a *nonsexist* as well as a nonracial society. This feminist consciousness was born from the organizing of women who were actively involved in the struggles against apartheid and for trade unions, in consumer and rent boycotts; and in *both* armed organizations and peace movements. The Women's Charter of the Federation of South African Women, a group of the ANC, set forth a feminist nationalist position—before the 1994 government transition to majority rule—that provided the framework for the new constitution and its emphasis on eradicating sexism. Mangaliso explores the possibilities of a society with a traditional culture incorporating a progressive, feminist political platform and notes that much of the feminist agenda will be determined by economic transformations—particularly in the division of labor in the household and in the presence of women in the formal governmental sectors of power.

The efforts toward democratization in a number of Asian states seem to have made a difference for women. The effects of the reinstitution of democratic forms in the late 1980s in the Philippines led to a proliferation of feminist movements during the 1990s: feminist nationalist, socialist/Marxist, and radical. Lynn Kwiatkowski and I show how the left-wing, progressive movements in the Philippines developed a feminist nationalist agenda that did not prioritize gender, class, or national issues but, rather continually argued for their simultaneous constructions within the social actions of localized agendas and communities. Cordillera feminist nationalism emphasized its own forms of ethnonationalism—asserting regional cultural integrity with the economic and political sovereignty agendas of the larger women's movement. Trade union women (factory and service-sector workers) emphasized class/labor/trade union agendas at their workplace sites because these affected women, but worked in conjunction with larger labor, nationalist, and community issues of the male-dominated progressive and militant labor movements. Health workers broadened biomedical ideas about health care to link issues of nationalism and feminism to models of care—so that prostitution, for example, gets linked to the trafficking in women, which is linked to the neocolonial and class-based nature of Philippine society. The grassroots organizing among poor women was unprecedented during the 1980s, and the increasingly "feminist" tone of such organizing helped encourage the proliferation of feminist nationalism, which was manifest in the strength of the large and vocal presence of Philippine women at the 1995 Beijing conference.

South Korea saw a rise during the 1980s and 1990s in feminist organizing among students, trade union women, elites, and others who linked women's issues to larger national issues, such as the unification of Korea. Alice Yun Chai argues that feminists understood they needed to operate autonomously but also in cooperation with larger societal (and global) struggles. South Korean feminists, like their progressive Philippine counterparts, created "umbrella" structures to bring together diverse, and localized women's organizations, which could then take on other social issues and causes: issues of working-class, urban poor, and rural women, violence against women in all its forms, and the unification of the nation. The emphasis of "women's rights as human rights" challenged the traditional structures which had encouraged sexual and economic exploitation, and put the exploitation into larger analyses of the global political economy—an element of this movement shared by Philippine feminist nationalists. Both cases demonstrated the "integrative"/holistic nature of feminist politics.

Haunani-Kay Trask argues that feminism and nationalism in Hawai'i share more with indigenous populations in the Pacific Islands than with the United States, where feminism has been "informed by the long genocidal heritage that created the United States." Hers is the voice of the activist who argues that "First World feminist theory is incapable of addressing indigenous women's cultural worlds." Hawaiian nationalists vary on their relation to the United States—some want complete secession, others a "nation within a nation," where native Hawiians would have sole voting citizenship rights.[34] But feminists in the Pacific Islands have been organizing against occupation, environmental degradation, nuclear testing, sex tourism, and the effects of development policies on women.[35]

The Americas demonstrate differing histories. Norma Stoltz Chinchilla examines the relationship of feminism and nationalism to the revolutionary movements of Central America. Chinchilla argues that "in contrast to the United States and much of Western Europe, there [are] no social leftists who are not convinced radical nationalists" because of the economic needs for social justice. Women revolutionaries are "examining critically, for the first time, the conditions that favored or inhibited their access to lasting improvements in more equal gender relations." Chinchilla analyzes their critiques of the lack of a gendered analysis of the movements, the role of masculinist culture in the vanguard party, the principle of obedience to authority, and the role of civil society in the creation of a new society. Through these critiques feminist nationalism is being constructed "in the direction of greater democracy, tolerance, and respect for daily life."

The final two cases focus on nationalism in the relationships of minorities to majority societies: Québec's nationalism in relation to greater Canada, Chicana nationalism in relation to U.S. society and culture. In Québec, sociologists Patrice LeClerc and I show how feminist nationalists struggled with the contradictions created between nationalism and feminism. Yet from the "Quiet Revolution" of the 1960s, feminists were able to "mainstream" women's concerns, ensuring them a place in governmental policy. Nationalism continues to motivate votes for secession from Canada in the mid-1990s, and there is some feeling that it may be only a matter of time before Québec secedes and forms its own nation-state. The feminist agenda as it became institutionalized in the Québec government never wavered, and Québec feminist nationalists believe that their provincial government's policies on women are more progressive than the federal government's, and that these rights will be preserved with or without secession. Yet nationalist concerns over a low Québec birthrate would crop up to challenge feminist concerns with how the government would continue to treat the movement. There were always contradictions, but comparatively speaking, Québec seems to far outrun other countries in concerns over women's issues.

Feminist nationalism in the United States is very much alive in multi-cultural and ethnonationalist debates over the nature of internal colonialism. Alma Garcia focuses on the struggles over class, ethnic, and racial oppression for women of Mexican heritage, Chicanas, which took form in a feminist nationalist discourse during the 1960s and 1970s. This discourse grew out of the farmworker and student social movements. Echoing Chatterjee on early Indian nationalism, the Chicano family became the site of resistance to oppression in the development of a cultural nationalism. Like Philippine feminists, who sought to balance demands of class, nationality, and gender with family, Chicanas distinguished their critique from the individualism of liberal mainstream American feminism. Whereas Philippine feminists focus their critiques on the effects of external neocolonialism (primarily from the United States), Chicanas developed a discourse over the nature of internal colonialism to challenge what they perceived to be Anglo-American cultural and ideological hegemony. Part of this was to develop ethnic identity and pride, part to use as an organizing tool to unite Chicanos around issues affecting their lives—be it farmworkers' trade union rights or affirmative action. The struggle, for Chicanas, was on forming consensus over a feminist nationalism in an era of dramatically changing social roles and aspirations.

Other Cases

The parameters of a single anthology do not allow for a consideration of every contemporary feminist nationalist movement. At the NGO (non-governmental organization) Forum at the Beijing conference, feminists presented a number of panels and workshops on feminist nationalist struggles. Those not discussed here include East Timor, Tibet, Chechniya, Rwanda, Western Sahara, and Israel, among others.

With the invasion of East Timor by Indonesia in 1975, Timorese women began organizing with men in an anticolonial movement against the Indonesians. According to activist accounts, women's involvement in the National Armed Forces for the Liberation of East Timor (with its armed wing) and the political National Council of Maubere Resistance took women out of traditional family structures, subjected them to rape and prostitution, and forced birth control programs by the Indonesian family planning programs. They are organizing against human rights abuses and to encourage international involvement on women's rights.[36]

In other parts of Asia, women have been organizing outside Tibet and in international solidarity with human rights networks against the Chinese occupation there and its forced population program.[37] Russian mothers fought to keep their sons out of Afghanistan and Chechniya. In Africa, feminist nationalists such as Monique Mujawamariya, who founded a battered women's shelter in Kigali, have been organizing in Rwanda in response to the war and forced migration there.[38] In the Western Sahara, L'Union Nationale des Femmes Sahraquies (UNFS; National Union of Sahrawi Women) organized for women's rights as part of the Front POLISARIO, a political movement that has been struggling for the independence of Western Sahara from Morocco. The UNFS was organized in the refugee camps in 1979 to represent women's issues, including implementation of the 1985 Nairobi UN women's conference platforms, while it continues to work for independence with the larger POLISARIO.[39] Other movements can be found—such as the ongoing struggles of the "enclaved" women of Cyprus.[40] Additionally, research on women and nationalism has highlighted how national issues like the population policies of Israel affect women in nationalist states.[41]

These cases, I believe, demonstrate that there is such a cross-cultural, or global, phenomenon as feminist nationalism. Some movements have risen and fallen depending on cultural repression, or state policies. Many seem to have been motivated by the increasing literacy and wage work of women worldwide, who have used their economic power and education to spur social-movement organizing around specific women's interests. The past twenty years of the United Nations' efforts for women have helped tremendously in providing states with strategies for social change and a consensus and discourse on women's rights. Many women have used these efforts to legitimate their organizing for social change.

Lois A. West

Toward a Theory of Feminist Nationalism

Activists in these contemporary feminist nationalist movements share their desire to work out the contradictions in women's struggling for women's rights within contexts that have denied them rights as citizens at the same time that they are working on various nationalist struggles rooted in their kin, ethnic, religious, or regional group. This is what defines them as "feminist nationalist" movements: social movements simultaneously seeking rights for women and rights for nationalists within a variety of social, economic, and political contexts. This definition encompasses a much larger framework than viewing nationalism within limiting terms of "culture" (various groups could fight for a region yet not share a culture) or "ethnicity" (many struggles have religious or ethnic components) or even economics when it lacks a cultural component.

What is interesting is that for all that has been written about the relationship between nationalism, culture, or ethnicity in relation to women, gender is still not constructed as a central component of nationalism. This book is an attempt to incorporate gender, viewed here as the struggle for women's rights, into a definition of nationalism that places women at the center and acknowledges feminist nationalism as a process of interaction developed between women and men, and not solely by men. Where there is a "primordial" form of nationalism linked to violence, racism, and militarism, then its construction as a gendered phenomenon may yet identify it as a particular kind of masculinized phenomenon. This does not mean women do not maintain primordial nationalism, only that its construction may be more of a masculine enterprise. How this is so remains to be analyzed.

Elsewhere, I have offered three ideal types of feminist nationalist movements: historical, national liberation social movements; movements against neocolonialism; and identity-rights movements that wage struggles internal to their societies.[42] The first type arises in colonial contexts when nationalist movements seek independence from external, imperial control. The Indian women's movement against British colonialism is one example.

In contexts where colonialism has formally ended but neocolonialism remained, some feminist nationalist movements begin historically and turn into decolonization movements. Nationalist movement actors view their sovereignty as compromised by neocolonial political and economic relations, and women balance nationalist with feminist struggles. The current leftist movements in the Philippines present a case in point, Palestine another.

A third type of feminist nationalism are movements against internal neocolonialism or for identity rights. Groups (whether majority or minority) struggle for a political voice or land rights, or, to have a particular cultural or economic demand met. Contemporary cases include minority rights movements by Chicanas or African-Americans in the United States, and the feminist movement led by women of Quebec. Both the Hawiian and Quebec movements appear to be identity rights and decolonization movements.

There are undoubtedly other ways to schematize these movements, and movements may incorporate elements of all three types. Given the complexities of the nationalist movements today, one welcomes a further differentiation, which is why I have argued for a gendered cultural relativism: the relativizing of the struggles of feminists and nationalists to their historical, cultural, social, and economic time and place. However, the complexities are even more troublesome in the nationalist movements that are more primordial in nature, such as those one finds in the former Yugoslavia. Can those movements, which have elements of fascism or racism not unlike the nationalism of Nazi Germany, really incorporate variants of feminism? Can you have primordial feminist nationalist movements, as women in the former Yugoslavia ask? One needs to separate the elements of feminism from nationalism in such cases.

How is feminism constructing nationalism? Struggles against the oppression of women and for rights equal to those of men place women as central to the discourse. Women redefine feminism with nationalism and civil rights by redefining the private and public realms as not mutually exclusive and binary but as complementary and unitary. Work and the struggle for nation are not prioritized over family/leisure and the struggle for women. They are dealt with simultaneously, as women deal with family and work/leisure simultaneously. "Mixed" realities are managed, and women are actors, not simply reactors. Further, while women struggle within specific cultures, economies, polities, and societies, there is a quickly growing internationalization of feminism. As technology progresses and as elites in even the poorest of countries are able to integrate the technologies, the world grows closer. Women's marginalization in both the development of nation-states and in wars has led to an advantage, as Virginia Woolf notes above: women see the world globally in terms of antimilitarism. She asks for her country and for women what she would have for the whole world. Armed feminists in guerilla movements are not antimilitarist, but where women have children, they certainly are. From women's standpoint, sovereignty, identity, self-determination are more than nation-state, they are family and peace.

Thus, I propose a dialectical model in which state structures (including civil law) interact with culture (including customary law, religion, language, and ethnicity, which incorporates race), geography/territory, social movements, families, and individual actors. Within this framework, gender is an integral part of each structure and not simply a variable. This means not apprehending gender as a taken-for-granted reality but as a key component defining each of these elements of nationality and of nationalism itself. The social movement is "doing gender" and "doing nationalism" simultaneously. Although forces push social movement actors to prioritize issues and time, in the movements proposed here, one cannot add simple gender as a concept or variable. Gender is fundamental to the definition of each of these components. Thus, using Woolf's conception, women have no states and may not identify with the war-making capacities of men, but women *are* the nation-state, the culture, the family, as integral as men to these definitions, only defined in different terms and activities. We can define feminism as the social movement activities that seek women's rights, but examination of gender's relationship to nationalism reveals that feminism is integral to it.

Further, with the globalization of social movements, as well as economies, we need to look at feminism as its own kind of nationalism. Women have struggled for women's rights usually within narrow national contexts such as for the right to vote. Until the United Nations Decade for Women, women did not operate in a global setting. Now that feminism has become globalized, could it become nationalized as an ideology without borders? A cultural nationalism that unites women around the world on issues like inequalities worldwide in the division of labor—particularly in the home? But class and colonial issues still divide women. Women who have cracked the "glass ceiling" of corporate life or who were born into wealthy families may not see their interests tied to those of poorer women in either their own communities or abroad. Poorer women are their servants, not their equals. And in that way, class may override many other interests. Yet the globalization of capitalist economics may mean the increasing use of women's contingent labor. All economies have depended on women's unpaid household labor. Imagine the revolutionary possibilities of a global women's movement which would go on strike—refusing to provide that labor!

There are loose ends of analysis here. I have not examined how the cultural isolation and individualism perpetuated by developing capitalism promotes a liberalism in which women's rights can prosper in one form, but perhaps a colonial form. The questions have been raised. How the answers work themselves out remains to be seen.

Notes

I am grateful to Marilyn Hoder-Salmon, Jack Brodsky, Jim Ito-Adler, Arend Holtslag, and Miraan Sa for comments on this chapter, and to the American Council for Learned Societies and Florida International University for grants to attend the 1995 U.N. Beijing Women's Conferences.

1. Virginia Woolf, *Three Guineas* (New York: Harbinger Book, 1938), pp. 107–109.

2. United Nations, *Report of the Fourth World Conference on Women* (Beijing, 4–5 September 1995), New York: United Nations, 1996: p. 5. There are many indicators of the perpetuation of global women's inequality. See United Nations, *The World's Women, 1995: Trends and Statistics* (New York: United Nations, 1995); United Nations Development Programme, *Human Development Report, 1995* (New York: Oxford University Press, 1995).

3. Joey Sprague and Mary K. Zimmerman, "Overcoming Dualisms: A Feminist Agenda for Sociological Methodology," *Theory on Gender, Feminism on Theory*, ed. Paula England (New York: Aldine de Gruyter, 1993), pp. 255–280.

4. See the classic Stacey and Thorne article, which argues that the studying of women as one "variable" in sociology has limited the discipline's ability to understand gender. Judith Stacey and Barrie Thorne, "The Missing Feminist Revolution in Sociology," *Social Problems* 32, no. 4 (1985): 301–316.

5. See J. Ann Tickner on gender's impact on economic nationalism in *Gender in International Relations* (New York: Columbia University Press, 1992), pp. 78–96.

6. United Nations, *Report of the Fourth World Conference on Women*, p. 6.

7. See Lois A. West, "Feminist Nationalist Social Movements: Beyond Universalism and Towards a Gendered Cultural Relativism," *Women's Studies International* 15, nos. 5/6 (1992): 563–579.

8. I highlight the gendered language. John Hutchinson and Anthony D. Smith, introduction *Nationalism* (Oxford: Oxford University Press, 1994), p. 4.

9. Louis Snyder, *Encyclopedia of Nationalism* (New York: Paragon, 1990), p. 245.

10. Ernest Renan "What Is a Nation?" in *Nation and Narration*, ed. Homi K. Bhabha (London: Routledge, 1990), pp. 8–10.

11. Partha Chatterjee, *The Nation and Its Fragments: Colonial and Postcolonial Histories* (Princeton: Princeton University Press, 1993), p. 9. See also the issue "Women and Religious Nationalism in India," *Bulletin of Concerned Asian Scholars* 25, no. 4 (October–December 1993).

12. V. Spike Peterson, "The Politics of Identification in the Context of Globalization," *Women's Studies International Forum*, 19, 1/2 (1996): 5–16.

13. See Synder, *Encyclopedia of Nationalism*.

14. John Breuilly, *Nationalism and the State* (Chicago: University of Chicago Press, 1982).

15. Daniel Druckman, "Nationalism, Patriotism and Group Loyalty: A Social Psychological Perspective," *Mershon International Studies Review* 38 (1994): 43–68.

16. For example, see Yale H. Ferguson's review essay, "Ethnicity, Nationalism, and Polities Great and Small," *Mershon International Studies Review* 38 (1994): 1241–246. Gurr has no gender component of his "ethnopolitical conflicts" for 1993–1994, but he has a nice list of them; see Ted Robert Gurr, "Peoples Against States: Ethnopolitical Conflict and the Changing World System," *International Studies Quarterly* 38, 3 (1994): 347–377. Also, the review essay of Will Kymlicka, "Misunderstanding Nationalism," *Dissent*, Winter 1995, pp. 130–137.

17. Linda Racioppi and Katherine O'Sullivan. See, "Nationalism Engendered: A Critique of Approaches to Nationalism" (unpublished paper, Michigan State University, 1995).

18. For this treatment, see "Women: The Oppressed Majority," in Richard T. Schaefer, *Racial and Ethnic Groups* (New York: HarperCollins College Publishers, 1996).

19. Sylvia Walby, "Woman and Nation," *International Journal of Comparative Sociology* 33, nos. 1–2 (1992): 81.

20. Nira Yuval-Davis and Floya Anthias, *Woman-Nation-State* (New York: St. Martin's Press, 1989), p. 7.

21. Fiona Wilson and Bodil Folke Frederiksen, "Introduction: Ethnicity, Gender and the Subversion of Nationalism," in *Ethnicity, Gender and the Subversion of Nationalism*, ed. Fiona Wilson and Bodil Folke Frederiksen (London: Frank Cass, 1995).

22. Cynthia Enloe, *Bananas, Beaches and Bases: Making Feminist Sense of International Politics* (Berkeley: University of California Press, 1990), p. 44.

23. Kumari Jayawaradena, *Feminism and Nationalism in the Third World* (London: Zed Books, 1986), p. 2.

24. Ibid., p. 260.

25. V. Spike Peterson, "The Politics of Identity and Gendered Nationalism,"

in *Foreign Policy Analysis: Continuity and Change in Its Second Generation*, ed. Laura Neack, Jeanné A.K. Hey and Patrick J. Haney (Englewood Cliffs, NJ: Prentice-Hall, 1995) p. 193.

26. R. W. Connell, "The State, Gender, and Sexual Politics: Theory and Appraisal," *Theory and Society* 19 (1990): 523.

27. George l. Moose, *Nationalism and Sexuality: Middle-Class Morality and Sexual Norms in Modern Europe* (Madison: University of Wisconsin Press, 1985), pp. 167, 170.

28. See Gisela Kaplan, *Contemporary Western European Feminism* (New York: New York University Press, 1992).

29. See also Mary Nash, "Political Culture, Catalan Nationalism, and the Women's Movement in Early Twentieth-Century Spain," *Women's Studies International Forum* 19, 1/2 (1996): 45–54; Ellen Marakowitz, "Gender and National Identity in Finland," *Women's Studies International Forum* 19, 1/2 (1996): 55–63.

30. There has been a proliferating literature on this. For example, see Maria B. Olujic, "Sexual Coercion and Torture in Former Yugoslavia," *Cultural Survival Quarterly* 19, no. 1 (1995): 43–45; Manuela Dobos, "Mass Rapes Committed by Serbs Are War Crimes," in *Nationalism and Ethnic Conflict*, ed. Bruno Leone (San Diego: Greenhaven Press, 1994), pp. 128–134; Silva Mexnaric, "Gender as an Ethno-Marker: Rape, War, and Identity Politics in the Former Yugoslavia," in *Identity Politics and Women*, ed. Valentine Moghadam (Boulder: Westview Press, 1994), pp. 76–97.

31. United Nations, *Report of the Fourth World Conference on Women*, pp. 61, 63.

32. Valentine Moghadam, "Introduction and Overview: Gender Dynamics of Nationalism, Revolution and Islamization," in *Gender and National Identity*, ed. Moghadam (London: Zed Books, 1994).

33. See Sherna Berger Gluck, *An American Feminist in Palestine* (Philadelphia: Temple University Press, 1994).

34. Annie Nakao, "Sovereign Sisters," *San Francisco Examiner Image*, June 29, 1993, pp. 12–17. See the publications of University of Hawai'i professor and founder of Ka Lahui, a sovereignty movement, Haunani-Kay Trask, including *From a Native Daughter: Colonialism and Sovereignty in Hawai'i* (Monroe, Maine: Common Courage Press, 1993).

35. See Tina Takashy, Grassroots, Women NGOs of the Pacific, *Beneath Paradise: See Us, Hear Us, Beijing '95* (Victoria, Australia: International Women's Development Agency, 1993); 'Atu Emberson-Bain, *Sustainable Development or Malignant Growth? Perspectives of Pacific Island Women* (Suva, Fiji: Maram Publications, 1994). At the 1995 UN NGO Forum on Women, Susanna Ounei-Small presented the situation of Kanak women, who did not believe that concerns of their people were seriously addressed in the accords with the French in the late 1980s. She sees domestic violence, rape, and the division of labor that keeps women in subordinate roles as due to the neocolonial relationships forged in

New Caledonia/Kanaky under occupation by the French. Susanna Ounei-Small, "The 'Peace' Signed With Our Blood," in Emberson-Bain, *Sustainable Development*, pp. 199–211. The grassroots women's movement in Palau/Belau has been struggling to maintain the nuclear-free Constitution against what it sees as U.S. neocolonial desire for military access. Cita Morei, "In Defense of Our Nuclear-Free Constitution," in Emberson-Bain, *Sustainable Development*, pp. 219–222.

36. Ceu Brites, Ines Almeida, Benilda Brites, and Odete Goncalves, "East Timor Resistance: 20 Years On" (paper presented at the UN NGO Forum, September 1995, Beijing). See also CNRM East Timor, National Council of Maubere Resistance, "A Message to the Beijing Conference from the East Timorese Women," Eworld, on-line, September 6, 1995; Emma Franks, "Women and Resistance in East Timor: 'The centre, as they say, knows itself by the margins.' " *Women's Studies International Forum* 19, 1/2 (1996): 155–168.

37. International Committee of Lawyers for Tibet, "Denial of Tibetan Women's Right to Reproductive Freedom" (San Francisco: ICLT, August 1, 1995).

38. Monique Mujawamariya, "Rwanda: An Activist Reflects on Her Nation's Trauma and Recovery," *Ms.* 5, no. 3 (December 1994): 10–15, quoted in Cynthia Enloe, "When Feminists Think About Rwanda," *Cultural Survival Quarterly* 19, no. 1 (Spring 1995): 26–29.

39. L'Union Nationale des Femmes Sahraouies UNFS, Comité national préparatoire de la Conférence mondiale des femmes, "Beijing 1995, Egalité, Développément, Paix" (Suisse: Mouvement Chrétien pour la Paix, 1995).

40. Free Unitary Karpass Association, "The Enclaved: Those Who Stayed Behind," (Nicosia, 1994); Women's Organization of the Democratic Party of Cyprus, "The Women of Cyprus Demand Justice and Freedom for Their Country," (1995); Floya Anthias, "Women and Nationalism in Cyprus," in Yuval-Davis and Anthias, *Woman-Nation-State*, pp. 150–167.

41. See Nira Yuval-Davis, "National Reproduction and 'the Demographic race' in Israel," in Yuval-Davis and Anthias, *Woman-Nation-State*, pp. 92–109; also the article on similar issues in South Africa in the same volume.

42. West, "Feminist Nationalist Social Movements."

Europe

Feminism and Nationalism:
The European Case

Gisela Kaplan

Feminism and nationalism are almost always incompatible ideological positions within the European context. The agenda for this chapter is to highlight the relationship between feminism and modern forms of citizenship against nationalism and antidemocratic forces. The chapter is divided into four parts. Part 1 broadly traces the historical development of nationalism in Europe across its different traditions. Part 2, cryptically titled " 'The Angel of History,' " narrates mainstream and subversive trends (that is, suffragette/emancipationist movements) from the 1870s to the 1930s. It argues against Lovenduski's assessment that the "history of women's emancipation has been a history of false starts and broken promises,"[1] and attempts to show how little chance at the time feminist ideas had in the turmoil of failing or barely nascent democracies and peace.

Part 3 looks to examples of new or different alliances in which feminism and nationalism were not mutually exclusive. So extraordinary and unusual is the alliance between feminism and nationalism in Europe that I was able to find only two examples: nineteenth-century Italy and twentieth-century Finland. To preempt the question why I have not chosen other countries for exemplification, I like to stress at the onset that these two countries have not been selected by me but are the *only* two examples in (western) European history where a confluence of feminism and nationalism has occurred. They remain exceptional cases and are re-counted here in a paradigmatic fashion, arguing that under very special historical circumstances nationalism and feminism may not be inimical. Part 4 deals with the state of the European Union and argues that the current move centripetally away from the nation-state toward globaliza-tion (supranational federation) on the one hand and regionalization on the other has created new constellations, which have begun to supersede nationalism as conceived in the nineteenth century. Hence, feminism faces very new challenges. In this introduction I propose to provide some definitions first in order to help set the scene for historically very com-plex, changing, and partly ambiguous phenomena in Europe.

The Origins and the Meaning of Feminism in Europe

Feminism and the language of participatory democracy have their origins in Europe, in two interrelated traditions. One commenced in England in the seventeenth century. Between 1647 and 1649 the English Levellers, radicals destined for execution, drafted a constitution that they called Agreement of the People. More than one hundred years later that Agreement had travelled across the Atlantic and became the basis for the American Declaration of In-dependence in 1776. The Declaration of Independence in turn was the ba-sis for the feminist Declaration of Sentiments, presented by Elizabeth Cady Stanton in the United States in 1848.[2] Indeed, it was closely modeled on that document, as was the ensuing feminist Declaration of Rights for Women of 1876, which demanded justice and equality, and most notably, "that all the civil and political rights that belong to citizens of the United States be guaranteed to us and our daughters forever." These ideas on both sides of the Atlantic were the basis of international feminism. It was Hannah Arendt's contention that, among other things, the Declaration of Independ-ence was a profound political act because it constituted a new political community.[3] Likewise, feminism, be it in Europe or the United States could be dubbed a new political community.

The other part of the English-speaking feminist tradition begins with a link to the French Revolution and the Enlightenment through Mary Wollstonecraft (1759–1797). Still of special interest today is her *Vindication of the Rights of Women* (1792). Wollstonecraft belonged to the small circle of radicals supporting the French Revolution, but not without critical reference to the role of women beyond that revolution. She was particularly critical of Jean Jacques Rousseau's (1712–1778) misogyny and sex-role assignments.[4] Her critique is a starting point for the long line of liberal feminism, at least in English speaking countries.

Feminism is a term that came into use in Europe in the early twentieth century. It has defied unequivocal definition, partly because of a multitude of feminist groupings based on different theoretical and disciplinary backgrounds,[5] and debate about the term continued well into the 1980s. Feminism usually appears with additional labels to indicate specific ideological positions (for example, socialist, liberal, Marxist, radical). Broadly, feminism certainly was, and still is, a political challenge,[6] and/or a blueprint for political action.[7] Much of feminist practice and theory holds that gender inequality fundamentally contradicts notions such as equality, freedom, citizenship, and justice. Feminism is an argument for women's autonomy and signifies a standpoint of *dissent*, containing the hope for a liberation of women with a view toward changing all human relationships for the better.[8] The term *feminist* has not been used in every European country. In some places—curiously, even where progressive action and social change took place rather rapidly, such as in the Netherlands and Denmark—it has at times had derogatory connotations. Women had to create their own public space and, as it were, their own tradition. Many European feminists consciously adopted a posture of disrespect and disregard for the European history of ideas because these ideas had played "a key role in justifying women's subordination and public invisibility."[9] For instance, in the history of European jurisprudence (and philosophy) the boundaries of the private and public realms were very clearly drawn. From ancient times onward, political life "has been conceptualized in opposition to the mundane world of necessity, the body, the sexual passions, and birth."[10] Authoritative philosophers such as Rousseau or Hegel expressed cognizance of women's ability for love and nurturing but argued, therefore, that women had to be excluded from the public realm of citizenship *because* they are caretakers "of affectivity, desire, and the body." By contrast, the public realm was reserved exclusively for men as a space determined by rational and impartial thought. The separation of the two spheres over centuries was anything but arbitrary.[11] In practice, it achieved two things: on one hand, relegating woman to the private sphere and therefore barring her from public life; on the other, privatizing pluralism, dissent, and diversity, thereby ensuring that anything she might have to say could be viewed as private opinion and privatized dissent. Arendt turned the table on those who implied that political action was reserved for men. She argued that since Plato, the Western tradition of political thought has been a *philosopher's* tradition and hence fundamentally apolitical. The very people, she argued, who engage in political thought have been men of contemplation rather than of political action. Hence, theorists have no business telling practitioners how to think.[12]

The Link of Feminism to Citizenship

In the broadest sense, modern feminist claims in western Europe were an expansion of citizenship claims made during the French Revolution. Citizenship traditions in individual European countries have varied widely. However, Bryan Turner has reminded us that there are basic active-passive dimensions to citizenship that hold true even across different traditions. He argues that citizenship concepts can grow either from above or from below. The passive dimension of citizenship stems from the descending view of king or ruler as the all-powerful sovereign whose subjects are recipients of privileges. In the ascending view, in which citizenship develops from below, citizenship means freedom and the bearing of active citizenship rights.[13] The French Revolution was clearly a fight for active citizenship rights, with some rather limited success in nineteenth-century Europe. Among the noteworthy moments of the latter part of the nineteenth century are the suffragette (or in Europe usually referred to as emancipationist movements) and the socialist movements in which the "privatized dissent" of women became public despite state opposition and prohibitions.

In fact, up to the twentieth century most European governments, even the English government,[14] were inimical to active citizenship and would or did react against *any* expressions of discontent, whether staged by men or women. For women, the state largely functioned as the maker or defender of a "*Kinder, Küche, Kirche*" ideology.[15] By the 1920s or 1930s, those views had gained the upper hand. A number of European countries then saw a rapid decline in public space and public self-expression. This was a consequence of dictatorial regimes, be these fascist (Spain, Portugal, Italy) or national-socialist (Germany, Austria).

Reclaiming public space and public opinion everywhere in Europe first required an end to dictatorships and to the fascist ideology at the end of World War II, and thereafter a process of liberalization. That process was arrested by the late 1960s. New social movements began where existing formal organizations left off; namely, to expand, redefine, and democratize social spaces in which new forms of democratic association have emerged.[16] Within the women's movements but not only in that context, the concept of a collective identity implied collective action.[17] Generally, feminists aligned themselves with parties of the Left as political groups above suspicion of fascist leanings. Admittedly, the more radical proponents of the western European movements, such as communist, anarchist, utopian, socialist, and communitarian groups, have had few inheritors, not so much of their ideas as in the practice of their ideas. Bourgeois, liberal feminist reform movements have fared better because their methods and goals were more manageable within existing structures. They were also less threatening and demanding.[18]

The Definition of Nationalism
in the European Context

The term *nationalism* in the European context requires more detailed appreciation, for it has undergone profound changes as a consequence of historical events. "Nationalism," as Kedourie states categorically in the opening of his book of the same title, "is a doctrine invented in Europe at the beginning of the nineteenth century."[19] We may not agree with the date given, but a European invention it was nevertheless. Indeed, the very history of Europe since the French Revolution (1789) may be described as the history of the rise and development of political nationalism,[20] and as one of its strongest forces. As a force, it was not a static or an easily identifiable phenomenon by any means. It underwent significant changes and adaptations, having been warped and shaped by some of the most extraordinary events. It came to mean and signify different things to different countries, and its applications led to different solutions and aberrations.

Initially in Europe, in some senses, nationalism functioned as a positive force. National unity for the sake of achieving political self-determination (as in the case of Germany) was also associated with economic maneuverability and growth of a strengthened bourgeoisie. In this aspect, nationalism was capable of functioning as a force of an *ascending* citizenship. In its worst form, it defied and despised anything foreign and created a climate in which it became legitimate to dominate other nations, and to exploit, punish, and persecute other peoples.

7

Nationalism, in the way in which it degenerated in western Europe, was also again identifiable with a *descending* concept of citizenship as a passive role.

Plamenatz argued that nationalism was a reaction of peoples who feel culturally at a disadvantage.[21] Outside Europe, nationalism was largely a reaction to Western power and dominance. The Chinese, for instance, were "infused with despair and strident bitterness,"[22] at the European encroachments on their realm more than one hundred years ago. In response, they developed an anticolonial nationalism, built on fear of enslavement and of dismemberment of their country. But inside Europe, nationalism was an ideology that could serve as a legitimation for the subjugation of others.

In Europe's history, nationalism has functioned in both positive and negative ways. The Italian revolutionary Giuseppe Mazzini and the Hungarian Lajos Kossuth were both highly regarded, even venerated, proponents of nationalism among European radicals and English liberals, but Mussolini and Hitler were also nationalists. This confusion about where nationalism belongs politically in Europe[23] has led to the mistaken belief, I feel, that there is "no major ideology of the modern world with which nationalism is entirely incompatible."[24] In my opinion, there is at least one ideology with which nationalism has been incompatible in most western European countries, and that is feminism.

In western Europe today the term *nationalism*, at the very least, carries derogatory connotations, not just for feminists. It is generally regarded as an exaggerated feeling of national consciousness that is blind to the claims and rights of other nations. In the past and the present it has been and is relatively rare for feminists to align themselves with groups and ideologies promoting nationalism. If they did so, their alignment tended to be confined to very special political local events. In general, feminists of the nineteenth century and the twentieth have found the ideological packages wrapped in nationalism problematic, if not diametrically opposed, to their own views and aims. Allowing for some noteworthy exceptions, then, at best contemporary western European feminism has enjoyed an extremely uneasy relationship with the idea of nationalism. In some countries its complete rejection was based on good historical reasons, which will be outlined in this chapter. There are some occasions, however, as we shall see later, in which nationalism briefly combined with feminism toward goals of self-determination and liberation.

Part 1. The Historical Development of Nationalism

In Europe, "nationalism," so one writer argued, "begins as Sleeping Beauty and ends as Frankenstein's monster."[25] Minogue's metaphor for the development of European political nationalism from the nineteenth to the twentieth century is not entirely overstated. The idea of nationalism, for all the connotations that it has in Europe today, began its career as a progressive, liberatory political force.

Out of its idiosyncrasies, its countless interpretations, and the dearth of material written and published then and now, perhaps two main views are fairly uncontested ingredients of post–French Revolutionary nationalism. One view is that a nation would be built on self-determination. Kant said in his *Religion Within the Boundaries of Reason Alone* that "one must be free in order to learn how to use one's powers freely."[26] Freedom here referred not to the freedom of princes but to the freedom of the state (a nation) as against that of other nations. The second view is that a nation is not shaped and functioning because of a sovereign at the helm, a practice of absolutism and enlightened despotism, but because the people *are* the nation. Rousseau was perhaps the first to draw an explicit link between population and state, making both politically interdependent. These revolutionary ideas of freedom and self-determination have neither disappeared nor lost value in modern interpretations of nationalism, although they are now usually found in developing nations rather than within Europe itself, and then often as a reaction to the exploitative imperialist ravages of European nations. In nineteenth-century Europe, the idea of nationalism occupied a firm place within liberalism *and* humanitarianism.[27] Indeed, John Stuart Mill identified the principle of nationality as a clause of liberalism itself.[28]

Nationalism's other, dark side developed in Europe in concert with imperialism and the racial and eugenic theories expounded in the second half of the nineteenth century. To an extent, leaving aside economic issues, nationalism was a precondition for imperialism. Not all political thinkers and practitioners merely believed in the wisdom and freedom of their own nation-state and the progressive forces within the confines of their nationality. Aggressive nationalism adopted an air of supremacy, believing one's own culture to be superior and therefore believing oneself obliged to spread one's own values to others. Nationalism became tinged and dominated by the idea of a "national mission." For instance, the British believed that they had to educate and train other "inferior" nations (that is, the "white man's burden"); Russians automatically assumed leadership of the Pan-Slavic movement; the Germans and French thought of their heritage as "Aryans" as undoubtedly superior; and Spain believed it was the guardian and defender of Christendom.

In terms of technological progress, the two nations that were most advanced by the middle of the nineteenth century were Britain and France. It is no accident that the impulse for the new imperialist writings came from the two countries in which industrialization had taken off earlier than anywhere else. Among the most respected proponents of racist imperialist ideas were the Frenchman Joseph Arthur, Comte de Gobineau (1816–1882) and the Englishman Houston Stewart Chamberlain (1855–1927). Gobineau's cumbersomely pompous and yet popular work *Essai sur linégalité des races humaines*, written between 1852 and 1855, proceeded to "prove" not only that "whites" were superior to the "black" and "yellow" races but that civilization had progressed only when "Aryans" had taken the lead. Chamberlain proposed very similar views of race in his widely influential *The Foundations of the 19th Century* (1899). In Britain, as Arendt argued,[29] imperialism combined several forces destructive of the political sphere: expansion for its own sake, which was itself built on racism (that is, regarding other peoples as inferior and therefore not having any moral qualms about subjugating native populations in Africa and elsewhere) and the development of bureaucracies to service overseas possessions. The issue in the colonies was not to establish responsible governments but to "administer" possessions gained by immoral means. Colonial governments created an atmosphere in which racial domination became historically justifiable destiny. Colonialism taught that violence alone can establish racial supremacy.[30]

This rise of racism, imperialism, and, as an obverse side to imperialism, movements such as Pan-Slavism and Pan-Germanism provided the raw material for totalitarianism in the twentieth century and undermined and eventually dismantled the structure and self-understanding of nation-states.[31] The imperialist, racist ideas traveled from developed nation-states (France and Britain) to political entities far removed from being nation-states (Russia and Germany). The translation of the imperialist ideas into very different political structures led to an inverted imperialism that was based solely on race as a source for the legitimate claim of the right to nationality. Hence, in the case of Russian and German territories, the expansionary claims were vindicated not by institutions and political structures but solely by racial claims. The Pan-Slavic and Pan-Germanic movements were thus inimical even to the creation of nation-states because political boundaries could be ignored when viewed along some fabricated racial unity. While the imperialist ideas of France, Britain and others wreaked havoc overseas (largely in Africa and Asia), the adoption of racial and imperialist ideas in Russia and Germany were inflammatory at home. In Germany, Gobineau's and Chamberlain's ideas were quickly developed further; however, here they were being directed not just against other peoples but against anything foreign, weak, sick, or different *within the Germans' own* culture. The enemy—the weaker, the inferior— was not just out there but within. With a writer like Ernst Haeckel the line is drawn directly to Nazi biopolicies.[32] Haeckel adopted the new social Darwinism and seriously proposed the active elimination of groups of people and of anyone whose life somehow polluted, threatened, or unbalanced the national "gene pool." Nazis, later, actively decided whose life was worth sustaining or not; in the name of "racial hygiene," the mentally and physically handicapped, the politically recalcitrant, homosexuals, Jews, and Gypsies were systematically exterminated.[33]

In other words, the concept of nationalism quickly degenerated into a legitimation for power and narrowed its goals from broad political national aspirations into *völkisch*, ethnically based, principles. The idea of individual rights, political democracy, and humanitarian values as a part of a liberal nationalism, the actual *raison d'être* of nation-states, gradually gave way to the idea of the supremacy of the state over the individual. The state was not created to protect individual liberty, but the individual had to serve the state. In other words, the impetus as power from below was quickly turned into its obverse, as power from above.

Nationalism became the ideology that forged "crowds into congregations,"[34] created symbols of near-religious sacrosanctity, and raised the real or imagined threat of self-annihilation to a blueprint for destruction and bloodshed. It served a petty bourgeoisie to derive from it a sense of superiority and a legitimation for the brutal oppression of other peoples. The "common good" was defined purely in terms of the existence and power of the state—a view that justified aggressive and assertive measures internationally and curtailment of individual freedoms nationally.

We have shown elsewhere that the new racial theories, "proving" the immutable and unalterable inferiority of non-Europeans, also led biologists, anthropologists, and other natural scientists to theories that proposed the utter and immutable inferiority of women.[35] Indeed, in an attempt to substantiate male white superiority, "inferior" status of race was often likened to differences between the sexes. The new nationalistic pathos, whether with some genuine grievances or not, was intrinsically a *masculinist* culture. Thus P. H. Pearse, the Irish revolutionary, exclaimed in 1916: "Bloodshed is a cleansing and sanctifying thing and the nation which regards it as a final horror has lost its manhood. There are many things more horrible than bloodshed; and slavery is one of them."[36]

Ultimately, the proof of "manhood" of a nation required the invention of state enemies and the abolition of political democracy. As we know, after World War I (1914–1918), Stalinism in the Soviet Union, national socialism in Germany (Hitler), fascism in Italy (Mussolini), and the fascist dictatorships of Portugal (Salazar) and of Spain (under Franco) eventually achieved precisely that.

Part 2. The "Angel of History"

2.1 Mainstream Trends

Feminism in Europe, from its nineteenth-century movements to today, has suffered experiences not unlike those of Walter Benjamin's "Angel of History." Benjamin, caught in the pessimism and apocalyptic visions of those few who fully understood the nightmare of totalitarianism to come, wrote of the "angel of history":

> His face is turned towards the past. Where we perceive a chain of events, he sees one single catastrophe which keeps piling wreckage upon wreckage and hurls it in front of his feet. The angel would like to stay, awaken the dead, and make whole what has been smashed. But a storm is blowing from Paradise; it has got caught in his wings with such violence that the angel can no longer close them. This storm irresistibly propels him into the future to which his back is turned, while the pile of debris before him grows skyward. This storm is what we call progress.[37]

Women of the nineteenth century were like Benjamin's "Angel of History." A "storm" of progress (industrialization) lifted them up and allowed them to see the wreckage accumulated in its name. The Industrial Revolution saw poor women turned into chattel, functioning as the cheapest labor of the new entrepreneurial capitalism. Women (married women) in the strengthening middle and upper strata of the bourgeoisie were, as Balzac so aptly wrote in 1829, slaves "whom one must be able to set on a throne" (*La Physiologie du Mariage*); that is, women were safely deposited in the golden cage of home and served as much as a status symbol of acquired wealth and leisure time as a toy at their husbands' disposal. They were asked to submit dutifully and gratefully to the unchallenged and legally sanctioned sole rule of the husband.

Notwithstanding these repressive trends, there had also been the French Revolution with its claims of citizenship and *egalité*, and a whole host of radical ideas had been aired for long enough by writers and thinkers famous enough not to go unnoticed in women's drawing rooms. The uprisings and ideas of the 1830s and of 1848 further fueled the rising discontent. Saint-Simon, the founder of French socialism, had preached a new equality and he and the Saint-Simonists had led to a veritable cult of women. They are credited with the publication of the first feminist journal, *La Femme Nouvelle*. Flora Tristan, even before Marx and Engels, began to condemn the plight of the working classes, specifically of women, and women everywhere in central and western Europe began to organize.[38] In France, 1848 saw the publication of the first feminist daily, *La voix des femmes* (Women's voice), and the founding of numerous revolutionary clubs for women. In England, radical movements such as the Owenites and Utopians advocated equality for women. In German territories, Louise Otto-Peters began her feminist career with her essay "The Participation of Women in Matters of State" (1846), culminating in 1848 in the founding of the *Women's Newspaper* and in the *Address of a German Girl*, in which she particularly spoke of the predicaments of working-class women. Louise Aston, the nearest German equivalent of George Sand, founded the Club for Emancipated Women, and in her poetry collection of 1846, (the title of which translates as "Wild Roses"), she openly proclaimed her right to "free love." In Vienna, 1848 witnessed the first large-scale demonstration by women factory workers, followed by the founding of the Viennese Democratic Women's Association.[39] In Sweden, a law of 1845 permitted inheritance of property and assets by both men and women. To an extent, the radicalism of the first part of the nineteenth century had something to do with the new liberalism, and thus with nationalism, more than simply by implication. To illustrate, John Stuart Mill was not just an ardent defender of nationalism but one of the early defenders of women's rights. It was he who, in 1866, submitted to parliament a signed petition for women's enfranchisement.

The second half of the nineteenth century was characterized by two major trends. One was the explicit effort to eradicate radical forces. The openness and promise of the 1830s and 1840s was all too brief an interlude, a moment's reprieve from the oppression until the dust of left-wing radical stirrings settled and the reactionary forces were firmly in control. The failed European revolution of 1848 is also the failed first attempt by women to gain some measure of self-control (over their properties, their children, their lives), and some degree of political emancipation. Apart from the very slow inroads into education and positive educational policy decisions that were generally not revoked, many other progressive ideas disappeared again. Restrictive legislation was put into place, especially in central Europe, some of which was explicitly directed against women's rights; for example, women's right to assemble for political purposes. From 1852, Louise Otto-Peterson was prohibited by law to publish the *Women's Newspaper,* and Louise Aston, like many dissenters of the time, had to leave Prussia. The women's rebellion in Vienna was brutally suppressed. The brief period of liberalism in France (1860–1870) ended in the bloodshed of the Paris Commune (1871) and in the defeat, imprisonment, exile, or death of radicals and feminists (the "*pétroleuses*"). Radicals of central and western Europe migrated to England, to the United States, and even to Australia.

The other trend in the second half of the nineteenth century and the early twentieth was characterized by a consolidation of reactionary political forces, by single-minded attempts for expansion, profit, and power. France and England strove to expand their overseas posessions. In German territories, nationalism without a nation in 1871[40] finally led to the unification of German territories under Prussia's (Bismarck's) leadership. Nationalism and unification were understood in terms of national interests in which the individual's rights and needs were of no concern at all. Any progressive ideas were quashed and the political left-wing parties and writers imprisoned or exiled; August Bebel wrote his famous *Women and Socialism* in prison. Under Tsar Alexander II (1855–1881) Russia swiftly expanded its territory in Asia (the Caucasus). All European imperialist powers, chiefly England, France, Russia, and Spain, but also Belgium and the Netherlands, now had to contend with opposition from powers outside Europe that had quickly gained in status and power: the United States and Japan. It was in the late nineteenth century to the early twentieth that industrialization and the scramble for new territories forged a new world politics and world economy.

In this period of consolidation of nation-states, population policies or biopolicies, as we now call them, also came into vogue. Eugenics, "racial purity" and a new demonstrative self-assertion demanded that one's own culture and "race" be protected from decline, "miscegenation" (that is, general "pollution," and attacks from "inferior races"), by a strong and assertive population policy. This seemingly urgent task for governments resulted in reproduction policies that directly affected women. It needs to be stressed that the new European political nationalism of the late nineteenth century and early twentieth was responsible for introducing the first secular antiabortion and anticontraception laws in history.

It cannot be emphasized strongly enough that "nationalism" was the direct cause of the creation of laws that condemned and forced millions of women for the first time in history to bear and keep unwanted children. Of course, church laws had existed before (and in the late nineteenth century the Vatican became more powerful than it had been in centuries), but the state had had very little direct control and say in matters of childbearing. Abortions, infanticide, and setting children out as foundlings had all been widely practiced methods of ridding oneself of unwanted children. One of the first legal changes that Bismarck, for instance, introduced in 1871, was the notorious paragraph 218 (actually 218–220) of the Penal Code, a law that German women still were fighting in the 1970s and that has not yet disappeared from the Penal Code. It made abortion punishable by up to five years' imprisonment and imposed a ten-year prison term on anyone assisting a woman in an abortion.[41] In the Netherlands, the first law to be explicit about abortion was passed in 1836. As late as 1911, the law was tightened, making abortion a crime in all cases except for severe medical reasons.[42] In Italy, Mussolini adopted the code of one of his ministers (the Rocco Code) in the 1920s. Similar laws were set in place all over Europe, wherever nationalism and the new racial ideologies had taken hold. Indeed, the idea of "populate or perish" was intrinsically tied to nationalism, to the fears of the new nations *and* to their assertiveness.

It is hardly surprising that women, who alone fully understood the enormity of state intervention, were also the first to find these antiabortion laws oppressive in the extreme. Depending on the speed of industrialization in each country concerned, it was soon recognized that the harsh penal codes imposed an impossible burden on working-class women who had to produce children they could not feed, and who could barely find the strength to carry them to full term. The biological processes of reproduction were often not well understood, and contraception was not known, not available, or not reliable. Abstinence from sexual activity, late marriage, or abortion were the only widely practiced social remedies to conception. However, more working-class women got

15

married, and tended to get married earlier, than middle-class women because adult independence was financially possible only with a partner.

Indeed, statistics from around the turn of the century show that as many as 30 percent of middle-class women had never been married by the age of forty. Moreover, more children stayed alive because of the advances in medicine in the late nineteenth century. The Dutch medical practitioner Aletta Jacobs (1854–1929), was one of the first women to devote her energies entirely to women's reproductive health problems. She established a free clinic for poor women in Amsterdam and also pioneered the introduction of birth control methods where this appeared to be medically or socially advisable.[43] But no critic succeeded against the powers of international competition, warfare, and ruthless nationalistic state management.

2.2 Subversive Energies

It took little time for astute women to realize that the implications of the idea of nationalism worked very much against them, their welfare, their (potential) rights, their quality of life, and their views. Then the suffragette movement spread throughout western Europe. All the prohibitions put into place after the failure of 1848 were ultimately futile. It is an immutable fact that people's will to freedom cannot be squashed once they have had the minutest taste of it. At the same time that reactionary forces won the day in Europe, a radical tradition, despite being forced underground or severely curtailed, became stronger and precisely because of the asperity with which that tradition was sought to be eradicated. Karl Marx and Friedrich Engels's writings had begun to make a lasting impact, and socialism, communism, and a number of other radical groups gained in strength and membership.

By and large, the ideology of nationalism could *not* furnish women with a vehicle for protest. Nationalism in Europe had turned too quickly into anti-individuality and against active participation, successfully overlaying the democratic grid on which it might have been built. Women's choices were then to side with ideologies that clearly identified individual and group oppression. Such radical ideas were available. One of their chief ingredients, however, was that from the outset they were *international* in orientation. That such "internationalism" was still largely Eurocentric is a separate problem, but at least it was transnational and clearly *antinationalistic*.

Symptomatic of this shift of radical ideas from functioning locally to their appeal in an "international" forum was *The Communist Manifesto* written and distributed by Marx and Engels in London in 1847–1848. "Workers of the world unite" was a blueprint for action that not just ignored national boundaries but consciously made a statement against nationalism. Problems of class oppression were no longer specific to one nation. Women's oppression also then was not a national but, rather, a universal concern. Hence, these two strands of traditions, for a while at least, could enter into a new partnership. In 1864 the First International took place in London and was attended by a substantial number of women. In 1878 the First International Congress for Women's Rights was held, and in 1892 the first international congress to label itself feminist took place.[44] In 1889 the Second International, on specific request by the German Socialists, saw perhaps the most important union between international socialism and feminism ever to be forged in a general political platform. This was largely due to the work of Clara Zetkin (1857–1933), who became the leader of the national and international proletarian women's movement (and had to leave Germany because of her radicalism). During the congress at the Second International she gave a paper that, as is generally agreed, was instrumental in incorporating women and women's issues in the socialist movement. Indeed, once published as *The Contemporary Women Workers and Women's Question* (1889), it formed the basis of the women's emancipation theory of the party.[45] As Boulding rightly argued:

> By 1880 they [women of the West] were prepared to bypass the nationalistic struggles of Europe and forge alternative structures for the solution of what they already perceived to be global, not national problems, of social justice and human welfare. Although they had begun nationally in associations for peace, in anti-slavery organizations , , , , by the 1880s they were prepared to act internationally. In the international socialist movement as elsewhere they stood for decentralism, non-violence and grassroots activity on behalf of human welfare.[46]

Organizationally, international feminism spread rapidly. In 1888 the International Council of Women was formed by American feminists. At its 1899 congress in London, several countries were represented by their own national councils, such as Denmark, Holland, Great Britain, Ireland, Germany, and Sweden. There were also delegates from Austria, Switzerland, Italy, Norway, and Russia, and observers from France and Belgium. In 1904 the International Women's Suffrage Alliance became the International Alliance of Women.

Let me repeat: European feminism was *not* comfortable within the confines of the nation-state. It generally did not embrace nationalism but stood in defiance of it. Many women had to leave their own countries in order to pursue feminist goals. Yet the "angels of history" were not to fly forward into the future. The Western world moved toward war and often enough this absorbed the energies of feminists. Bertha von Suttner (1843–1914), the first recipient of the Nobel Peace Prize, founded an Austrian and German pacifist organization in 1891. Her book, *Down with the Weapons,* initially published in 1889, was translated into almost every European language and had gone through more than thirty editions and reprints by 1910.[47] French writer Hélène Brion, known for her feminist critique of socialist and unionist insensitivity to women's issues (*La voie féministe: femme, ose être!* [The feminist way: woman, dare to be!], was tried for pacifist propaganda and imprisoned in 1918. At a time of revival of strong nationalistic sentiments in France and an ongoing nationalistic sentiment in Britain and Germany, these lone voices of women were not able to stem the tide of international politics.

2.3 Republican and Democratic Reprieve

There was a period in early-twentieth-century western European history when feminists could return to their countries and attempt to build at home on the ideas they had developed and promulgated in an international forum. Indeed, 1918, which marked the end of World War I, was a crucial year in modern European history. It saw some substantial changes in Europe's political landscape, many of which, however, were quickly contested again. Iceland had just won independence from Denmark and proclaimed itself as a monarchy (1918), Finland had gained independence from Russia (1917). With the collapse of the Habsburg Empire (1918) and the reshuffle of political borders at the end of World War I, Austria entered European politics as a republic and as an independent country for the first time, a republic that folded with Hitler's annexation in 1934. Likewise, Yugoslavia emerged as a new kingdom, and Hungary, Czechoslovakia, and Poland were proclaimed independent republics. A little later Greece entered an eleven-year period of republicanism (1924–1935), until the monarchy was restored and the new prime minister Metaxas began to exercise dictatorial powers, throwing Greece into one of the bloodiest and most devastating periods in its history. Portugal's troubled republic—forty-four governments and eight presidents—lasted for sixteen years (1910–1926); in that time women were awarded equal rights, strong radical feminist groups sprung up, and the rhetoric then had a good deal in common with that which occurred after Portugal's so-called Carnation Revolution of 1974. Spain's republican era (1931–1939) was thwarted by the Falangist Party and Franco, ending the Spanish Civil War, and ending as well a very lively period of national renewal, progressive reform legislation, and left-wing party activity.[48] Not only were women highly represented in left-wing party activity but they formed their own radical, anarchist, syndicalist and feminist organizations. They gained civil rights and actively took part in their society. All these rights were revoked in 1939, and returned again only after Franco's death in 1975. Germany's Weimar Republic lasted only fifteen years (1918–1933).

In the period 1918–1933, views and laws concerning women, especially in relation to love and sex (for example, the use of contraceptives among working-class women), and work were to some extent successfully challenged. For instance, in Germany in 1926, incarceration penalties for abortion were changed from time in high-security prisons (*Zuchthäuser*) to time in low-security prisons. In 1931 a spectacular "I have aborted" campaign against the abortion law was publicly staged, and there was every indication that the law might have been modified or repealed had the Nazis not won the election. Writing from Stockholm, the Russian feminist Alexandra Kollontaj fervently defended women's right to sexual and social liberty. Polish-born Rosa Luxemburg, the founder of democratic communism, coined the famous thesis "Freedom is always the freedom of the dissenter," and her most popular work, *Reform and Revolution* (1899), like the writings of Kollontaj, left a lasting imprint on European feminist thought (even though she was said to have once declared that feminism was for old ladies). Both women became important sources of inspiration for many new-wave feminist movements in the 1970s, chiefly in Italy.[49]

In every country trialing democratic governments, a sudden burst of activities showed that action was taken to right the wrongs and put into place legal and social structures that would fulfill democratic ideals. Among these ideals were concerns about women's status. During this period, women in some countries were enfranchised. In Finland, women gained the vote in 1906; in Norway in 1913; in Denmark and Iceland, in 1915; in Luxembourg and Poland, in 1918; in Sweden, Germany, Czechoslovakia, and the Netherlands, in 1919; in Ireland in 1922; in Britain, in 1928; and in Spain, in 1931. In most Scandinavian countries, the right to vote built on already substantial rights for women that were not generally available in other parts of Europe. For a brief period, then, women were considered equal before the law and, in most democratic countries, had rights to employment and property. It is unlikely that *any* feminists of that period would have considered themselves nationalistic. Indeed, one invariably precluded the other. They saw instead that their role in democratic nation-states had to be that of a citizen with a right to participation.

2.4 Totalitarianism and Fascism

The doors for emancipation closed almost as quickly as they had opened. Most republics and monarchies degenerated into dictatorships and right-wing ideologies. Fascism and national socialism swept through Europe from the mid-1920s onward. It is important to realize that the new *nationalist* right-wing movements were instrumental in abolishing every freedom women had just gained in the brief spells of democracy. The constitutions of most western European countries of the mid- to late 1930s said nothing of women and/or actively deprived them of the most basic and fundamental liberties. Except for Scandinavian countries, first and foremost Sweden, women were not allowed to keep their own property and income, and had no control over their children, assets or any aspect of their lives. Many European state laws expressly permitted husbands to chastise their wives. The Portuguese Penal Code went so far as implicitly to permit a husband to kill his unfaithful wife; the crime had no prison sentence attached to it, merely the stipulation that its perpetrator had to leave his province for three months.[50] In Spain, legislation reverted to the legal codes of 1839 (Commercial Code) and 1889 (Civil Code). Once again, ecclesiastical tribunals became the sole arbiters on love, marriage, sexuality, and child custody, and the "ghost of the Inquisition moved through the lives of many unfortunate women."[51] Mussolini, founder of the Italian fascist party, ensured that women were housebound in every way. Husbands could even accuse their wives in court if they had "strayed" too far from the house. Men were allowed to rape women without legal repercussions. Every birth, death, and life decision was entirely in the hands of the husband, father, or any male relative in the family deemed to be its "head." In Germany, the "*Kinder, Küche, Kirche*" ideology combined again with lofty nationalistic tunes: the German woman was a source of comfort, pride, and Germanic sobriety if she stayed at home and produced children.[52] In all dictatorships, fascist and totalitarian regimes, women were the producers of children, be this to provide cannon fodder (Mussolini), to help "invigorate the race" (Hitler), or to work as servants of men (Salazar, Franco). Biology indeed became destiny.[53]

World War II (1939–1945) then added for women the nightmare of enforced conscriptions into labor camps, war factories, and "breeding" programs (for example, the German *Lebensborn)*, and the horrors of concentration camps, forced sterilization, starvation, and death. Perhaps there has been no time in European history in which the contempt for women has ever reached such psychotic heights as in the first half of this century. Misogyny is not sufficient to explain, and not entirely appropriate in elucidating, the perverse attitudes toward women at the time, oscillating as they did between extreme nationalistic pathos, a sickly sexual attraction and even asexual veneration, and a psychopathy similar to that of sexual serial killers. The untold and unsung stories of women's suffering and their personal tragedies have almost no equal to those consciously inflicted on women in the twentieth century—in the name of nationalism and nationalistic assertiveness.

In terms of the connection between feminism and nationalism, a very special constellation needs to be mentioned here, one which occurred only in Germany. *Feminism* was of course staunchly opposed to national socialism but often *women* who had a particular interest in women's issues were not. Ironically, it was under the Nazi movement, as a distinctly *nationalistic* movement, that women were officially hailed as being of particular value, honor, and unassailable sanctity as wives and mothers. In 1933, in the very year of Hitler's seizing of power, Karl Beyer entitled his book on women's issues *Die Gleichstellung der Frauen im Nationalsozialischen Deutschland* (the equality of women in national socialist Germany). In it he proclaimed that for the first time since Germanic tribal times, and only under this new nationalistic ideology, women had been raised to a status of *equality*, to an exalted position within society. Equality, in the Nazi jargon, had of course absolutely nothing to do with social or legal equality. It was based on purely biological and racial grounds. Beyer exclaimed that "all man's work would wither without the nourishing juices and strength that rise out of womanhood and motherhood. . . . Without the equality of women no German people can exist."[54] There was, then, a role and even a pedestal for women (that should read: for women prepared to marry and bear children, provided they were of impeccable "Aryan" stock, preferably blond and blue-eyed, and "unblemished" sexually). Countless women responded favorably to the call by the *Fuhrer.*

Indeed, there *were* many women who were ardently interested in women's issues and equally ardently embraced national socialism in the firm belief that it had the answer for women's liberation or what they perceived as liberation. But these were not feminists.

It is clear that in Nazi Germany women responded in the first instance to the *nationalistic* call. In Hitler's Germany, *every* German was to be a proud German once again. The mass propaganda machine pounded in that one message. Young people saw the arrival of Hitler as the arrival of a national liberator: "Germany is awakening. . . . everywhere the people are rising up . . . for Hitler, Father, for freedom and bread."[55] He was the leader who would wipe away the repugnant Treaty of Versailles (1919), which the historian Golo Mann in agreement with Hitler described as late as 1964 as an "unspeakable instrument for the subjugation, exploitation and constant offence of Germany."[56] And Hitler was the leader who publicly acknowledged the importance of women, so many thought.

There were certainly *no* feminists among those women who embraced the new *nationalistic* ideologies. There were no feminists who supported Franco, Salazar, Metaxas, Pilsudski, Mussolini, or Hitler. These feminists belonged invariably to political camps of the Left, which were systematically hounded, tortured, imprisoned, and killed—and obliterated from the national culture. In a sense, the bleak European history does not stop in 1945. Many of the antiwomen laws instigated under right-wing terror were not rescinded for decades after the dictators had gone. It took until the 1960s in Italy and West Germany, and even until the 1970s in Austria, before the most misogynist and/or fascist laws were removed. In Portugal, the nation and women were freed in 1974; in Spain, with the death of Franco (1975), and in Greece, as recently as the fall of the junta and the election of the PASOK government in 1981. It is only from then on that the horrible metaphor of the "angel of history" has begun to lose its meaning. But these events also signaled the end of overtly nationalistic ideologies and governments.

Feminism in western Europe, from its overt political beginnings in the nineteenth century to the present, has been affected by nationalism in the sense that as a consequence of nationalistic programs, feminism is aligned with parties of the Left.[57] Thus, Europe has developed very little of the "liberal" feminism of the United States. Instead, western European feminism tends to be more radical and more marked by the language and ideas of Marxism, Leninism, communism, and socialism than in Western industrialized nations outside Europe.

In its *strategies* of political action, feminism in Europe has been vastly influenced by the negative experiences under right-wing terror. In Franco's Spain, for instance, women had been meticulously segregated from men in all areas of life. So effective was this division that female factory workers had no idea of the work and life of male factory workers. Their different conditions of employment became apparent only after Franco's death and the fall of the Falange Party. This segregation of women into entirely different spheres made Spanish feminists wish for coeducation and gender-shared living and working spaces. Never again would they want to be isolated on the grounds of gender. In Italy and Germany, feminists were equally eager to avoid any structural or other similarity with former fascist women's groups. The new German feminist, movement adamantly rejected any hierarchization. The most obvious feature of West Germany's new-wave movement was its autonomy: without a center of power, without hierarchy, without obvious formal organization, and without formal spokespersons it had clearly responded against the tight Nazi organization of women's groups and women's activities throughout the Third Reich. Even the term *movement* had been tainted by fascist governments, who used it to underpin and demonstrate their legitimacy, that is, to point to the mass support for their ideology. In Italy, feminists were adamant that they ought to battle for reform and change through the political parties, and/or in conjunction with men, because fascist governments had shown that even the largest segregated women's organizations were completely and utterly ineffectual in the political arena.[58] Italian women were determined that their claims remained on the programme of political parties. Thus, even in the aftermath of the worst aberrations of nationalism this century, feminists have responded by staying clear of any suggestion, idea, action, structure, and goal that somehow fitted the nationalistic ideology of their country in the past.

Part 3. Feminism and Nationalism: The Exceptional Cases

There are some positive European examples of the relationship between nationalism and feminism, more than have so far been implied. But such examples are often a brief or even chance encounter between the two ideologies, occurring when specific trends intersected in a country or happened more by accident than design, when women were catapulted into the political foreground, and these women *were* feminists. This is not to be confused with acts of patriotism. In Italy and France, women were given the right to vote as acknowledgment of and as the nation's reward for their outstanding services in the resistance against Nazi domination in 1944 and 1945, respectively. In both countries, women had played a dominant role during the war and, in the absence of men, often the only role in keeping underground movements against the Nazis alive.[59] At the time of national crisis, it was recognized that without the courageous acts of women, much would have been lost.

3.1 Italy

In most cases, to reverse Minogue's metaphor used above, feminism as a new set of beliefs in the equality of women remained a sleeping beauty at a time of nationalist revival. Embalmed, venerated, and treasured, it remained under a glass dome in full view of anyone who wanted to visit the shrine. This was certainly the case in Italy. Italian northern city culture of the Renaissance and beyond had boasted many women in leading cultural and academic positions. They occupied chairs at Italian universities—and one may take note that these chairs were largely in fields of science[60]—were leaders in the arts and in famous salons.

During the period of the *risorgimento* (national reawakening) from 1815 to 1870, however, women's issues as well as notable public female figures disappeared almost entirely. It seemed as if the period of most intense nationalism, led by such liberal and capable men as Guiseppe Garibaldi (1807–1882), Guiseppe Mazzini (1805–1872), and Camillo Count Benso di Cavour (1810–1861), was mutually exclusive with women's issues, let alone feminism.

But there were exceptions. In northern Italian provinces, the Casati law of 1861 permitted women to become teachers, and there were some women who combined ardent nationalism with feminism. The most noteworthy of these were Anita Garibaldi, the wife of the revolutionary leader of the *risorgimento* movement, and Cristina di Belgiojoso. In 1866 Belgiojoso published the first critical feminist account of women's position, *Scritto sulla condizione della donne* (writings on the condition of women), but it remained almost without repercussions, largely because Italy was constantly at war in order to achieve its independence from the French Bourbons, who ruled the South; from the House of Habsburg, who ruled the North; and from the Vatican, which ruled the center of

Italy. Thus, in 1859 the Italian Unification War unified cities and a large part of the Vatican lands, and succeeded in expelling the Bourbons from Naples and Sicily. In 1866 Garibaldi led troops against the Austrian Habsburgs in the German War, which wrested Venice from the Habsburgs, in addition to the Lombardy captured before, and in 1862 and 1867, against the Vatican. The Vatican fell in 1871 when, because of the outbreak of war between the German and French, Napoleon had to withdraw from Rome his troops who had protected the pope since 1849.

In the Italy of the nineteenth century, nationalism and feminism were however not necessarily incompatible or pitted against each other. The latter was merely postponed in favor of the urgent need for unification. Italy faced the huge task of restructuring and internally unifying Italian politics and society. The north and the south had been separate political entities for centuries and had developed substantially differently. The North began industrialization relatively early in the second half of the nineteenth century; the South remained agricultural and backward. It was in the North where socialist ideas, unionism, and feminism took root and expanded very quickly. In the forefront of concern for Italian feminists were, at first, not the typical bourgeois middle-class issues of enfranchisement, property, custody, and assets legal reform, as in other countries. Instead, they saw their most urgent task as helping working-class women who labored under the most appalling conditions in the northern factories. Socialist influence ensured the formation of working-women's groups and politically active groups intent on improving working conditions. In 1889 female textile workers formed the first union, and in 1890–1891, Milano had its first women-workers' association. At that time, strike actions became more frequent; rice pickers in the Emilia, for instance, rose on several occasions, first in 1883.[61]

There were feminists of impressive caliber and leadership, capable of turning the plight of working women into a matter of public debate and national concern. Thus, Anna Kuliscioff addressed the nation before the 1897 elections, calling the dismal conditions of the 1.5 million working women a national disgrace. Just eight years after Clara Zetkin's famous merger of socialist and feminist ideals at the Second International in Paris, Kuliscioff achieved inclusion of the legal and political equality between men and women into the political program of the Italian Socialist Party. Perhaps even more important was the work of Anna Maria Mozzoni, who had already advocated women's rights before the unification of Italy. She was able to break through the class nexus by pointing out that the goal had to be the liberation of every woman, for she was exploited not only in the labor force but also in the home. The ideal of women's liberation from *any* form of oppression in 1881 led her to found a league for the promotion of women's interests. This is the organization that has been identified as the feminist-socialist forerunner of the Udi (Unione Donne Italiane), which was to play an important role in Italian life after World War II. By 1897, when the Italian nation was a mere sixteen years old, the first National Women's Association was formed in Rome. Two years later Milan saw the first National Women's Union, and 1903 the National Council of Italian Women.

The first two decades of the twentieth century were times of extreme labor unrest in Italy. Be this in the new workers' movement, in the radical parties, on the union floor, in some of the largest mass strikes in the world of that time, or in massive antiwar demonstrations, Italian society at large was highly politicized and prepared to participate actively in the country's political fate. It is probably not exaggerative to argue that nationalistic ideals were as much a part of worker radicalism as class-specific interests. Of great importance also was the founding of the Communist Party in the 1920s, on the eve of Mussolini's fascist dictatorship. The Communist Party at once took up the feminist issues. Significantly, it treated the *questione femminile* (women's question) not just as an urgent *social* issue but also as "one of the great unresolved *national* questions" (emphasis added).[62]

It has already been said that, with Mussolini, a very different nationalism became the order of the day and women's organizations and all parties of the Left were eventually ousted. A severe antidemocratic period began, reflected also in antiwoman legislation and in the persecution of writers and thinkers, who, such as Antonio Gramsci and Camilla Ravera, went to prison, and often to their death. We also know that Italian feminism and radicalism did not disappear, despite the severe oppression of any leftist ideologies. If anything, at least underground they gained in strength and in conviction and this eventually (1940–1945) led to the formation of well-organized partisan/resistance fighting groups throughout the country, in which large numbers of women actively worked, risked and gave their lives.

These *partigiani* (partisans) in World War II acquired some fame in the postwar years. Italians even called the *partigiani* fights their second *risorgimento*. And indeed, in matters of national renewal, of (re-)building Italian society after the humiliations of World War II, the partisans had done a great deal to offer the nation an acceptable alternative vision. Immediately after the war, it was under the leadership of the Socialist Party and the Communist Party that a republican constitution was drawn up. Palmiro Togliatti, the leader of the Communist Party, continued to champion women's rights, and in these first postwar years (1945–1946), the idealism, nationalist rhetoric, the professed goals of egalitarianism, and a just society were not all empty promises. In 1946, 53 percent of all voters were women and twenty-two women became delegates in the constituent assembly. The women who became active in politics were more often than not feminists who had taken an active part in the communist-led resistance movement during the war. Indeed, women's presence in politics after the war well exceeded that of most western European countries. In this second *risorgimento*, Italy experienced a *heightened* national consciousness. The vocabulary of the *political* parties that drafted the new Italian constitution in 1945 was rather similar to that of the feminists, who, more often than not, had also been partisans. Both argued for liberty, for participatory democracy, and for the end of oppression on the grounds of class or gender.

The link between nationalism and feminism in the Italian case can be easily misread and misrepresented. Nationalism in Italy meant two things: One meaning of nationalism was derived from the desire to unify Italy and to rid the country of the hated foreign rulers. However, under Mussolini, nationalism was used quite differently, as the justification for dictatorial rule. Italy is perhaps the only western European country, excepting Scandinavian countries, where women's issues, up to the present time, have remained on the political agenda of the nation. Feminism is certainly part of the landscape of national renewal.

3.2 Finland

The developments in Finland deserve special mention because they constitute a special case in European history. Finland today is the one country in the world with the highest employment of women in politics and in the professions, and possibly with the highest overall employment rate of women in any country; the most equal pay distribution between men and women; and possibly the greatest degree of emancipation among women. However, Finnish women, and indeed Finnish governments, do not spare themselves self-criticism. It was Elina Haavio-Mannila who edited the important book *Unfinished Democracy,* and the Statistical Bureau in Finland that published a gendered interpretation of its own society,

concluding that women fared not at all well in terms of the country's professed aims at equality.[63] Be this as it may, the statistics are very favorable
in comparison to the rest of western Europe, indeed to the rest of the
world. And the question arises why an outpost of Europe, largely agricultural up to the second half of this century, sparsely populated (it now
has a population of only five million), and rather marginal to European
and world events, has achieved such outstanding results in gender terms.
The first countries in the world to give women the vote were New
Zealand (1893) and Australia (1902). Within Europe, however, Finland
was the first country to enfranchise women (1906). At that time, Finland
was not a separate country but a grand duchy under Russian rule.

I elaborate on these historical developments here in order to elucidate
one of the very rare cases in Europe in which feminism and nationalism
went together. It is one instance of an intersection of events that allowed
women to develop an ideological position at the time, or even before, a
political national platform had developed or fully matured. Expressed differently, Finland was unlike other nations, which either subscribed to nationalism because they were concerned exclusively with securing
independence, as Ireland,[64] or did so to expand own territory and power,
as England. In Finland, the rhetoric for self-determination was *coeval* with
goals of achieving prosperity and social progress, and it seems that the
combination of these two goals from the outset will create an environment that is very differently predisposed to social issues, and to women's
issues, than in cases in which that combination of goals is absent.

Until 1809 the Finnish territories had been under Swedish rule for
seven hundred years. In the Peace of Hamina that relationship was severed
and Finland was turned into a Russian province under Tsar Alexander I.
Initially, the new Russian orientation worked well and the Finnish aristocracy not only was loyal to the tsar but was able to enter into service in
the Russian empire. But gradually the relationship deteriorated, partly because the Finnish aristocracy became insolvent and partly because of Russian chauvinism that no longer looked very favorably on the provincial
peers. The Finns were thus left in a vacuum, still speaking Swedish (among
the educated) but no longer Swedish, not speaking Russian but under
Russian suzerainty. Matti Klinge explains that being no longer Swedish
and unable to become Russians, the Finns responded in a fairly low key:
"Let us be Finns."[65] That concept required some major adjustments. For
instance, Finnish was almost exclusively the language of peasants: it was
not used anywhere in official circles, in government, administration, and

the military, or among the educated. It was often not even known as a second language. After the secession from Sweden, a slow process of rebuilding a linguistically specific Finnish heritage began. In 1831, the first Finnish literary society was founded in Helsinki and it set about discovering and uncovering a national culture in folklore, poetry (The Elk Hunters), and epic stories such as the *Kalevala*. Finnish had to be introduced in schools and taught to the aristocracy. In 1850 the first professor of the Finnish language was appointed, and in 1863 Finnish was proclaimed the official language together with Swedish.[66] This literally meant that Finnish nationalists, usually derived from the educated classes and the aristocracy, consciously decided to forgo their mother tongue (Swedish).

In terms of the revival of Finnish as a culture, it was important to get as many children to school as possible, also from peasant stock. Before 1870 only 7 percent of students were from peasant backgrounds; by 1880 the percentage had already doubled and it continued to increase through the last decades of the century.[67] To my knowledge, there was no gender distinction made, and girls were able to enter schools quite early. The issue of national revival (after more than seven hundred years!) among such a low number of people (just over two million in 1880) simply did not permit exclusion of females. From 1886 on, women were able to get a university education. It is also noteworthy that in the same period a slow but steady urbanization took place, creating a small yet visible middle class for the first time. Between 1870 and 1910, the urban population trebled, although even then it was still under 15 percent of the total population. Moreover, the university in Helsinki and its students began to play an increasingly important role in this emerging Finnish nationalism.

Finnish nationalists were keen on strengthening the Finnish national character by means of language and culture, and the liberals began to emphasize the need of Finnish political independence. Both strands of nationalism, in whatever form they appeared in the political parties, had little if any broad support in the country as a whole. It appealed to the wealthy peasantry but otherwise stayed confined within the "narrow milieu of the political and cultural elite."[68]

Mass movements were largely unknown in Finland in the nineteenth century, a working class did not come into being until the early twentieth century, and its peasantry, unlike its European mainland counterparts, had never known serfdom or the brutal oppression that followed the abolition of serfdom (a Swedish influence). However, in 1899 the Finnish Labor Party was founded and within the span of a mere six years had captured substantial support from the countryside. The Russian revolution of 1905–1906 further radicalized the party and its members into a more revolutionary Marxist ideology than before. The radicalization was helped by a more militant presence of Russia in the Finnish province. For instance, in 1900 a Russian decree ordered that Russian become the principal language of Finnish administration, and a year later, a military service law ordered the absorption of the Finnish military into the Russian Empire. Both decrees fueled Finnish resistance and undoubtedly helped to intensify support for political nationalism. In 1910 Russian legislation stipulated that all laws of general state interest were to be made by Russian institutions.[69] This confrontational path of Russia vis-à-vis its Finnish province vastly accelerated Finnish determination for independence.

At the height of the socialist movement, which in 1906 had more than 100,000 members, women were enfranchised. By the first parliamentary election of 1907, the labor movement had firmly entered parliament (80 seats), and by 1916, the Finnish Marxist party was the first and only one in the world to win a clear majority (103 seats) in parliamentary elections before the Russian Revolution.[70] A year later, in 1917, the socialist movement managed to gain mass support for Finnish nationalism. The brief "War of Independence" momentarily succeeded in displacing class antagonisms and vested interests with national solidarity, and it succeeded in winning political independence from Russia that same year.

The role of women in the development of Finnish nationalism is as much marred by vested interests, class, and education factors as that of men. However, the first Finnish women's movement was in itself to some extent a proclamation of Finnish nationalism. In 1884, the Finnish Women's Association was formed, staking its role firmly within Finnish *national* events, even before the Labor Party was founded. Several other associations sprang to life shortly thereafter, and these organizations, unlike such groups in other European countries, *coincided* with the formation and consolidation of political parties and a new, distinctly *national* political platform. The Young Women's Union, for instance, fought hard to argue for equal pay, to gain women the vote, and to ensure that "many of its members" were sent to the first Finnish parliament.[71] The ideological platform of the new women's groups was certainly left-wing in orientation and in many ways already distinctly feminist.

Here, then, was a unique constellation of developing new political structures at the very time when women gathered for the first time to seek rights for themselves. There were Finnish women in parliament from

the very beginning. Women's presence in politics and in elected governments at a rate of 10 percent was more than unusual: in no other European country, and possibly in the world, were women in politics at that
time (1907) and in such numbers. It might also be noted that the participation of Finnish women in government in 1907 exceeded the percentage of women in politics in many European countries in 1991. That
position of women in public life, both in politics and in the labor force
(Finnish women made up 37 percent of the labor force in 1910), was
never lost again.[72]

In contradistinction to other European territories that also made a bid
for nationalism and political independence as nation-states, such as Italy
and Germany, there were no comparable entrenched political parties and
it is true to some extent that Finnish nationalism did not have to grapple
with well-entrenched regional politics, at least not on the scale as in German and Italian territories, nor for the same reasons. The outmoded
three-tier voting system, which had benefited the aristocracy and left
one-third of the Finnish population without a vote, was overthrown and
in its place suffrage was made universal. It was not a matter of unification
but a matter of gaining independence. In that sense Haavio-Mannila was
right in arguing, somewhat cynically, that the entry of Finnish women
into politics earlier than anywhere else in the world was precisely possible
because new political structures were only beginning to evolve and had
not yet become a male bastion.[73]

The Finnish case refutes the notion that women do not like politics
because of its structure and formality. Rather, it exemplifies that some of
the very real barriers for women's entry into politics are barriers created
purely on gender antagonism alone. In Finland, the time when the general political, social, and economic climate supported the ideals for a
thorough transformation of society fell together with women's claims for
rights and for a change in gender relations. In other words, women's issues, if perhaps only surreptitiously, had become part of national issues.

Part 4. Regional "Nationalism" and Feminism

In present-day Europe, there is another trend worth noting. European
unification, symbolized and given effect by the Maastricht Treaty in 1993,
has given rise to new trends. Globalization and regionalism are two divergent but complementary responses away from or even against the na-

31

tion-state and national identity. As yet the theoretical framework for a supranational, let alone global, citizenship is far from view. If present trends continue, national identities may become anachronistic and hence eventually superfluous (in agreement with Bryan Turner).[74]

In Europe, there are interesting developments in this direction. For instance, supranational alliances have raised the issue of regionalism in a new way. In the past, nation-states were forged largely by enforcing limits or even by suppressing particularism. A leveling of the nation-states in favor of a large federative entity of the European Communities should eventually diminish the former importance of nation-states. National borders are an anathema to effective capitalism, and Europe is removing as many of them as it can manage. In such a substantial structural shift, particularism and regionalism get a new lease on life.

Regional claims for self-assertion have taken on the format of *nationalist* claims in some instances. One of the earliest examples even prior to formation of the European Union occurred in the Basque lands and in Catalonia in Spain. Franco's repressive measures against the ETA (*Euskadi Ta Azkatasum*, Basque Lands and Liberty), led to international attention and outrage.[75] Basque nationalism has been fought for by men and women alike, both with their own radical agendas. Here, to some extent, the revolutionary idea of liberation from domination has led to a marriage with feminism. One suspects that the reason for this alliance is similar to that of the Finnish nationalists. In each case, the number of dissenters was too small to ignore women as potential and real allies.

We may well see more examples of regional "nationalism" in concert with feminism in future, if and where there is some evidence of "oppression" of individual liberty and the movement strong enough to gain grassroots support. Moreover, some radical groups, as we know, have inadvertently preached regionalism for some decades now. For example, environmentalist groups have coined the slogan "small is beautiful," some have even proposed the backward-looking (nonprogressive) yearning for "the community," the village, the premedieval harmony with nature sustainable in small kin or clan groups.

The reactionary tendencies of nationalism, so well practiced in Europe for such a long time, have now led to an unholy alliance of the worst aspects of provincialism with the hollow sounds of a lofty nationalism. Within the context of the waning importance of the nation-state the "Frankenstein's monster" has reawakened, exemplified by the radical right-wing organizations that have made headlines over the past two decades: be this the British National Front, the West German Republikaner, the French National Front, Italian neo-fascism, or the revival of racism right across Europe.[76] There is indeed a dark side to Europe.[77]

As we know, the rise of reactionary forces, even if they are seemingly directed against specific "isms" or groups, has always harmed women. In these cases, feminists will remain well above and outside regionalism and nationalism, becoming once again an oppositional force, and they will continue to attempt to influence the thinking at the European summit level, where, at this moment, considerable efforts have led to supranational feminist organizations and to guidelines protecting basic rights of women.

In 1988, Helen D'Ancona declared that the European Community was the legislatively most progressive political community for women in the world.[78] From the point of view of legislature this may well be true, but what does this mean in reality? My reading of current opinions and literature suggests only qualified support for the achievements of the European Community in terms of the 1979 UN Declaration for the Elimination of all Forms of Discrimination Against Women. "The deficiency of the EECT and its amendments," Fritz Fabricius rightly argued, "is that they do not contemplate any legal-normative basis on which social policies may be formulated."[79] Hence, sociopolitical issues fall far short of the benefits that the European Union might have rendered to its members. This design creates blind spots in the areas of work that *do* fall within the province of the *European* planning and implementation. Among these blind spots are many of the highly relevant and important social preconditions and/or consequences of work. Women especially are affected by consideration or lack thereof of the social context in which work is sought and maintained.

Moreover, at European summit levels the political climate of opinion in recent years has shifted from a social democratic preponderance in favor of conservative forces. This is reflected in attitude changes. Once these were prowork, proindependence of women, and hence proinfrastructure development (such as kindergartens and other service provisions), and now there are more assertive conservative attitudes in favor of proprivacy, profamily and anti-infrastructure developments. Feminist members of the various units at the European parliamentary level, however, were largely recruited from around or within the field of experienced feminist lobbyists, administrators, academicians, and politicians. They usually now find themselves fighting the same battles of opposition that were fought twenty years ago. In the Session Documents of the European Parliament (European Network), of January 1994, the minutes

33

record that, *de jure*, women in Europe today face no barriers in the public domain as citizens, in political parties, by politicians or even in the private sector. *De facto*, however, women continue to be "grossly and persistently underrepresented."[80]

In a recent report of the Global Summit of Women, "Women and Political Leadership," one of the explicit strategies for women's participation in politics was expressed in the following terms:

Point 2: To encourage elected women representatives at all levels to create caucuses between women of all parties, regardless of affiliation and across party lines, in order to lobby, pass legislation and encourage increasing numbers of women into politics.

Point 3: To encourage women to vote for male as well as female representatives that push legislation that upholds women's rights and supports their agenda.[81]

The International Alliance of Women Politicians was established in 1994 and will be operational for the next Global Summit meeting in Barcelona in 1996. It seems to me that the numbers game here has gone far beyond representative functions and traditional party politics, especially if women are willing to enunciate a common cause *across* party lines. The European administration and government leave much to be desired if this numbers game is the measuring stick that is applied. Women have certainly forged a presence in national governments (see figure below) but one notes that they have done not nearly as well as in Finland, which has continued to provide the lead in the world with respect to women in politics.[82]

The link here between nationalism and feminism seems to reconfirm that unless women's overall feminist agenda is firmly embedded at the center of political life, women will continue to lose out. In the public policy area, progress on women's equality has been arrested to an extent that leading female politicians gathered in the Committee on Women's Rights in 1993 around the slogan "The democratic deficit in question." Indeed, the meeting's project was to expose, emphasize, question, and challenge the deficits of the emerging European democracy. At the conclusion of this meeting, they felt the need to devise another "declaration," the now-famous Athens Declaration, reminiscent of manifestos in the nineteenth century, such as the Declaration of Rights for Women of 1876, referred to at the beginning of this chapter. The Athens Declaration

PERCENTAGE OF WOMEN IN
GOVERNMENT/EC MEMBER STATES

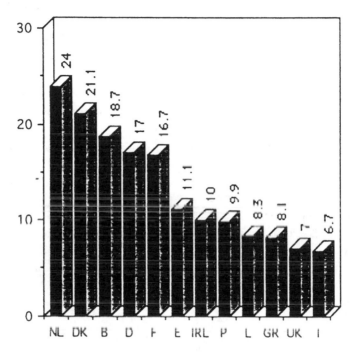

Source: European Network Women in Decision-Making, 1992, Year of data:
IRL and NL, 1989, DK, 1990, E and P, 1991; remainder, 1992, p. 65.

argues for nothing less than coresponsibility of women (Hannah Arendt's term[84]). It is noteworthy that, apart from the UK, the only western European countries which made *full* allowance for women's rights and women's equality in all areas of life (employment, and family and marriage) were Portugal, Spain, and Italy. Even *de jure* women's rights are not yet firmly installed, let alone *de facto*.

Klaus von Dohnanyi, state secretary of the Foreign Office in Bonn (1976–1981), argued that the nationalism of the nation-states pre-1945, which was military in orientation and symbolized by flags, soldiers, and weapon, is passé for good. His optimism is reassuring. He also suggested, however, that in the new supranational alignment of nations within the European Communities, the *social* systems of each nation will inevitably be bound more strongly to national/local forces.[85] Internationalism, once the backbone of leftist organizations and of feminism for the sake of the *op- pressed* and *exploited*, has experienced a remarkable volte-face in the postin- dustrial world. Internationalism, in its redefined role as a yardstick for *economic* activity, has shed much of its former ideological political role. It is at least possible that issues such as women's status in society will lose out in two important ways: internationally losing clout because international- ism has shifted into a different gear, and at the same time losing out na- tionally because here the important politics are played only in relation to supra-national events, and the *social* system of a country will lose in im- portance. Alternatively, if Europe stops short of the unification it once conceived and remains what de Gaulle saw as a state-centered confederate European Union, a "*L'Europe des Patries*," which Denis de Rougemont dubbed an "Association of Misanthropes,"[86] the old nationalistic flavor would not disappear. In this case one would not expect women's status and "coresponsibility" to improve. It would not be the first time in history that women were the chief casualties of important political changes. But per- haps, this time, the well-formed feminist organizations and the new awareness and the new political skills of women will prevent the possibil- ity that women fall between the nets of international and national con- cerns in future.

Notes

1. Joni Lovenduski, *Women and European Politics: Contemporary Feminism and Public Policy* (Brighton, Sussex: Harvester Press, Wheatsheaf Books, 1986), p. 57.

2. Mary Ann B. Oakley, *Elizabeth Cady Stanton* (New York: Feminist Press, 1972).

3. Hannah Arendt, *The Human Condition* (Chicago: University of Chicago Press, 1959), pp. 155, 200; Hannah Arendt, *On Revolution* (New York: Penguin Books, 1963), p. 130; B. Honig, "Toward an Agonistic Feminism: Hannah Arendt and the Politics of Identity," in *Feminists Theorize the Political*, ed. Judith Butler and Joan W. Scott (New York: Routledge, 1992), pp. 215–238.

4. Gisela Kaplan, "Accounting for Difference: A Review of Feminism and Political Theory" (major review of the field), *Political Theory Newsletter* 5, no. 2 (September 1993): 140–164.

5. Rosemarie Tong, *Feminist Thought: A Comprehensive Introduction* (London: Unwin Hyman, 1989).

6. Vicky Randall, "Feminism and Political Analysis," *Political Studies* 39 (September 1991): 513–532.

7. Donna Hawxhurst and Sue Morrow, *Living Our Visions: Building Feminist Community* (Tempe, AZ: Fourth World, 1984).

8. Hester Eisenstein, *Contemporary Feminist Thought* (London: Allen & Unwin, 1984), p. xiv.

9. Diana Coole, "Re-reading Political Theory from a Woman's Perspective," *Political Studies* 34 (March 1986): 29.

10. Carole Pateman, "The Fraternal Social Contract," in *Civil Society and the State: New European Perspectives*, ed. J. Keane (London: Verso, 1988), p. 115. See also Jean Elshtain, *Public Man, Private Woman: Women in Social and Political Thought* (Princeton: Princeton University Press, 1981).

11. Iris Marion Young, "Impartiality and the Civil Public: Some Implications of Feminist Critiques of Moral and Political Theory," in *Feminism as Critique*, ed. S. Benhabib and D. Cornell, special issue of *Praxis International* 5 (January 1986): 382, 387–389; Pateman, "The Fraternal Social Contract," p. 115.

12. Gisela Kaplan, "Hannah Arendt," in *Social Theory: A Guide to Central Thinkers*, ed. P. Beilharz (Boston: Allen & Unwin: Kaplan & Kessler, 1989).

13. Bryan Turner, "Outline of a Theory of Citizenship," in *Dimensions of Radical Democracy, Pluralism, Citizenship, Community*, ed. Chantal Mouffe (London: Verso, 1992), p. 52.

14. Constance Rover, *Women's Suffrage and Party Politics in Britain, 1866–1914* (London: Routledge & Kegan Paul, 1967).

15. Renate Bridenthal, Atina Grossmann, and Marion Kaplan, eds., *When Biology Became Destiny: Women in Weimar and Nazi Germany* (Boston: Houghton Mifflin, 1984).

16. Andrew Arato and Jean Cohen, "Social Movements, Civil Society, and the Problem of Sovereignty," *Praxis International* 4, no. 3 (October 1984): 269.

17. A. Pizzorno, "Political Exchange and Collective Identity in Industrial Conflict," in *The Resurgence of Class Conflict in Western Europe Since 1968*, ed. C. Crouch and A. Pizzorno (London: Macmillan, 1978).

18. Seyla Benhabib and Drucilla Cornell, eds., *Feminism as Critique: Essays on the Politics of Gender in Late-Capitalist Societies* (Cambridge: Polity Press, 1987), pp. 367ff.

19. Elie Kedourie, *Nationalism* (London: Hutchinson, 1978), p. 9.

20. Eugene Kamenka, "Introduction: Political Nationalism—The Evolution of the Idea," in *Nationalism: The Nature and Evolution of an Idea*, ed. E. Kamenka (Canberra: Australian University Press, 1973), p. 3.

21. John Plamenatz, "Two Types of Nationalism," in Kamenka, *Nationalism*, p. 3.

22. Wang Gungwu, "Nationalism in Asia," in Kamenka, *Nationalism*, p. 88.

23. Kedourie, *Nationalism*, p. 90.

24. K. R. Minogue, *Nationalism* (London: B. T. Batsford, 1967), p. 19.

25. Ibid., p. 7.

26. Immanuel Kant, *Religion Within the Boundary of Reason Alone* (Edinburgh: T. Clark, 1838).

27. Kedourie, *Nationalism*, p. 89.

28. Minogue, *Nationalism*, p. 134.

29. Hannah Arendt, *The Origins of Totalitarianism* (New York: Harcourt Brace Jovanovich, 1951).

30. See Gisela Kaplan and L. J. Rogers, "Race and Gender Fallacies: The Paucity of Determinist Explanations of Difference," in *Challenging Racism and Sexism: Alternatives to Genetic Determinism*, Genes and Gender Series, vol. 7, ed. E. Tobach and B. Rosoff (New York: Feminist Press at the City University of New York, 1994).

31. Arendt, *The Origins of Totalitarianism*.

32. See Ernst Haeckel's most important work, *The Riddles of the Universe at the Close of the Nineteenth Century* (New York: Harper, 1900).

33. Bridenthal, Grossmann, and Kaplan, *When Biology Became Destiny*; Gisela Kaplan, "Irreducible 'Human Nature': Nazi Views on Jews and Women," in Tobach and Rosoff, *Challenging Racism and Sexism*.

34. George L. Mosse, "Mass Politics and the Political Liturgy of Nationalism," in Kamenka, *Nationalism*, p. 39.

35. Kaplan and Rogers, "Race and Gender Fallacies."

36. Citation in F. X. Martin, "The Evolution of a Myth—The Easter Rising, Dublin 1916," in Kamenka, *Nationalism*, p. 74.

37. Walter Benjamin, *Illuminations* (London: Cape, 1970), pp. 259f.

38. Flora Tristan, *The London Journal of Flora Tristan*, trans. and introd. J. Hawkes (London: Virago, 1982).

39. Daniela Weiland, *Geschichte der Frauenemanzipation in Deutschland und Österreich*, Hermes Handlexikon (Düsseldorf: Econ Taschenbuchverlag, 1983).

40. Johannes Willms, *Nationalismus ohne Nation: Deutsche Geschichte von 1789–1914* (Nationalism without nation) (Düsseldorf: Claasen Willms, 1983).

41. Richard J. Evans, *The Feminist Movement in Germany, 1894–1933* (London: Sage, 1976).

42. Colin Francome, *Abortion Freedom: A Worldwide Movement* (London: Allen & Unwin, 1984), p. 135.

43. I. J. Brugmans, *Paardenkracht en Mensenmacht* (Den Haag: Nÿhoff, 1961), p. 287.

44. Elaine Marks and Isabel de Courtivron, eds., *New French Feminisms: An Anthology* (New York: Schocken Books, 1981), p. 21.

45. Weiland, *Geschichte der Frauenemanzipation in Deutschland und Österreich*, p. 290.

46. E. Boulding, *Women in the Twentieth Century World* (London: Sage, 1977), p. 213.

47. Weiland, *Geschichte der Frauenemanzipation in Deutschland und Österreich*.

48. Victor Alba, *Transition in Spain: From Franco to Democracy*, trans. B. Lotito (New Brunswick, NJ: Transaction Books, 1978).

49. Lucia Chiavola Birnbaum, *Liberazione della donna: Feminism in Italy* (Mid-

dletown, CT: Wesleyan University Press, 1986); Gisela Kaplan, *Contemporary Western European Feminism* (Sydney: Allen & Unwin; New York: New York University Press; London: UCL, 1992).

50. Madelena Barbosa, "Women in Portugal," in *The Women's Liberation Movement—Europe and North America*, ed. J. Bradshaw, special issue of *Women's Studies International Quarterly* 4, no. 4 (1981): 477.

51. Lidia Falcón, "Women Are the Conscience of Our Country," in *Sisterhood Is Global*, ed. R. Morgan (Garden City, NY: Anchor Press/Doubleday, 1984), p. 628.

52. Jill Stephenson, *Women in Nazi Society*, (London: Croom Helm, 1975); Gisela Kaplan and Carole E. Adams, "Early Women Supporters of National Socialism," in *The Attractions of Fascism: Social Psychology and Aesthetics of the 'Triumph of the Right'*, ed. J. Milfull (New York: Oxford; Munich: Berg, 1990), pp. 186–204.

53. Bridenthal, Grossmann, and Kaplan, *When Biology Became Destiny*.

54. Breyer, 1933, p. 21, cited in Kaplan and Adams, "Early Women Supporters of National Socialism," p. 201.

55. Wieck citation in Silke Hesse, "Fascism and the Hypertrophy of Male Adolescence," in Milfull, *The Attractions of Fascism*, p. 167.

56. Cited in Bernt Engelmann, *Einig Gergen Recht und Freiheit: Deutsches Antigeschichtsbuch 2. Teil* (United against justice and freedom) (Frankfurt/M: Fischer, 1977), p. 167.

57. Jan Slaughter and Robert Kern, *European Women on the Left: Socialism and Feminism, and the Problems Faced by Political Women, 1880 to the Present* (Westport, CT: Greenwood Press, 1981.)

58. Liana Glaab, *Die unbekannte Italienerin: Aufbruch in die Emanzipation* (Freiburg/BR., Basel, Wien: Herder Verlag, 1980), p. 38.

59. Susan Bassnet, *Feminist Experiences: The Women's Movement in Four Cultures* (London: Allen & Unwin, 1986), p. 104

60. Theodore Stanton, ed., *The Woman Question in Europe: A Series of Original Essays* (New York: Source Book Press, 1970); Kaplan, *Contemporary Western European Feminism*.

61. Rosanna Fiocchetto, "Die Geschichte der italienischen Frauenbewegung," in *Italien der Frauen*, ed. M. Savier and R. Fiocchetto (Munich: Frauenoffensive, 1988), p. 24.

62. Judith Adler Hellman, *Journeys Among Women: Feminism in Five Italian Cities* (Cambridge, Oxford: Polity Press in association with Basil Blackwell Hellman, 1987), p. 29.

63. Nordic Council of Ministers, *Kvinnor och män i Norden. Fakta om jämställdheten* (Copenhagen: Nordic Council of Ministers, 1988).

64. E. Rumpf and A. C. Hepburn, *Nationalism and Socialism in Twentieth-Century Ireland* (Liverpool: Liverpool University Press, 1977), p. 219.

65. Matti Klinge, "Let Us Be Finns," in *The Roots of Nationalism Studies in Northern Europe*, ed. R. Mitchison (Edinburgh: John Donald, 1980), pp. 67–76.

66. Ibid., p. 70.

67. D. G. Kirby, *Finland in the Twentieth Century* (London: C. Hurst, 1979), p. 9.

68. Ibid., p. 19.

69. Ibid., p. 34.

70. Ibid., p. 33.

71. Elina Juusola-Halonen, "The Women's Liberation Movement in Finland," *Women's Studies International Quarterly*, 4, no. 4 (1981): 454.

72. Nordic Council of Ministers, *Kvinnor och män i Norden*, p. 118.

73. Elina Haavio-Mannila, "How Women Become Political Actors: Female Candidates in Finnish Elections," *Scandinavian Political Studies*, ns.s., 2, no. 4 (1979); Lovenduski, *Women and European Politics*, p. 153.

74. Turner, "Outline of a Theory of Citizenship," pp. 33–62.

75. Alba, *Transition in Spain*, p. 244.

76. Institute of Jewish Affairs, *Political Extremism and the Threat to Democracy in Europe*, Report for the European Centre for Research and Action on Racism and Antisemitism (London, 1994).

77. Geoffrey Harris, *The Dark Side of Europe* (Edinburgh: Edinburgh University Press, 1990).

78. Helen D'Ancona, "Statement bei dem EG-Seminar 'Die institutionellen Voraussetzungen für die Gleichberechtigung von Mann und Frau in den Mitgliedsstaaten der EG' " (The institutional preconditions for equality between men and women in the member states of the EC) (Hannover: *IFG-Dikumentation*, 1988), pp. 171–179.

79. Fritz Fabricius, *Human Rights and European Politics: The Legal-Political Status of Workers in the European Community* (Oxford: UK, and Providence, RI: Berg, 1992), p. 6

80. European Parliament, Session Doc., January 27, 1994, p. 6.

81. Katalin Koncz, "Global Summit of Women: 'Women and Political Leadership,' A Participant's Report," *European Network for Women's Studies Newsletter*, no. 10, April 6–8, 1994, p. 7.

82. United Nations press release (UNIS/WOM/358), "Women in Politics: Finland Leads the Way," May 22, 1991; see also figure, part 4.

83. Gisela Kaplan, "Pluralism and Citizenship: The Case of Gender in European Politics," in *Citizenship and National Identity in Europe*, ed. P. Murray and L. Holmes (London: Dartmouth Publications, 1966).

84. Gisela Kaplan and Clive S. Kessler, eds. *Hannah Arendt: Thinking, Judging, Freedom* (Boston: Allen & Unwin, 1989).

85. Klaus von Dohnanyi, *Brief und die Deutschen Demokratischen Revolutionäre* (Munich: Knaur Verlag, 1990), p. 124.

86. Cited in Etienne Tassin, "Europe: A Political Community?" in Mouffe, *Dimensions of Radical Democracy, Pluralism, Citizenship, Community*, pp. 169–192.

Women on the Margin:
The Women's Movements in Northern Ireland, 1973–1995

Carmel Roulston

I

The "second wave" of feminism made its appearance in Northern Ireland a little later than elsewhere in Europe or the British Isles. As was the case in some other countries, many of the activists who created women's groups in Northern Ireland had already been involved in political and social movements which challenged the existing social and political structures. In Northern Ireland much social unrest had its roots in battles over the national identity and constitutional future of this small "province": battles that have been both an effect and a cause of such intense divisions among the population that the creation of a movement claiming to represent the interests of all women always appeared problematic. In many countries that experienced a revival of feminism in the 1960s and 1970s, divisions among second-wave feminists became common as women's movements were accused of "false universalism" and "ethnocentrism." In Northern Ireland in the 1970s and 1980s, disputes focused upon how "true" feminists should respond to the "national question" of whether Northern Ireland should remain British or become part of a United Ireland, and on how "feminists" should react to the revival of the Irish Republican Army as a group using armed force to create a United Ireland.

Armed conflict has, of course, been a feature of the history of British and Irish relations, as have ideological disputes over how to describe the conflict accurately. Ireland was gradually colonized by England/Britain in a process that might be said to have reached completion by the passing of the Act of Union, creating the United Kingdom of Great Britain and Ireland, which came into force on January 1, 1801. Over the centuries various movements of resistance to Ireland's subordination had arisen. In the nineteenth century, new nationalist movements emerged, campaigning for Irish independence from Britain, for the rights of Irish peasants against British landlords, and for religious rights for Catholics against the established Anglican Church. Nineteenth-century nationalist groups employed parliamentary, passive- and violent-resistance tactics. Frustration with the failure of efforts to secure a *Home Rule Bill,* granting autonomy to Ireland, in the parliament at Westminster gave impetus to armed republican nationalism, which aimed for a fully independent Ireland with no ties to Britain's parliament or monarchy. Following the ill-fated Easter Rising of 1916, militant republicanism gained more support. When the Sinn Fein (Gaelic for "ourselves alone") party declared the creation of an independent Irish parliament (Dail Eireann) in 1918, clashes between British forces and republicans escalated into a war of independence which was ended in 1921 by a truce, which it was hoped in Britain would result in a permanent settlement of "The Irish Questions."

The British government, however, attempted to set the terms of the settlement by passing, in 1920, the Government of Ireland Act, which allowed the creation of two autonomous parliaments in Ireland, one in Belfast, the other in Dublin. The Belfast parliament was intended to deal with independence and separatism. Those who supported unionism were Protestants, often descendants of English and Scottish people who had settled in Ireland; they had strong reservations about the influence of Catholicism on Irish nationalism. Though described by Irish nationalists as "planters," many of these communities had lived in Ireland from the sixteenth century and regarded themselves as having rights to protection as British citizens, earned over decades of loyalty to the monarchy and the Reformation. By 1920, unionism had become weaker in Ireland as a whole but had become a considerable force in the northeastern counties, part of the historic province of Ulster. The industrial revolution had created there a distinct working-class community, the majority of whose members opposed nationalism, in common with farmers, landowners, professional middle-class people, and industrialists. Unionists did not want an autonomous parliament in Belfast, preferring to remain integrated into the British state; from 1912 on, a paramilitary force armed to resist home rule was maintained in Ulster.

Eventually, a compromise was reached that in some respects was unsatisfactory for all Irish participants. The Northern Ireland parliament located at Stormont in Belfast was to govern the six northeastern counties. The border between Northern Ireland and the Irish Free State was drawn so as to ensure a Protestant and unionist majority in the northern state. There was, however, a substantial Catholic and nationalist minority, many of them implacably opposed to the "partition" of Ireland. There was also resistance in the South of Ireland to the Treaty that was intended to resolve the conflicts. A civil war was waged for two years as militant republicans tried to undo partition and achieve complete independence, not just home rule for all of Ireland. Eventually, stability was achieved; in 1948 the Irish Free State became a republic, severing all links with the British Commonwealth but reiterating the aspiration to unite all of Ireland in one, united state.

The Unionist government in Northern Ireland, fearful of abandonment by Britain and of being overwhelmed by nationalism, created a political community in which the Catholic minority was represented as dangerous, alien, and potentially treacherous. Repressive legislation, electoral gerrymandering, and religious discrimination were employed to reinforce the Unionist power base. By the 1960s, however, it seemed as though both communities had outlived the hostilities of the past. The IRA, now a tiny force, illegal in both Northern Ireland and the Irish Republic, had attempted a renewed military campaign in the North in 1956, which was overcome with relative ease and which had been opposed by most Catholics. As a result, the IRA and Sinn Fein began to reevaluate their militarist strategies, and to evolve a politics of peaceful change. A new Unionist prime minister—in the face of opposition from within the Protestant community and his own party—opened discussions with the government of the Irish Republic and appeared to be sympathetic to Catholic expressions of grievance at the unequal treatment they had received from Unionist-dominated political institutions over the years.

When, in 1968, Catholic political groups created a civil rights movement, presenting demands for protection from discrimination in the allocation of public-sector housing and jobs and protesting against the use of emergency legislation against Catholics, hopes for harmony were shattered. Extreme Unionists and other loyalist parties saw the movements as a subtle means of reviving Irish republicanism; the repression of the movement led to sectarian conflict, which polarized the Catholic and Protestant communities as much as they had been in 1920. As the conflict became more violent, the British government sent in troops to keep the peace and traditional nationalists in the North and the South of Ireland returned to the strategy of using military force to unite Ireland. The Provisional IRA was created and loyalists' paramilitary groups were formed. From 1970 on, the small community of Northern Ireland endured the multifaceted armed conflict, with random murders of civilians, bombs in shopping centers and bars, politicians shot down and British troops and Northern Irish security forces routinely targeted. The sectarian aspects of the conflict meant that religious segregation in housing was resumed, and for certain Catholic and Protestant communities, the paramilitary groups acquired the status of defenders and controllers.

When the Northern Ireland government responded to the deteriorating situation by introducing internment in prison camps for those suspected of paramilitary violence, the conflict escalated dramatically, in part because most of those interned were Catholics, many of them nationalist activists who were not actually engaged in paramilitary violence. The Unionist government lost control of the situation. The British government—to Unionist and loyalist outrage in 1972—closed down the Stormont Parliament and introduced a system of direct rule of Northern Ireland by Westminster politicians and a civil service department, the Northern Ireland Office. Elected local councils lost many of their powers. Successive British administrations have endeavored to bring about a resolution of this situation with up until the most recent "peace process"—very little success. The "troubles" that began in the 1970s resurrected the divisions of previous generations; it has been difficult to achieve a compromise when all parties have disagreed even on how to define the problem.[1]

It was against this background of escalating civil strife that a movement for women's rights began to emerge in the 1970s, influenced by feminist movements in the United States, Britain, and the Irish Republic, as well as by awareness of the unfairness of treatment of women in Northern Ireland. As was the case in the United States and elsewhere, women activists in civil rights and leftist student movements began to ponder on the sexism of these reputedly radical groups. "Shouting 'one man, one vote' just didn't sound right" recalled one female student activist "but I didn't know why."[2]

In the 1960s and early 1970s, women in Northern Ireland had a standard of living that was similar to that of the industrial regions of the United Kingdom, although attitudes about gender equality were more conservative. More women were joining the labor force as the public sector expanded and new multinational plants moved in to replace the declining textile and garment industries. The work force was, however, highly segregated and equal pay was not an issue taken seriously by anyone except some trade unionists. Although women were often the family breadwinners in areas of high male unemployment, even where their work was accepted as skilled, their pay rates were not as high as for men's work.[3] Women breadwinners were often also solely responsible for child care and domestic labor. Day nurseries had been established during World War II to allow manufacturers to employ female labor but were closed, in spite of opposition soon after the end of the war.[4] Because of unemployment, dependence on social security was high, and the high cost of essential commodities, such as fuel, meant that poverty was widespread. The legal status of women in Northern Ireland was in some respects worse than that of women in Britain. The Northern Ireland Parliament at Stormont had autonomy in domestic matters and, dominated as it was by men of strong religious convictions, it would on occasions refuse to introduce reforms that might offend religious sensibilities. The 1967 Abortion Act was rejected, as was a measure aimed at making divorce easier to obtain. Direct rule from Westminster was welcomed by some radicals and reformers as an opportunity to achieve changes previously blocked by the local parliament.

As the civil rights movement faded (many of its demands having been granted) and mass involvement in politics was undermined by IRA and loyalist violence and increasing sectarianism, consciousness of women's needs began to take form. The early 1970s saw a more active participation by women in community-based groups. The introduction of internment brought women in Catholic areas into the foreground for a time. Women in both Catholic and Protestant areas also mobilized against paramilitary violence on occasion. Poverty and poor housing also provoked campaigns in which women took initiatives. As Buckley and Lonergan point out, women became involved in such campaigns as the guardians of family life and in the interests of the community rather than as fighters for women's benefit. Women, especially mothers, were seen as having a unique insight into the needs of the community and a special role to play in protecting or promoting the interests of the community.[5] In spite of the fact that

movements based on such ideologies have often been short-lived or transformed into something alien to the ideals of their founders, such ideologies persist and resurface periodically. The mobilization of women is often
achieved by reference to their responsibilities in and for the family rather
than by appealing to their individual needs or interests.

Against this background of community organization, and drawing
upon a tradition of trade-union agitation for women's rights, some formally organized feminist groups began to appear in the 1970s. The first
group formed was based in a working-class community, Belfast's Ormeau
Road. This group campaigned against poor housing conditions in the
area and against the poverty suffered by its inhabitants, using direct action
and lobbying with some success.[6] In 1974 a consciousness-raising group
appeared in the small town of Coleraine, involving women from the New
University of Ulster and from the town itself. The Coleraine Women's
Group quickly became a campaigning as well as a discussion group, focusing public attention on the existence of domestic violence against
women and on the related problems of the lone mother.[7] Their campaigns sparked a response to domestic violence from women throughout
Northern Ireland; within a short time, a Northern Ireland Women's Aid
Federation was formed, lobbying for law reform to protect the victims of
violent male partners and providing emergency assistance to women
seeking refuge from abuse.

University women were also involved in a women's liberation group set
up in Belfast in 1974. The following year, some of the members of this
group joined in the creation of the Northern Ireland Women's Rights
Movement (NIWRM), which was proposed by some women members of
the Communist Party of Ireland, who wanted to take advantage of the
publicity surrounding the opening of the UN Decade for Women to create a movement in Northern Ireland. Other members included women
from the Civil Rights Association (which continued to exist in an attenu-
ated form), trade union activists, women from the part of the Republican
movement that had abandoned militarism in the 1960s, and individual
women interested in feminism. It was hoped that the NIWRM might become the nucleus of a mass movement of working-class women and
"middle-class feminists"; the structure envisaged followed a rather bureaucratic model of a federation of women's groups and sympathetic affiliated
organizations. This organized mobilization did not come into being; however, twenty years later, there are hundreds of women's groups of various
types and sizes throughout Northern Ireland, relating to one another

through multiple unstructured networks. The founding group itself could not easily have become a nucleus; it was undermined by disagreements that soon resulted in division.[8]

II

It was perhaps inevitable that splits and disputes would emerge among women activists in Northern Ireland; women's movements and feminist groups in almost every country have become fragmented by differences over theory and priorities. The fact that Northern Ireland's population is relatively small   1.5 million, 51 percent females—may have made unity more necessary but not any more likely. Almost as soon as the NIWRM was formed, conflict surfaced over the structure of the movement; the bureaucratic model proposed did not appeal to some of the radical feminists who had initially been attracted. Quite apart from their distaste for the idea of a women's group with membership cards, annual general meetings, and an executive committee, was the problem that the affiliate structure meant that male delegates might be sent by, for example, a trade union to some of the meetings. For some, this was unacceptable: women's groups should be autonomous and for women only. At a special meeting to resolve this issue, the majority preferred to retain the original structure; many of the members were trade union activists who felt that an absolute women only policy would mean the movement might be taken less seriously. Some were amazed at the very idea of women activists' requiring separate forums and meetings. As a result, a small number of women decided to devote their energies elsewhere and created the Socialist Women's Group (SWG). Although it was intended that the two groups would cooperate with each other, they became more rather than less distant as time passed.[9]

One of the most important factors in this distancing was how feminists could or should position themselves in relation to unionism, nationalism, and republicanism. By 1976 feminists were being divided by "the national question." Such disharmony was not a recent phenomenon in Irish history. At the turn of the century, nationalist women and other feminists were bitterly divided over whether a votes-for-women clause should be added to the proposed home rule bill. Later, the sentiments of nationalist women were outraged by the activities of the British Women's Social and Political Union, which decided that pressure should be put on Unionist leaders to accept women's suffrage; accordingly, branches were set up in Ulster.[10] It would be misleading to accept the suggestion that women in the 1970s were "reproducing the same debates as those of sixty years ago."[11] However, it was clear that setting priorities and defining a core interest for women was proving to be difficult in a context where many of the women likely to be attracted to feminist politics held conflicting views on the best solution to Northern Ireland's ethnic conflicts.

The NIWRM attempted to deal with this difficulty by adopting an approach that had been employed by trade unions: asking members to leave their commitment to nationalism or unionism or whatever "at the door" and focus upon "women issues." In an unusual reversal of radical feminism, the "political" issues relating to statehood were designated as "personal." The approach had enabled trade unionism to function;[12] feminism, however, directs itself toward such radical change that the avoidance of taboo subjects may not always be possible or appropriate. Socialist parties in Ireland had floundered because of "the national question"; feminism was to be no more fortunate.

The SWG was critical of the "nonposition" that the NIWRM hoped to follow. Its members were, for the most part, involved in or sympathetic to the Trotskyist left, which tended to offer qualified support to the IRA's ambition to achieve a united Ireland. In its manifesto of 1976, the SWG argued that full liberation (not defined) for Irish women could come only through the creation of a united socialist Ireland;[13] it rejected the "reformism" of the NIWRM because it failed to pose the question of the legitimacy of the government of whom reforms were demanded. The objective of drawing women into a unified movement might be worthy and admirable, but it would be a "false" unity if it failed to challenge prejudices and sectarianism. In addition, the reformist orientation of the NIWRM meant that it was reluctant to raise the issue of abortion lest doing so would cause unnecessary division, and, for the same reason, it was not prepared to reject male delegates who might be proposed by trade unions.[14]

Although it argued that British imperialism was the fundamental cause of women's oppression in both states in Ireland, the SWG did not approve of the military campaigns being conducted by the IRA. Its aim of winning working-class support for feminism led the SWG to identify women's groups in working-class districts that it could support or assist. Its activities began to focus on Catholic areas, drawn there in part because of an assumption that Catholic women, having experienced a tradition of rebellion and resistance to unionism and imperialism, would be more receptive to radical ideas about gender roles than their Protestant sisters, whose defense of a conservative ideology—unionism—was assumed likely to make them resistant to feminism.

One of the groups in which many Catholic women in Belfast were involved at this time was the Relatives Action Committee (RAC) created by the families of people who had been convicted of and imprisoned for terrorist offenses. Its function was to demand that the prisoners have special rights as "political prisoners." The RAC was a classic example of the type of group discussed by Buckley and Lonergan, set up and maintained by women to campaign on behalf of family members or the "community." In the end, SWG members became less enthusiastic about its potential when its leadership and direction were taken over by the Republican movement, so that it no longer functioned even as a medium through which women could exercise influence. A rather different women-initiated group was beginning to find that a shared commitment to women's liberation did not guarantee agreement. The group dissolved in 1977, with some members pursuing a policy of stronger support for republicanism, and others trying again to create an autonomous, radical women's group. The Belfast Women's Collective (BWC) was announced in 1988. It was now suggested that by describing themselves as socialist, the SWG "was in fact alienating those women it mostly wished to work with." A more open group was needed that would cater to all women, "whether they regarded themselves as socialists or not." Accordingly, the BWC would have no manifesto or program and would be open to all women interested in working on women's issues. It would continue to work mainly in Catholic West Belfast but would also talk to women from other areas.[15]

The BWC was still critical of the NIWRM, which was becoming more established if not significantly larger. Having won some local government funding for a women's center, the NIWRM was attempting at this time to provide resources and support for women's groups throughout Belfast. The women's center was open to all those involved in campaigns for women's benefit; from time to time, "unity" meetings were held to allow the differences between the various groups to be aired. Comparison of the ideas and actions of the BWC and the NIWRM, in retrospect, shows that they had much in common. Both wanted to be open to all women, and both campaigned for equal pay, child care, health, sexuality, and fertility control, and against violence and poverty. Both condemned state and paramilitary violence, both lobbied members of Parliament, ministers, local councilors, and civil servants on women's issues. Both were prepared to accept that laws passed at Westminster might improve the lives of women in Northern Ireland. But the BWC, even without a formal manifesto, was uneasy with the idea that it was acceptable to avoid having a policy on Northern Ireland's political future. Many members of the NIWRM were, in fact, sympathetic to the idea of Irish unity; others were deeply opposed to Irish nationalism. They restrained their disagreements for the purpose of effective work on women's issues, but they were not always altogether happy with the situation. Perhaps because of its greater resources and more functional approach, the NIWRM again outlived its rival; the tensions between republicanism and socialism brought an end to the BWC in 1981.

III

The decision to dissolve the BWC was taken partly because the tension between republicanism/nationalism and feminism became particularly acute for feminists during the period of the campaign for political status for prisoners convicted of terrorist offenses. From 1972 on, all those sentenced to imprisonment for terrorist crimes had been granted certain privileges as a result of protests by male Republican prisoners. These privileges—the right to wear clothes of their choice rather than prison uniforms; to refuse to do prison work, to be grouped with other members of their paramilitary organization under the control of a "commanding officer"—were granted to both Loyalist and Republican prisoners and were known as "political status." In the mid-1970s, a Labour government with a tougher line on security decided to phase out these privileges and restore normal prison discipline for all those convicted of terrorist offences. The secretary of state responsible for implementing the new policy has been described as having "a slightly theatrical attitude to his own administration, embellishing its essentially pedestrian features through a series of confrontations between himself and the local forces of darkness and unreason."[16] Certainly, the restoration of "law and order" in the prisons became symbolic of the government's efforts to restore the rule of law in Northern Ireland. For the IRA, resistance to criminalization became symbolic of its claims to legitimacy as the vanguard of the "national liberation struggle." All prisoners sentenced after March 1, 1976, were to be held in newly built blocks of individual cells—which became known as

"H-blocks" because of their lay-out—rather than in compounds and would be expected to wear the prison uniform and do prison work. The second and third changes were seen as important by the prison authorities as a means of preventing the wearing of paramilitary uniforms and the practices of military drills and training. A campaign against the new regulations both inside and outside the prisons was launched as soon as the first prisoners were expected to conform to them. Within the prisons, the protest went through various stages. Refusal to wear the prison uniform led to the prisoners' being left without clothes; this was followed by a refusal to wash or leave cells to work. The authorities retaliated by leaving the men in their uncleaned cells all day. Finally, the IRA resorted to hunger strikes, which had been used successfully in 1972 and harked back to a heroic tradition in Irish resistance to Britain. A hunger strike was begun and abandoned in 1980. Another strike began in 1981. After ten prisoners had died and communities had reached a point of near-hysteria, a compromise allowed some concessions on work, clothes, and visiting but fell short of according political status.[17]

The prison protest and hunger strike affected everyone. Community tensions and sectarian conflict increased. The situation became an issue of particular importance for women's groups because of the involvement of some feminists with the Relatives Action Campaign and because some IRA women prisoners joined the protest. The women's protest was not highlighted by the IRA leadership, partly because the women enjoyed better conditions than male prisoners and also partly because less public ity in general was given to women "on active service." Publicity for the women's protest was achieved through the efforts of the group Women Against Imperialism (WAI). WAI had been set up by some of the former members of the Socialist Women's Group who had not joined the Belfast Women's Collective. The WAI believed that the "anti-imperialist struggle" was the central issue for women in Northern Ireland. It worked exclusively with women in the Republican areas of Belfast and Derry, continuing an association with the women in the Relatives Action Campaign and also working with women members of Sinn Fein. They saw themselves as the nucleus of an autonomous women's movement within the wider Republican movement.[18]

The women prisoners' protest followed the same pattern as that of the men, escalating through protest and punishment until the women, too, were on a "dirty" protest. (Some of the women joined the brief hunger strike in 1980, but were refused permission by the IRA leadership to take part in the 1981–1982 fast.) On International Women's Day, 1979, WAI picketed outside Armagh's women's prison, calling on other women's groups to support the prison protest because not only was the demand for political status just but the Armagh prisoners had suffered at the hands of male prison staff. Sanitary napkins had been withheld, for example, in response to the women's no-wash protest, hence making their conditions much more unpleasant than the men's. Other forms of harassment, such as punitive strip searches were also alleged. Two members of WAI were themselves imprisoned for refusal to pay fines imposed as a result of the demonstration. They in turn joined the protest in prison, attempting to interest their fellow prisoners in feminism.

WAI's call for support for the women prisoners met with a mixed response from other women's groups. Attitudes toward the basic demand for political status, obviously, depended upon attitudes toward the IRA's military campaign. Opposition to the sexual harassment of the women prisoners was difficult to express without being co-opted by the movement for political status. The response of the Belfast Women's Collective illustrates the difficulties for feminists. Its members initially supported the women's protest, joining demonstrations at the prison and elsewhere. The BWI, however, in time became unhappy with the manner in which the campaign was handled and the lack of autonomy for feminists within it. Disagreements over the issue led to the dissolution of the BWC in 1981, its members moving into single-issue campaigns.[19]

The NIWRM did not split or fold over the protest issue, but there were deeply felt differences about it, reflecting the conflicting perspectives of its members on Northern Ireland politics. The majority were distressed by the hunger strike and opposed to the ways in which prisoners were treated; others were deeply opposed to the idea of political status and the implications of supporting a campaign initiated by the IRA. After much agonizing, the NIWRM decided, once again, to have no policy on the issue of political status but agreed that there should be a discussion of the treatment of women in prison and a strategy for reform devised.[20] In fact, no major campaign developed on this issue.

The debate about the political status issue was also conducted within the wider women's movement. Monthly meetings open to women in any group and to individual women had been initiated to encourage discussion and to expand support for campaigns. Here, too, political status, the legitimacy of the IRA campaign of violence, and the plight of the Armagh women were debated, often with great acrimony but without clear resolution. Against the background of young men starving to death and the Thatcher government's denying all responsibility, discussions of the situation in the prisons became highly emotional. Those who did not accept the legitimacy of political status and who were reluctant to support the women prisoners in a movement that was headed by the IRA were accused of "betrayal" or of being "pro-British" or "pro-Imperialist."[21] Dublin-based journalist Nell McCafferty demonstrates the tone: "The menstrual blood on the walls of Armagh prison smells to high heaven. How can we turn up our noses at it?"[22]

IV

In spite of the bitterness generated by these debates, effective campaigning continued on a range of other issues. By 1979, some progress had been made. Employment protection legislation benefited part-time workers, of whom many were women. The Equal Opportunities Commission for Northern Ireland was set up, and divorce laws were improved. The Conservative government in 1980 introduced the Domestic Proceedings Order, which gave some protection to victims of domestic violence. Such legislative changes were accompanied by changes in attitudes and atmosphere. Thanks to the efforts of Women's Aid, the housing authority and the Department of Health and Social Security had begun to make provision for women forced out of their homes by violent men. The Belfast City Council granted some money to the NIWRM toward the cost of opening the city's first women's center. Direct rule had, clearly, its advantages for women, though all women were agreed that there was still a long way to go.

The advances made in women's rights and status achieved by 1979–1980 had been fought for by a relatively small number of women; only a few hundred were in any way involved in feminist politics or in women's groups. Approximately five hundred participated in the Women's Liberation Conference in 1977, but this included women from Britain and the Irish Republic. Individual groups were also small; the Socialist Women's Group and the Belfast Women's Collective each had no more than fifteen members at any one time. The NIWRM, with its trade-union backing, could call on larger numbers of women to support its campaigns, but the numbers attending meetings regularly were also relatively small. Some women participated in several groups, projects, or campaigns which meant an enormous drain on their physical, financial and emotional resources. Particularly noteworthy in this respect were the members of the lesbian community, who supported virtually every activity—political, social, or cultural. Their commitment was not always reciprocated by heterosexual women, few of whom gave more than verbal or moral support. An information pack for women produced in the 1980s made only a passing reference to lesbianism.[23] Any small shift in public attitudes toward lesbianism (and male homosexuality) can probably be attributed to the effects of United Kingdom membership in the European Community, with its stronger emphasis on individual liberties.

Although campaigns on various issues continued, the divisions that came so sharply into focus in 1982 have continued to affect the feminist community. On some issues, strong and effective campaigns have been built; on others disunity has prevailed. The Northern Ireland Women's Aid Federation has, after twenty years of extraordinary effort and commitment, created numerous refuges for women victims of domestic violence, influenced policy makers and transformed public attitudes toward men who inflict injuries on their partners. Creating a campaign to reform abortion laws in Northern Ireland proved more difficult, perhaps because prevailing religious ideologies make abortion a sensitive subject. At a meeting to launch a campaign to secure law reform on abortion, disagreement quickly surfaced over whether it was right to lobby the British Parliament on the issue because to do so would be to accept the legitimacy of British rule.

Throughout Northern Ireland, assisted by the efforts of women employed in local government, a remarkable network of women's groups and women's centers has been created in the past decade. These have tended to be grassroots groups in working-class communities and have therefore been—however reluctantly—segregated along the ethnic/religious lines that characterize much of public activity in Northern Ireland. However, initially through the resources provided by the NIWRM in its Women's Center and as a result of "unity" meetings held there, connections were made between Catholic and Protestant women's groups that have resulted in the creation of the Women's Information Group, which organizes exchanges of information, support for campaigns, sharing of resources and ideas. The vacuum created by the absence of effective local political institutions has brought about a complex structure of voluntary organizations that both fulfill functional roles by providing resources of various types to disadvantaged communities and also present policy ideas to ministers and civil servants. These organizations are often innovative and radical, and have an open, democratic structure. They support women's initiatives and draw many women into political activities. One of the uncertainties concerning the peace process is the effects of creating local, elected policy-making institutions that would be dominated by the traditional political parties, which up to the present have been slow to focus on the underrepresentation of women.[24] The possibility of the voluntary and community groups being displaced is not welcome to everyone.

One of the dramatic changes in feminist organization has been as a result of the decision by some members of Women Against Imperialism to join Sinn Fein in order to create a feminist consciousness within the republican movement. By the early 1990s, Sinn Fein's Women's Department had become very effective on certain issues. Women's centers have been opened in Catholic working-class areas, traditional male attitudes toward sexual preference, divorce, and contraception—though not abortion—have been very successfully challenged and a quota to ensure that women are represented in the policy-making bodies of the party has been introduced. It is clear, however, that although the Women's Department has great autonomy to influence and develop policy on "women's issues," women members have been less influential in the making of policy on the broader set of issues concerning the resolution of the conflict between unionism and nationalism, Britain and Ireland. The Sinn Fein leadership has made a point of including some women in the delegations to take part in talks and negotiations during the current "peace process," but the women delegates have been remarkably silent during press conferences and give the appearance of being relatively junior.

Some of the feminist members of Sinn Fein have recently expressed reservations about the party's strategy in the peace process, in part because the issues of women's rights and gender inequalities have not been raised by any parties to the negotiations. Nevertheless, the Women's Department of Sinn Fein continues to exhort other feminists to "build a women's movement in the 90s that once again links women's freedom with national liberation."[25] Many women, including those who do and those who do not identify themselves as feminists, share the desire to see a women's movement come into being that could draw women from all political, social, and religious backgrounds, not all of whom could accept the vision of national liberation proposed by Sinn Fein.

In the 1990s women in Northern Ireland enjoy some of the benefits of a growing awareness of gender inequalities but suffer the effects of the economic decline and the persistence of ideologies that serve to exclude women from power or control. Women have entered the spheres of paid employment and community work in great numbers, but there are few in leadership roles, with the exception of the voluntary sector. There have been changes: in 1960 fewer than 30 percent of married women worked outside the home, and only 12 percent of mothers with preschool children were in paid employment; in 1990 the figures were 60 percent and 43 percent, respectively. Women's careers are still restricted by factors such as the lack of affordable child care, the "poverty trap," and sexism, but it is clear that more and more women are aware of their rights and are using the law and the Equal Opportunities Commission to demand them.[26]

It is in the world of politics that change seems slowest. There are no women party leaders, no women members of the Parliament at Westminster, nor are there likely to be in the near future. Northern Ireland sends three representatives to the European Parliament, all are men and are likely to be men until the next elections three years hence. By comparison, the Irish Republic sends fifteen representatives to the European Parliament, four of whom are women; 13 percent of the members of Dail Eireann are women; and women hold some of the key offices of state, including minister of justice and, of course, president. Of the twenty-six local councils in Northern Ireland, three have no women members at all, and overall only 12 percent of councilors are women. There are signs of slow change. The larger nationalist party, the SDLP, declared in 1995, that it would develop a quota system to include women in its executive bodies. One of the small loyalist parties which have come to the fore since the loyalist paramilitary cease-fires—the Progressive Unionist Party—has declared a commitment to encourage women's participation. There is still a long way to go.

The absence of women and women's issues in the peace talks has led to worries that new institutions will be created that have no place for women. In the period during the cease-fires there were several conferences, meetings, and workshops convened to express anxieties about women's continued marginal status and identity issues of importance to women that should be addressed. But although the cease-fires opened the opportunity for a settlement of Northern Ireland's long-running ethnic, religious, and political conflicts, that settlement has not yet been reached. In the meantime, other cleavages, inequalities, and identities are accorded a lower priority. For Gerry Adams, "When the national question is resolved, then we can all have our diversity of attitudes, religions, hang-ups."[27] On the unionist/loyalist side, preserving the remnants of British identity takes the same precedence. To some extent, the majority of women share these preoccupations; any feminist movement that tries to disregard or dismiss them will not have wide appeal. So for the immediate future, Northern Irish women will have to be "qualified" feminists, fighting for space within and against their communities and hoping to be ready for the new political order.

Notes

1. P. Bew, and H. Patterson, *The British State and the Ulster Crisis*. (London. Verso, 1985).

2. Ronald Fraser, *1968: A Student Generation in Revolt* (London: Chatto & Windus, 1988).

3. See Michael McGuire, "Makin' Your Minutes: Women's Piecework in a Northern Ireland Telecommunications Plant," in *Gender in Irish Society*, ed. C. Curtin, P. Jackson, and B. O'Connor. (Galway: Galway University Press, 1987).

4. Liz McShane, "Day Nurseries in Northern Ireland, 1941–55," in *Gender in Irish Society*, ed. C. Curtin, P. Jackson, and B. O'Conner (Galway: Galway University Press, 1987).

5. See S. Buckley and P. Lonergan. "Women and the Troubles, 1969–1980" in *Terrorism in Ireland*, ed. Y. Alexander and A. O'Day (London: Croom Helm, 1984).

6. Sally Beltrage, *The Crack: A Belfast Year* (London. Andre Deutsch, 1907).

7. Margaret Ward. "Feminism in the North of Ireland: A Reflection," *Honest Ulsterman*, no. 83 (Summer 1987): 61.

8. Ibid.; Christina Loughran, "Armagh and Feminist Strategy," *Feminist Review*, no. 28 (1986).

9. Ward, "Feminist in the North of Ireland"; interviews with NIWRM members, Autumn 1986.

10. Margaret Ward, *Unmanageable Revolutionaries* (London: Pluto Press, 1983).

11. Women in Media, n.d., p. 60.

12. M. Goldrin, *Belfast: From Loyalty to Rebellion* (London: Laurence & Wishart, 1988).

13. Manifesto of Socialist Women's Group, 1976.

14. Manifesto of Socialist Women's Groups, 1977.

15. Belfast Women's Collective, *Women's Action* (newsletter), 1978.

16. Bew and Patterson, *The British State and the Ulster Crisis*.

17. Liam Clarke, *Broadening the Battlefield* (Dublin: Gill & Macmillan, 1987).

18. Loughran, "Armagh and Feminist Strategy."

19. Ward. "Feminism in the North of Ireland."

20. NIWRM minutes, Policy Statement, 1980; interviews with members and former members.

21. *Scarlet Women*, special Irish issue, June 1980.

22. Nell McCafferty, The Armagh Women *Irish Times*, August 1980.

23. Women in Media, "Picking up the Pieces: A Women's Resource Pack" (Belfast, n.d.).

24. C. Roulston, "Equal Opportunities for Women," in *Northern Ireland Politics*, ed. A. Aughey and D. Morrow (London; Longman, 1996).

25. M. Keane, "Sinn Fein Women's Conference," *Women in Struggle* (Dublin) 1 (1982).

26. J. Kramer and P. Montgomery, eds., *Working Women's Lives* (Belfast: EOCNI, 1993).

27. F. O'Connor, *In Search of a State: Catholics in Northern Ireland* (Belfast: Blackstaff Press, 1993).

Rape, Feminism, and Nationalism in the War in Yugoslav Successor States

Jill Benderly

The Yugoslav successor states bear witness to the destructive force of nationalism. "Ethnic cleansing" has turned more than a million people into refugees, killed tens of thousands, and resulted in rape, torture, separation of families, and widespread physical and psychological trauma.[1] During the nationalism driven wars that have raged in the region since 1991, feminists have provided some of the strongest opposition to the wars and strongest help for the survivors. Thus, one could say that post-Yugoslav feminism has an antinationalist character.

Although it appears that antiwar feminism in the successor states is automatically antinationalist, by looking a bit more closely, one finds one branch of feminism that is both antiwar and nationalist (or perhaps patriotic is a more accurate term). This branch was born in Croatia and also exists in Bosnia-Hercegovina (BiH). The Croatian feminist groups Kareta, Nona women's center, and Trešnjevka, and the women's organizations Bedem Ljubavi, Biser, and Žena BiH have all coalesced behind the perspective that the nations of Croatia and Bosnia-Hercegovina are being raped and victimized by Serbia, and thus are victim nations. These patriotic groups make common cause of "women as war victims" and "the nations of Croatia and Bosnia-Hercegovina as war victims" of the gynocide and genocide perpetrated by Serbia. According to their argument, the interests of Croatian and Bosnian women (stopping gynocide and genocide) overlap with the patriotic aims of their nations.

The questions that divide feminists between those who identify with their nation-state and those who oppose the objectives of their nation-state can be posed this way: Are all states in the conflict pursuing aggressive nationalism which should be opposed by feminists from all states? Or is Serbian nationalism the only ideology that is aggressive, expansionist, and genocidal, while the national identities of Croatia and Bosnia-Hercegovina are defensive in character and should be defended by feminists?

These two positions have divided feminists, particularly those in Zagreb, Croatia, into two bitterly opposed camps. The antinationalist Croatian feminists have overcome tremendous obstacles of separation, fear, and communication to stay connected with antinationalist feminists in Belgrade, Serbia. The patriotic Croatian feminists have, on the other hand, polemicized against Serbian feminists, calling them part of the enemy.

For the purposes of this chapter, I shall examine the relationship between feminism and nationalism among feminists in Zagreb and Belgrade. These two cities have had feminist movements active since the late 1970s, and I shall explore how the movements were affected by the changes in the region that culminated in war in 1991.[2]

Before 1991 feminist groups existed only in Serbia, Croatia, and Slovenia, and there mainly in the capital cities. Since then, small feminist groups have sprung up in far-flung parts of the Yugoslav successor states. All of the warring states have mobilized women into their national projects, most often by defining women's role as demographic (to give birth to more sons of the nation—do daughters count?) and service (taking care of the wounded, refugees, and displaced persons, and holding family life together while men serve at the front). In Bosnia-Hercegovina, women have also played an emerging role in the military, though mostly not in combat. In general, however, gender roles have become more polarized by nationalism and war.[3]

Yugoslav Feminism

Feminism in Yugoslavia has a long herstory. Developments in the feminist movement have been linked to those in the European women's movement since the first women's organizations were founded in the South Slav provinces of the Hapsburg Empire and in Serbia in the 1890s. The relationship between autonomous feminist organizations and Communist or Social Democratic parties has long been complex and conflictual. Women's active participation in the Yugoslav partisan struggle during World War II, particularly by the Antifascist Women's Front, created the possibility of a semiautonomous feminist organization influencing the newly-established socialist Yugoslavia. Instead, the women's organizations were reined in, and independent Yugoslav feminist voices were not heard again until the late 1970s.

From 1978 to 1986 feminism articulated a critique of self-managed socialism's unfulfilled promise of women's emancipation. This critique theorizes that all states constitute the "state subject" in a gendered way, so that citizenship is essentially a male project. Under Yugoslav socialism, while "the woman question" was purportedly solved by incorporating women into production and self-management, and by providing services to make this "social activity" of women possible, the unequal citizenship of women was never addressed, nor was the patriarchal nature of all states. There were polemics against this feminist position, but no attempt to silence it.

After 1986 feminist activism took shape as a new social movement (NSM). Although the feminist movement cooperated with other NSMs (especially where they were most developed, in Slovenia) and attempted to have an impact on "politics" as far as women's citizenship and rights were concerned, it also had a life of its own, building its own alternative culture, community, and network of initiatives in three Yugoslav republics.

Nationalism on the Horizon

Until the outbreak of war in 1991, feminist movements showed little interest in the independence of the republics, calling these matters "male politics," anticipating that new states would not be any more gender-neutral than Yugoslavia. In fact, between 1988 and 1991, feminists gave increasing attention to opposing nationalism (whether present among Communists, such as Slobodan Milošević in Serbia, or their opponents, such as the HDZ in Croatia or Demos in Slovenia). Feminists asserted that the construction of any nation, be it Yugoslavia or one of the republics, manipulates women.

In critiquing the impact of nationalism on women, Yugoslav antinationalist feminists developed an analysis, following the typology explicated by Anthias and Yuval-Davis, of the five ways women have tended to participate in ethnic and national processes and state practices: (1) as biological reproducers of members of ethnic collectivities; (2) as reproducers of the boundaries of ethnic/national groups; (3) as participating centrally in the ideological reproduction of the collectivity and as transmitters of its culture; (4) as signifiers of ethnic/national differences—as a focus and symbol in ideological discourses used in the construction, reproduction, and transformation of ethnic/national categories; (5) as participants in national, economic, political, and military struggles.[4]

Feminist theorists in Zagreb, Belgrade, and Ljubljana alike traced the pressures on women in increasingly nationalized civil society to fulfill the above roles. As the new nations emerged, the feminist argument extended. Ljubljana sociologist Renata Salecl argues:

> When the problem of patriarchal domination officially ceased to exist [under socialism], patriarchal domination became officially invisible—which also means that it became much more difficult to recognize its effects. As with nationalism, which officially did not exist, but nevertheless remained at work in a concealed way, patriarchal domination, although officially overcome, remained a surmise of political discourse. Thus, it was not difficult for the post-socialist moral majority to articulate patriarchy in a new way: to present the return to "natural" sexual roles as an attempt to introduce morality into a previously "immoral" social regime, and to reinterpret the moral majority ideology in a nationalist way.[5]

Feminism posed a strong challenge to rising nationalism in Yugoslavia by linking women's groups across republic lines and by critiquing the manipulation of reproductive rights for nationalistic demographic purposes. Antiabortion "right-to-life" initiatives were successfully blocked.

Women Against War

The new national entities had even more instrumentalist approaches to women than did the Yugoslav socialist state. In all the new national states women's roles are as symbol of the nation and mother of the nation. In the war, women's roles are as contested terrain: for one side, the object of rape, conquest, and "ethnic cleansing" by a national army; for the other side, the victim of such atrocities, both as "woman" and as national symbol.

Sociologist Žarana Papić from Belgrade describes women's position in all of the new states:

> With such totalitarian domination of nationalist ideologies the first victim is civil society itself. With civil society in danger, all human rights (and especially women's rights are in danger. . . . All nationalist ideologies in their political and military strategies are constructed and based on purposefully provoked, dominantly aggressive, openly violent and deadly oriented type of masculinity. . . . And its victims are not only the Other Enemy-Nations but equally Women as war-target, war-weapon, war-threat, war-revenge, war-pleasure-reward—as rape-objects. . . . Every aggressive, war-oriented nationalism (of which we are all victims) is, as a rule, based and primarily functions on the specific form of an undignified, violent patriarchal system, and strictly gendered order, in which men and women are separated into opposite zones: battle fields and shelter fields.[6]

Feminists in the republics have been among those best positioned to help women survivors of rape and "ethnic cleansing" in the wars since 1991: they were already providing social services for women through antiviolence hotlines and battered women's shelters. Feminists were also among those most actively involved in documenting the abuses and amassing evidence for the prosecution of war crimes. These small-scale, women-run self-help projects for refugees attempted to reconstruct some elements of civil society in the midst of an uncivil war.

When Slovenia and Croatia declared independence in the summer of 1991 and war broke out,[7] the peace movements across the Yugoslav successor states had their work cut out for them. Young men deserted the Yugoslav National Army in droves. Mothers of soldiers marched on parliaments and army headquarters to demand that their sons be sent home from military duty. At first, mothers from Serbia, Croatia, Bosnia, and elsewhere held coordinated antiwar protests.[8]

But as the war ravaged Croatia, cooperation—and even communication—between antiwar efforts in the various republics dwindled. With massacres and occupation shaping a defensive Croatian consciousness, it became easy for the Croatian government to co-opt popular "peace" sentiment, such as that of the mothers' movement's "Wall of Love" (Bedem Ljubavi). These mothers opposed their sons' call-up into the Yugoslav People's Army (JNA), but did not oppose their being drafted into the Croatian Defense Forces of President Franjo Tudjman.[9]

The Croatian peace and feminist movements also suffered bitter divisions between those who felt themselves to be part of a victimized Croatian nation and those who still opposed all nationalism. The former were more likely to cooperate with the government. The latter, grouped around the Antiwar Campaign—Croatia in Zagreb and its affiliates in other Croatian cities, had more trouble gaining public exposure because the government had done an effective job of throttling "disloyal" independent media.[10]

The issues of nationalism and nonnationalism were further complicated by the spread of the war into Bosnia. There, the Serbs were the most blatant "ethnic cleansers" but local Croatian militias and the Croatian government pursued their thirst for Bosnian and Hercegovinian territory.

In Belgrade the number of draft resisters was estimated in 1993 to be in the hundreds of thousands.[11] A significant portion of the populace—albeit a small proportion of the population of the rest of Serbia, who were beyond the reach of the political opposition and the independent media—grew tired of the war and the government of Slobodan Milošević. On the first anniversary of the war, Belgrade feminists led a crazy quilt of marchers—students, royalists, intellectuals—ringing alarm clocks and bells in front of Parliament to warn the regime to wake up to the truth.[12] Cigarettes and gasoline disappeared from the stores as international economic sanctions hit. Weapons, however, were still on the market, and the Serbian second economy was run by war profiteers, a mafia of paramilitary and military men.

Since the war began, a small band of Belgrade feminists dubbing themselves the Women in Black held silent vigils against the war. Standing in Belgrade's main street every week, they grew familiar with being spat upon and called traitors and whores.[13] In August 1993, Women in Black organized an antiwar protest in Vojvodina that drew two hundred women from all over the Yugoslav successor states as well as western Europe.

Help for Rape Survivors

When the news of rapes, forced pregnancies, and other war-related crimes against women emerged from the refugee camps in the summer of 1992, feminist journalists were among the first to pursue the story. Croatian writer Slavenka Drakulić termed the rapes "a method of ethnocide."[14] Bosnian women in the camps and in special army brothels had been subjected to gang rape and torture, sometimes in front of other detainees or their own families. Some were murdered after being raped. Others were detained for months after being impregnated so that they would give birth to "Serb babies."

The European Community, human rights groups, the United Nations, and the Bosnian and Croatian governments spent much of 1992 playing "the numbers game" about the extent of the rapes.[15] The first priority of feminist groups was to get out the information about the war crimes against women. Many later shifted gears to providing long-term assistance to women survivors.

Just as the Yugoslav war is the continuation of politics by other means, so rape is the continuation of the control of women's reproduction—by more violent means. The control of women's bodies in Eastern Europe had made abortion illegal and contraception utterly unavailable in Ceaucescu's Romania. Communist East Germany used the carrot instead of the stick to control women's bodies with *muttipolitik* (Mommy politics)—financial incentives for working mothers that allowed them to have their children and to work, too, but mainly in dead-end jobs. In Tito's Yugoslavia, this approach asserted that communism automatically emancipated women, but this "freedom" did not allow women to practice the heresy of feminism. In Serbia in 1990 it brought population control for Albanian women and curtailment of abortion for Serbian women. In Bosnia in 1992, it meant rape and forced pregnancy.

Anthropologist Gail Kligman puts the rapes in a long-term perspective, "Political self-determination in the region has always been linked to control of women's bodies. That was true for the communists, and it is true for the regimes that have followed them. Rape is more than a war crime, it is a weapon of war."[16]

Belgrade feminist Lepa Mladjenović has written about the ways nationalism has permeated every kind of relationship:

> Nationalist hatred has spread from the front line to family relationships as well. We consider the following war-related rapes: the rape of refugee women; the rape of wives and non-wives by war veterans; the rape of wives in interethnic marriages; and rape as a consequence of nationalist propaganda in the media (the post-TV news violence syndrome).[17]

Croatian feminist Vesna Kesić talks about the Croatian Movement for Demographic Renewal and its reduction of women to child bearers and child raisers. She analyzes the genocidal rape in the war as "a way for men to destroy the honor of other men and thus the society; it's not about sex [as in 'to the victor belong the spoils']."[18]

Discussions among feminists in the successor states offered opposing views of who is doing the raping and why. One view went out of its way to condemn men on all sides of the conflict for rapes, violence against women, and denial of reproductive rights. The other singled out the Serbian paramilitary forces and the "Yugoslav" army supporting them for perpetrating systematic rape and forced pregnancy as part of the strategy of "ethnic cleansing." As Helsinki Watch's Jeri Laber wrote,

> Although the rapes have been attributed to all sides in the war, the Serbian forces appear to be using rape on the largest scale and with impunity. Whether or not the order to rape comes from the highest authorities, the practice appears to be tacitly condoned, and even encouraged, at the local levels of command. The fact that the rapes often occur before witnesses indicates that the rapists have nothing to fear.[19]

The evidence pointed to a preponderance of genocidal rape by the Serbian paramilitary and army. However, in the the three-way war that unfolded, atrocities became abundant on all sides of the conflict. Even the UN peacekeeping forces appeared to be involved in the traffic in women.[20]

Nationalism Divides Feminists

Feminists in the Yugoslav successor states have split over their understanding of nationalism and patriotism. Two clusters of feminists in Zagreb worked on the issues of war-raped women. Croatia sheltered most of the war refugees from its own republic and from Bosnia-Hercegovina, so it became the most feasible site for work on this issue. The war severely exacerbated already-existing conflicts among the Zagreb feminist groups. In wartime, the political divisions among Croatian feminists took on a larger meaning: nonnationalism versus nationalism.

The four women's groups, Kareta (radical feminist group), Bedem Ljubavi (Wall of Love, a Croatian women's group), Zene BiH (a Bosnian refugee women's group), and Biser (International Initiative of Women of Bosnia-Hercegovina) have retained U.S. feminist attorney Catharine

MacKinnon. Their stand as Croatian and Bosnian women is that rape is a distinctly Serbian weapon for which all Serbs—even feminists who oppose the war—are culpable. They draw an analogy between nation as victim and woman as victim.

An excerpt from the "Open Letter" sent by these four groups to U.S. feminists gives a sense of their blanket condemnation of Serbs and non-nationalist feminists from Bosnia and Croatia, and the effect of nationalism on the four women's groups. The letter expressed their appreciation to a 1993 U.S speaking tour of antiwar women from Croatia, Serbia, and Bosnia-Hercegovina:

> [T]o place Muslim and Croatian women in forums which force on them women of the group committing the genocide, who do not even acknowledge that genocide is going on and who are trying to convince Muslim and Croatian women that it isn't happening, is to commit further violence against these women. This might be something like forcing Jewish women to "debate" with German women while the holocaust was still going on.[21]

At the June 1993 UN Human Rights Conference in Vienna, MacKinnon, going public with her hostility to Serbian feminists, made the following comment in response to a question posed by Belgrade feminist activist Nadezda Četković: "If you are in opposition to the regime in Serbia, why aren't you already dead?" MacKinnon wrote that the abundance of pornography in the Balkans induced genocidal rape in the war. Although there is evidence that videotapes of genocidal rape have been marketed, this shows porn as an effect, not a cause of the rapes.[22]

In contrast to the influence of nationalism on the actions of the aforementioned women's groups, the Zagreb Women's Lobby (the Center for Women War Victims and others) took a public stand against Croatian nationalism. In December 1992, it sent "a letter of intentions" to international women's and peace groups discussing strategy and explaining the kind of help needed.

> We fear that the process of helping raped women is turning in a strange direction, being taken over by governmental institutions. . . . We fear that the raped women could be used in political propaganda with the aim of spreading hatred and revenge, thus leading to further violence against women and to further victimization of survivors.[23]

The climate in Croatia brought severe attacks on the feminists who oppose nationalism. Five Croatian women writers and journalists who questioned Croatian nationalism and its effects on women were targets of a hate campaign whipped up by Zagreb's yellow press. These "five witches," who include well-known feminist writer Slavenka Drakulić, feminist philosopher Rada Iveković, and feminist editor and journalist Vesna Kesić, found their photos on Zagreb's front pages under headlines screaming that they were feminists, quislings, and Communists who "rape Croatia."[24]

Nonnationalist politics made it possible for a working relationship to be reestablished—delicately—among certain Croatian, Bosnian, and Serbian feminists, who frequently met at international conferences and communicated with one another by electronic mail.

However, nationalism also took its toll on feminists in Serbia. Women in Black activists Lepa Mladjenović and Vera Litricin shared some of their deepest feelings about the effect of the war:

> When the war started, nationalist hatred increased dramatically and the Serbian government began to produce propaganda and the notion of the Enemy. All of a sudden Slovenians became an enemy, then Croats, then Muslims, then Americans, Albanians and so on. Deep conflicts emerged in families, in workplaces, and women began to separate on that basis. Completely new questions appeared in women's groups. Can a feminist be a nationalist chauvinist? Can a pacifist be a nationalist? Is a weapon an instrument of defense? Should the groups take clear attitudes toward nationalist questions (and therefore the war) and in that way lose some women? Should the groups avoid the issue of nationalism altogether? Should the women merely sit down and confront their beliefs and see what happens? So nationalism made some women split within themselves. It also caused painful scars to Zagreb-Beograd feminist relationships.[25]

In 1995 the Bosnian war was struggling toward a peaceful settlement negotiated under duress by the same nationalist leaders who had started the war four years earlier. Yet an ever-expanding circle of women in the capital cities of Serbia, Croatia, and Bosnia-Hercegovina and in many other cities and towns throughout the region were working in their communities and across borders to achieve a deeper level of reconciliation. Women are using a variety of strategies to achieve that kind of peace. Women from Osijek, Croatia, in the Eastern Slavonia region heavily destroyed by heavy shelling at the frontline with Serbia, cooperate with women from

Serbia to organize meetings of divided families and friends from both sides of the cease-fire line. Meetings are held over the border in Hungary. Women from Kosova and Belgrade are cooperating to finance their groups by selling handicrafts in a secondhand shop.

Women shared experiences and strategies at a regional conference in Macedonia in June 1995. A woman peace activist from Vojvodina proposed a "Balkan Women's Parliament for Peace," and plans are on electronic mail. Women from all countries in the region caucused and held workshops together at the NGO Forum of the 1995 World Conference on Women in Huairou, China.

Each of the feminist organizations is attempting to alleviate the war's effects on women and children. The Medica Women's health center from Zenica, Bosnia-Hercegovina, describes its goal as

> to offer a place of refuge and new perspectives on life to traumatized women and their children in the war zone. . . . Violence, torture and rapes out of nationalist motives have triggered . . . revenge and are destroying the multi-ethnic coexistence of the Bosnian people which before had been completely natural. . . . Fifty Muslim, Croatian, and Serbian Bosnian women are working together in . . . one of the few places of refuge for traumatized refugee women and their children in the war zone. Here they are taken in thoughtfully in an atmosphere of solidarity.[26]

The goal of the Center for Peace, Nonviolence, and Human Rights in Osijek, Croatia, in the reality of violence and war, is

> to practice nonviolence in the work and growth of the group and in all its activities . . . and [to find] the impulse for life and work grounded on positive creative premises, no matter how hard. . . . This means taking into account all of the constituents of the actual social movement, especially those which seem to be a ballast, an obstacle, or even an enemy. . . . Sometimes the most one can do (often, it is as well the most valuable) is to . . . be there when a person mourns, accept and understand the bitterness of the ones being hurt, and express clearly and publicly your own attitude regarding the protection of human rights in your community.[27]

The goal of the Women in Black, Belgrade:

> It is the third year of the war and we are still in the streets. . . . For three

years our female presence kept saying to the Serbian regime: your politics is death, disaster and sorrow for those in whose name you are speaking, while the "national interests," are only the means to an end of power and destruction. . . . Women will remember, women are telling each other, and we are the witnesses of many crimes this regime is responsible for. Our women friends from all parts of the former Yugoslavia are still telling us about the suffering they endured and what they are going through now.

Nationalism had not separated all of us, a flow of trust still exists between women of all names. We the women who have gathered in the group Women in Black because of our pacifist and feminist beliefs, believe that peace is neither a manoeuvre nor a tactic, nor just the absence of war. For us the peace represents decisions brought without hate, for us the peace means requirements for a life without violence, conditions for a life together with others and those who are different from us. Our peace policy proves that it is possible to live together.[28]

Conclusion

Yugoslav feminism was a small beacon of opposition to nationalism before 1991. Women's groups from various republics built up a long-term cooperative relationship that endured longer than the Yugoslav federation. The basis for this antinationalism lay in the analysis that nationalism (whether in the form of nationalist movements or a nationalist state) manipulates women to become "mothers of the nation," and to relinquish any other form of agency.

Feminist activism in the period of 1989 to 1991 was focused to a great degree on identifying and resisting the effects of rising nationalism on women, particularly in the area of population and reproductive policy. Women's solidarity above and beyond national identity made feminism a fairly unique social movement in the period when most other movements had, to varying degrees, become nationalized by 1991.

Under pressure of war, however, some feminists ultimately reflected the nationalism of their states. Of course, there are varying types of nationalism in each Yugoslav successor state. In the ensuing war, Serbia appeared to play the role of aggressor and Croatia the role of victim. However, antinationalist feminists on both sides warned that the nationally constituted identities of both states were aggressive (as later was their taste for Bosnian-Hercegovinian territory).

There were divisions in the Croatian feminist movement in their views on women in war. Those who saw Croatia as a national state manipulative and dangerous to its women citizens located themselves in an oppositional position not only to the war but to the Tudjman regime. As "witches" they suffered the same sort of attacks as did their equally disloyal sisters in Serbia. Those who conflated "woman as victim" and "nation as victim" moved toward a sort of feminist nationalism, the patriotism of the victimized.

NOTES

1. Information presented in this chapter was gathered in Belgrade, Zagreb, and Ljubljana in 1986–1987, 1990, 1993, 1994–1996.

2. I will not treat the feminists from Slovenia in depth here, although they too began organizing in the 1980s. For a detailed account, see Vlasta Jalusic, "Troubles with Democracy: Women and Slovene Independence," in *Independent Slovenia: Origins, Movements, Prospects*, ed. Jill Denderly and Evan Kraft (New York: St. Martin's Press, 1994).

3. In Bosnia-Hercegovenia alone, 54 women's groups existed in 1995 of which at least four defined themselves as feminist. To complicate matters further, one must take a quick look at the parts of the former Yugoslavia not often in the headlines. In the province of Kosova, which was under Serbian martial law from 1989, more than 90 percent of the population is ethnically Albanian. Women's movements are new here and the small clusters of feminists are torn between the struggles for women's rights and national liberation, a tension that resembles Third World feminisms. Feminism is virtually brand new in the republic of Macedonia. Feminism does not really exist in Montenegro, a remote and highly patriarchal former Yugoslav republic now allied with Serbia. In Vojvodina, another province allied with Serbia, feminism has been primarily antiwar in character.

4. Nira Yuval-Davis and Floya Anthias, eds., *Woman-Nation-State* (New York: St. Martin's Press, 1989).

5. Renata Salecl, "Nationalism and Disavowal of Patriarchal Domination in Post-Socialism" (paper presented at the forum Gender, Nationalism, and Democratization: Policy Initiatives for Central and Eastern Europe, Washington, D.C., October 1993).

6. Žarana Papić, "Nationalism, War and Gender: Ex-Femininity and Ex-Masculinity of Ex-Yugoslavian Ex-Citizens" (paper presented at the forum Gender, Nationalism, and Democratization, Washington, D.C., October 1993).

7. For accounts of the war and its causes, see Laura Silber, *Yugoslavia: Death of a Nation* (New York: TV Books/Penguin USA, 1996); Mark Thompson, *A Pa-*

per House: The Ending of Yugoslavia (New York: Pantheon Books, 1992); Brian Hall, *The Impossible Country: A Journey Through the Last Days of Yugoslavia* (Boston: David Godine, 1994).

8. Žene za Mir (Women for Peace), Belgrade 1993; "Koliko su puta prevarene," (How deceitful are the ways.) *Danas*, July 9, 1991.

9. Interview with Slavenka Drakulić, December 1991.

10. Issues of *Arkzin*, 1991; interviews with Tomaž Mastnak, Marko Hren, Lynne Jones, and Slavenka Drakulić.

11. Interview with Vesna Pesić, director of the Center for Anti-War Action, Belgrade, summer 1993.

12. *Vreme*, July 1992; letter from Lepa Mladjenović, July 1992.

13. Lepa Mladjenović, and Vera Litricin, "Belgrade Feminists 1992; Separation, Guilt and Identity Crisis, *Žena za Mir*, 1992.

14. Slavenka Drakulić, "Women Hide Behind a Wall of Silence," *Nation*, September 6, 1992.

15. Aryeh Neier, "Watching Rights," *Nation*, March 1, 1993; Jeri Laber, "Bosnia: Questions about Rape," *New York Review of Books*, March 25, 1993.

16. Gail Kligman, presentation at the forum of the Washington, D.C., Ad Hoc Women's Coalition Against War Crimes in the Former Yugoslavia, February 17, 1993.

17. Lepa Mladjenović, "Universal Soldier," *Žene za Žene* (1993).

18. Interview with Vesna Kesić, October 1993.

19. Laber, "Bosnia."

20. Anecdotal evidence reported by Marijana Sanjack, executive director, Medica Zenica, interview July 1993.

21. Kareta, Biser, Bedem Ljubavi, and Žene BiH, fax to author, March 1993.

22. Catharine A. MacKinnon, "Turning Rape into Pornography: Postmodern Genocide," *Ms.*, July–August 1993.

23. Zabreb Women's Lobby, "Letter of Intentions," e-mail, December 1992.

24. "Croatia's Feminists Rape Croatia," *Globus* (Zagreb), December 11, 1992, p. 1.

25. Lepa Mladjenović and Vera Litricin, "Belgrade Feminists, 1992: Separation, Guilt and Identity Crisis," *Žene za Mir*, Belgrade, 1992.

26. Medica Zenica, "Surviving the Violence" (1994).

27. Osijek Center for Peace, Nonviolence and Human Rights, Bulletin 94, February 1995.

28. Women in Black, *Women for Peace* (Belgrade, 1995).

Middle East/Central Asia/Africa

Nationalist Agendas and Women's Rights
Conflicts in Afghanistan in the Twentieth Century

Valentine M. Moghadam

The case of Afghanistan is illustrative of the dilemmas feminists face in assessing the merits of nationalist movements in terms of their gender dynamics and outcomes for women. In the 1980s, two opposing movements —one Marxist-modernizing; the other Islamist-traditionalist—fought a long bloody war over divergent nationalist agendas and conceptions of "women's place." Although the Islamist movement was explicitly antifeminist, it received more international support (even from many European feminists) than did the modernizing government, because the mujahideen were perceived as attempting to liberate their country from Soviet domination. If there was a "feminist nationalist social movement," to use Lois West's term, in Afghanistan, I argue that it describes the efforts of the Marxists—men and women in and around the government and party—to modernize Afghanistan and enhance the status of the female population.

The 1980s conflict was not the first in Afghan history to be fought over "the woman question." In the early twentieth century, efforts by reformers and nationalists to improve the status of women, to establish an education system, and to modernize the economy and society met with the fierce resistance of traditionalists and ulema (Islamic clergy).

This chapter seeks to explain why women's rights and women's emancipation have been such vexed issues in Afghanistan, and in so doing provides a historical perspective on the Woman Question. I hope to show that notwithstanding the neglect of the gender dimension in nearly all accounts of the 1980s conflict in Afghanistan, the woman question was an integral part of the conflict between the tribal-Islamist mujahideen and the ruling People's Democratic Party of Afghanistan (PDPA), which came to power in the Saur (April) Revolution of 1978. The attempts by the PDPA to improve and enhance the status of women followed a Third World pattern of linking modernization, development, and socialism with women's emancipation. Civil war in Afghanistan was to a great extent a battle between modern revolutionaries and traditional social groups. At the center of the battle was the question of women. The conflict in the 1980s, then, was a continuation of the conflict in the 1920s.

I will argue here that the issue of women's rights in Afghanistan has been historically constrained by (a) the patriarchal nature of gender and social relations deeply embedded in traditional communities, and (b) the existence of a weak central state, that has been unable, since at least the beginning of this century, to implement modernizing programs and goals in the face of "tribal feudalism." The two are interconnected, for the state's weakness is correlated with a strong (if fragmented) society resistant to state bureaucratic expansion, civil authority, regulation, monopoly of the means of violence, and extraction—the business of modern states. These factors were behind the defeat of the modernizing nationalists in the 1920s. In the 1980s, war, the fundamentalist backlash, and a hostile international setting forced the Afghan leadership to shift from social revolution to national reconciliation, relegating the emancipation of women to a more stable future. And in April 1992 the government of Afghanistan collapsed and the mujahideen assumed control.

Part I of this chapter describes social structure in Afghanistan. Part II describes the early efforts to reform and modernize Afghan society. Part III describes the second major effort by modernizing nationalists to develop and transform the society—the Saur Revolution of 1978. Part IV reflects on feminism, nationalism, and "gendered cultural relativism."[1]

Part I. Social Structure in Afghanistan

Historically, the population of Afghanistan has been fragmented into myriad ethnic, linguistic, religious, kin-based, and regional groupings.[2] Afghan nationalism, properly speaking, is at best incipient because the concept of a nation-state, or of a national identity, is absent for much of the population, and has been promoted primarily by modernizing elites since the nineteenth century.[3] During most of the country's recent history, the fragmented groupings composed warring factions. Battles were fought principally over land and water, sometimes women and "honor," usually sheer power—or what Massell, writing of early-twentieth-century Central Asia, described as primordial cleavages and conflicts.[4]

One of the few commonalities in this diverse country is Islam. Afghan Islam is a unique combination of practices and precepts from the *Sharia* (Islamic canon law as delineated in religious texts) and tribal customs, particularly Pushtunwali, the tribal code of the Pushtuns, who constitute about half the population. On certain issues, Pushtunwali and Islam disagree.[5] For example, the absence of inheritance rights for females is contrary to Islamic law but integral to the complex web of the tribal exchange system. Contrary to the Islamic ban on usury, there has been widespread usury, a practice that has kept rural households in perpetual indebtedness. Exorbitant expenditure in marriages (for example, on dower such as *sheer-baha* and *walwar*) has also contributed to the rural household's debt accumulation. The Islamic dower, the *mahr*, (a payment due from groom to bride that is an essential part of the formal Islamic marriage contract), has been abused. In the Quran it is a nominal fee, and in many Muslim countries its purpose is to provide a kind of social insurance for the wife in the event of divorce or widowhood. In the Afghan patriarchal context, the *mahr* (or *walwar* in Pashtu) is the payment to the bride's father as compensation for the loss of his daughter's labor in the household unit.[6]

Afghan rural and poor women work extraordinarily hard, but their ability to contribute substantially to household survival or the family income takes place within a patriarchal context of women's subordination and intrahousehold inequality. In such a context, a woman's labor power is controlled and allocated by someone else, the products of her labor are managed by others, and she receives no remuneration for work performed. In areas where carpet making is a commercial enterprise, male kin are allowed to exploit women's labor without any wage payment, as Afshar has found for Iran and Berik has described for Turkey. In extended patriarchal, patrilineal households, as Kandiyoti has argued, collective (male) interests dictate strict control of a woman's labour deployment throughout her lifetime.[7]

Contemporary Afghanistan is situated in what the demographer John Caldwell has called "the patriarchal belt," and is an extreme case of what

Kandiyoti calls "classic patriarchy."[8] This belt stretches from northern Africa across the Middle East to the northern plains of the Indian subcontinent and parts of (rural) China. Here the patriarchal extended family is the central social unit, in which the senior man has authority over everyone else, including younger men. Women are subject to distinct forms of control and subordination, including extremely restrictive codes of behavior, rigid gender segregation, and a powerful ideology linking family honor to female virtue, as described by Kabeer with respect to Bangladesh. Young brides marry into large families, gain respect mainly through their sons, and late in life acquire power as mothers-in-law. In contemporary Muslim patriarchal societies, control over women is considered necessary in part because women are regarded as the potential source of social *fitna*, that is, disorder or anarchy.[9] These and other patriarchal societies (including northern India) are characterized by an adverse sex ratio, low female literacy and educational attainment, high fertility rates, high maternal mortality rates, and low female labor-force participation in the formal sector.[10]

Afghan patriarchy is tied to the prevalence of such forms of subsistence as nomadic pastoralism, herding and farming, and settled agriculture, all organized along patrilineal lines. Women and children tend to be assimilated into the concept of property and to belong to a male. This is particularly the case among Pashtuns, whose tribal culture, Pushtunwali, is highly masculinist. Tapper writes of the Durrani Pashtuns of north-central Afghanistan: "The members of the community discuss control of all resources—especially labour, land, and women—in terms of honor."[11] Note that "community" is the community of men, and that "women" are assimilated in the concept of "resources." Griffiths describes a conversation with the governor of a district in Kunduz, who explained with some pride

> how five or six women might work together for four or five months to make a patterned carpet . . . and how a man would pay a very good bride-price for a girl who was an accomplished carpet weaver. When I asked him who got the money for the carpets, he looked at me in astonishment and replied: "Why the man of course, the woman belongs to the man." This is the attitude which is the chief obstacle facing the champions of women's emancipation in Afghanistan.[12]

Veronica Doubleday, who lived in Herat on and off between 1972 and 1977, explains that women's complaints focused on two issues, which she came to see as related: sickness and the restrictions imposed by their seclusion. The women complained of backaches, lack of energy, and many other ailments, and said that sometimes their husbands would not let them to go a doctor. Some women complained specifically about their seclusion, which they called *qeit*, or confinement, imprisonment. Doubleday describes how, despite her desire to avoid Western ethnocentrism, she had to conclude that purdah was not simply about being segregated and veiled; it meant that men had complete control over the movements of their women, and it gave men ultimate power. She also tells of "the deep anxiety women experienced over illness."

> As mothers and nurturers of the family they had a vital responsibility, and yet they and their children were especially vulnerable since they depended upon their husbands for money for cures. It was iniquitous but true that men could deny women and children recourse to medical help, and it was no wonder that women placed importance upon methods such as divination or diet, which were at least accessible and within their control.[13]

Economic dependence on men, the practice of seclusion, and high maternal mortality may explain why census and surveys undertaken in 1967, 1972–1974, and 1979 revealed an unusually high ratio of males to females, which even exceeded the expected underreporting of females in a conservative Islamic society.[14]

And what of women's resistance, and their own aspirations? Writing in the early 1980s, Boesen reports that women resent male control of their sexuality and they rebel, pursuing extramarital affairs and covering up one another's activities. Such forms of resistance, however, do not challenge gender status ranking. Although Tapper has stated that a typical Afghan woman's wish is for a successful marriage with many sons, Doubleday's book on women in Herat reveals that women also have other aspirations, but that these are blocked.[15]

A final word on marriage and brideprice are necessary in order to put in perspective the marriage reforms. In a patriarchal context, marriage and brideprice are a transaction between households, an integral part of property relations and the exchange system, and an indicator of status. In Afghanistan, marriage, forced or voluntary, is a way of ending feuds, cementing a political alliance between families, increasing family prestige, or accumulating wealth. Mobility and migration patterns also revolve around the brideprice. Tapper has described how in the 1970s men from one region would travel to another to find inexpensive brides, and fathers would travel elsewhere to obtain higher prices for their daughters. The heaviest expenses any household has to bear are concerned with marriage. The choice of bride, the agreed brideprice, and the time taken to complete a marriage may visibly confirm or indeed increase a household's poverty. Tapper's description accords well with Massell's discussion of the importance of *Kalym* (brideprice) to overall property relations in early-twentieth-century Central Asia.[16] But it also reveals the extent to which the exchange of women for brideprice or in compensation for blood spilled treats women exclusively as reproducers and pawns in economic and political exchanges in a patriarchal context.

Afghanistan is a prototypical "weak state," inasmuch as the central authorities have been unable to realize their goals, or to regulate social relations and use resources in determined ways.[17] The existence of a weak modern state in a predominantly patriarchal and tribal society has had adverse implications for reform and development, as well as for the advancement of women. Since modernization began in the mid-nineteenth century, various governments and rulers have sought to discourage excessive expenditure on brideprice and marriage celebrations as a way of preventing rural indebtedness, and they have tried to extend education to girls. Various state initiatives during this century have invariably resulted in tribal rebellion against government authority.[18] Although Afghanistan was not immune to the general process of social change enveloping Muslim countries, it has seen far less transformation than in neighboring countries.

Britain's attempts to expand its sphere of influence outward from India led to two Anglo-Afghan wars (in 1839 and 1879), which contributed to the growth of a politico-religious nationalism and xenophobia. Moreover, the struggles strengthened the position of the Afghan tribes and the monarchy's dependence on their military might, and reinforced the position of the Afghan religious establishment. The formulation and propagation of the aims of Afghan nationalism and modernism came in the first two decades of the twentieth century, when a small group of educated Afghans sought to broaden the base of support for political and economic reform. Under the leadership of King Amanullah (1919–1929), the Young Afghans, like the Young Turks nearby, made ambitious modernization plans, explicitly including the emancipation of women in their agenda, as was the case in Ataturk's Turkey. Their ultimate failure, Gregorian notes, determined the course and nature of all future reforms and modernization programs in Afghanistan. According to Urban, the record of Afghanistan's leaders until 1978 was a pitiful one: they had failed to give the country any of the attributes of the modern centralized state, including a nationwide school system.[19]

Part II. Modernizing Nationalism: The Early Years

Reforms to improve the status of women began during the reign of Abdur Rahman Khan, who ascended the throne in 1880. He abolished a long-standing customary law that, in violation of Islamic law, bound a wife not only to her husband but to his entire family as well: a widow who wanted to remarry had to marry her dead husband's next of kin, often against her will.[20] Among Abdur Rahman's other measures was a law requiring the registration of marriages (*sabt*). He also modified a law pertaining to child marriages, permitting a girl who had been given in marriage before she had reached the age of puberty to refuse or accept her marriage ties when she attained maturity. Still another law allowed a wife to sue her husband for divorce or alimony in cases involving cruelty or nonsupport.[21]

Mahmud Tarzi (1866–1935), a royal adviser, was the first Afghan to take a positive stand on feminism, dedicating to famous women in history a series of articles that discussed the many abilities of women. Because in his view the health, welfare, and education of Afghan families were essential to Afghan progress, he attacked the extravagant expenditures incurred in connection with multiple marriages, which often financially ruined families.[22] His views were supported by the ruler, Habibullah Khan, who attempted to limit the burdensome expenses incurred in connection with marriage. To meet the costs, most Afghans had to borrow, at times paying as much as 75 percent interest. In 1922 Habibullah put a ceiling on the amount that could be spent, urging his people to abandon the customary public celebrations in favor of private parties. By establishing Habibiyeh College, Habibullah also sought to broaden the education system. Despite the founding of the Afghan Ministry of Education, government attempts to improve and standardize the curriculum were not totally successful. Gregorian writes that the mullahs, especially those outside Kabul, resented the government's control of education, the teacher-training center, and the teaching of English and of modern subjects in general, and vehemently resisted all further innovation.[23]

Habibullah Khan was assassinated in 1919, and his son, King Amanullah who ruled from 1919–1929, had the enormous task of convincing the religious establishment that modern secular education and Islam were not incompatible, and that the schools he built did not threaten the sanctity or spiritual message of Islam in Afghanistan.[24] His most audacious acts were to begin a study-abroad program for Afghan students and to open the first schools for girls.

In examining Amanullah's reform program and the organized resistance to it, one discovers parallels with the experience of the PDPA government some fifty years later. According to Gregorian, Amanullah's general program to improve the position of women was promoted by his wife, Queen Soraya (who founded the first women's magazine, *Ershad-e Niswan*), the reformer Mahmud Tarzi and his wife, the small intelligentsia, and the modernist and nationalist Young Afghans, who were impressed by developments in Turkey, Iran, and Egypt. In 1921 Amanullah enacted the Family Code, which undertook to regulate marriages and engagements. Child marriages and intermarriage between close kin were outlawed as contrary to Islamic principles. In the new code Amanullah reiterated Abdur Rahman's ruling that a widow was to be free of the domination of her husband's family. He followed his father's example and placed tight restrictions on wedding expenses, including dowries, and granted wives the right to appeal to the courts if their husbands did not adhere to Quranic tenets regarding marriage. In the fall of 1924, Afghan women were given the right to choose their husbands, a measure that incensed the traditionalists.[25]

The presence in Kabul of a considerable number of unveiled women, especially Turkish women who had abandoned the veil and adopted modern dress, undoubtedly encouraged the efforts of the new Afghan feminists. However, their greatest support came from Amanullah himself, who believed that the keystone of the future structure of new Afghanistan would be the emancipation of women.[26] The Afghan press, including bulletins of the War Office, took part in the emancipation campaign. In 1928, during the final months of his rule, Amanullah made a frontal assault on the institution of purdah, which "hid half the Afghan nation." Because of his efforts and the personal example of Queen Soraya, some one hundred Afghan women had reportedly discarded the veil by October 1928.

By this time, Afghan legislation was among the most progressive in the Muslim world. No other country had yet addressed the sensitive issues of child marriage and polygyny. Afghan family law on these issues became the model for similar reforms in Soviet Central Asia in 1926.[27] It is not surprising that the family law of 1921 was a major cause of the uprising instigated by the clergy in 1924.

The first organized reaction against Amanullah reforms was directed against the controversial administrative code, the Nizam-nameh, which he promulgated in 1923. Among other things, the code attempted to liberalize the position of women and to permit the government to regulate the various family problems formerly dealt with by the local mullah. A few traditionalist mullahs inveighed against the new code, asserting that it was contrary to the precepts of Islamic law. Their cause was picked up in 1924 by the Mangal tribe of the Khost region, and in March armed warfare broke out. The religious and tribal leaders were particularly exercised over the sections of the code that deprived men of full authority over wives and daughters, and they were further incensed at the opening of public schools for girls.

The Khost rebellion continued for more than nine months. Gregorian writes that both the rebels and the government side suffered enormous losses, and that the cost of the rebellion represented the total government receipts for two years. The king was forced to postpone various modernization projects and to revoke or modify many important sections of the Nizam-nameh; the schooling of girls, for example, was limited to the under-twelve age group. In 1928 the Loya Jirga, the traditional Afghan consultative body, rejected Amanullah's proposal to set a minimum age for marriage of eighteen for women and twenty for men. The Loya Jirga also vehemently opposed modern, Western education for Afghan girls in Afghanistan or outside it.

In the autumn of 1928, a group of female students was sent to Turkey for higher education, and the Association for the Protection of Women's Rights (Anjoman-i Hemayat-i Neswan) was established to help women fight domestic injustice and take a role in public life. The queen presided over several committees to strengthen the emancipation campaign. These unprecedented measures, which violated traditional norms, offended the religious leaders and their following, especially in rural areas. Reaction against the campaign for women's emancipation was a major factor in the outbreak of violent disturbances in November and December.

When the king banned the practice of polygyny among government officials, it caused an uproar among the religious establishment. A tribal revolt ensued, led by Bacha-i Saqqo, a Tajik rebel claiming Islamic credentials. As the political situation deteriorated, Amanullah was compelled to cancel most of his social reforms and to suspend his controversial administrative measures. The Afghan girls studying in Constantinople were to be recalled, and the schools for girls were to be closed; women were not to go unveiled or cut their hair; the mullahs were no longer to be required to obtain teaching certificates; compulsory military recruitment was to be abandoned; and the old tribal system was to be reinstated.[28]

As a last, desperate concession, the unhappy king agreed to the formation of a council of fifty notables, to be chosen from among "the most respected religious luminaries and tribal chieftains," and promised to abide by their advice as well as to conform to Islamic law as interpreted by the orthodox religious leaders. Any measure the government proposed to enact was to be ratified by this council. But in the end, all of these concessions were to no avail. The rebels attacked Kabul, and Amanullah abdicated and left Afghanistan.

Not until the 1950s were reforms attempted again. In 1950 a law was passed banning ostentatious life-cycle ceremonies. It prohibited many of the expensive aspects of birth, circumcision, marriage, and burial rituals but was difficult to enforce. The Marriage Law of 1971 once again tried to curb the indebtedness arising from the costs of marriage. The Civil Law of 1977 abolished child marriage and established sixteen as the minimum age of marriage for girls, but the law was ignored. Furthermore, it left the husband's right to unilateral divorce basically untouched.[29]

The above overview suggests the enormous difficulty faced by Afghan modernizers. The Afghan state had been too weak to implement reforms or to undertake modernization in an effective way, and was constantly confronted by religious and tribal forces seeking to prevent any change whatsoever, particularly in regard to their power. Nevertheless, as in many other Third World countries in the 1960s, a left-wing modernizing elite organized itself to address the country's problems and to steer Afghanistan away from its dependency on U.S. aid money.

III. The Saur Revolution and Women's Rights

In 1965 a group from the small Afghan intelligentsia formed the People's Democratic Party of Afghanistan (PDPA). Evoking the Amanullah experiment, the PDPA envisaged a national democratic government to liberate Afghanistan from backwardness. Among its demands were primary education in their mother tongue for all children and the development of the country's various languages and cultures. Its social demands included guarantees of the right to work, equal treatment for women, a forty-two-hour week, paid sickness and maternity leave, and a ban on child labor.

That same year, six women activists formed the Democratic Organization of Afghan Women (DOAW), whose main objectives were to eliminate illiteracy among women, forced marriage, and the brideprice. The 1964 Constitution had granted women the right to vote, and thus in the 1970s four women from the DOAW were elected to Parliament. Both the PDPA and the DOAW were eager for profound, extensive, and permanent social change.[30]

Among the most remarkable and influential of the DOAW activists was Anahita Ratebzad. In the 1950s she studied nursing in the United States, and then returned to Kabul as director and instructor of nursing at Women's Hospital. When the faculty for women at Kabul University was established, she entered the medical college and became a member of its teaching staff upon graduation in 1963. She joined the PDPA in 1965 and was one of the four female candidates for Parliament. In 1968 conservative members of Parliament proposed enactment of a law prohibiting Afghan girls from studying abroad. Hundreds of girls demonstrated in opposition. In 1970 two mullahs protested public evidence of female liberation such as miniskirts, women teachers, and schoolgirls by shooting at the legs of women in Western dress and splashing them with acid; among those who joined the mullahs was Gulbeddin Hekmatyar (who went on to be a leading figure in the mujahideen, one of the "freedom fighters" hailed by President Reagan). This time five thousand girls demonstrated.[31]

In April 1978, the PDPA seized power in what came to be called the 3aul (April) Revolution, and introduced a program to change the political and social structure of Afghan society. Three decrees were its main planks: Decree No. 6 was intended to put an end to land mortgage and indebtedness; No. 7 was designed to stop the payment of brideprice and give women more freedom of choice in marriage; and No. 8 consisted of rules and regulations for the confiscation and redistribution of land.[32] The decrees were complementary, but Decree No. 7 seems to have been the most controversial. On November 4, 1978, President Noor Mohammad Taraki declared: "Through the issuance of decrees no. 6 and 7, the hard-working peasants were freed from bonds of oppressors and moneylenders, ending the sale of girls for good as hereafter nobody would be entitled to sell any girl or woman in this country."[33] The six articles of Decree No. 7 were as follows:

Article 1. No one shall engage a girl or give her in marriage in exchange for cash or commodities.

Article 2. No one shall compel the bridegroom or his guardians to give holiday presents to the girl or her family.

Article 3. The girl or her guardian shall not take cash or commodities in the name of dower [*mahr*] in excess of ten dirham [Arabic coinage] according to Shari'at [Islamic law], which is not more than 300 afs. [about U.S. $10] on the basis of the bank rate of silver.

Article 4. Engagements and marriage shall take place with the full consent of the parties involved: (a) No one shall force marriage; (b) No one shall prevent the free marriage of a widow or force her into marriage because of family relationships [the levirate] or patriarchal ties; (c) No one shall prevent legal marriages on the pretext of engagement, forced engagement expenses, or by using force.

Article 5. Engagement and marriages for women under 16 and men under 18 are not permissible.

Article 6. (1) Violators shall be liable to imprisonment from six months to three years; (2) Cash or commodities accepted in violation of the provisions of this decree shall be confiscated.[34]

The PDPA government also embarked upon an aggressive literacy campaign that was led by the DOAW, whose function was to educate women, bring them out of seclusion, and initiate social programs. PDPA cadre established literacy classes for men, women, and children in villages, and by August 1979 the government had established six hundred new schools.[35]

The PDPA program was clearly audacious, aimed at the rapid transformation of a patriarchal society and a power structure based on tribal and landlord authority. Revolutionary change, state-building, and women's rights subsequently went hand in hand. This led one commentator to write:

> The novel character of the new regime [in Afghanistan] soon became apparent. It committed itself to land reform, to equality of the nationalities, to emancipating women, to a solution of the nomadic question. So it was that at a time and in a place suspected by few, and in a country renowned only for colonial war and narcotic plenitude, a revolutionary process of some description had begun.[36]

The emphasis on women's rights on the part of the PDPA reflected (a) its socialist/Marxist ideology; (b) its modernizing and egalitarian outlook; (c) its social base and origins (urban middle-class, professionals educated in the United States, the USSR, India, or western and eastern Europe; and (d) the influence of women members of the PDPA, such as Anahita Ratebzad. In 1976 Ratebzad had been elected to the central committee of the PDPA; after the Saur Revolution, she was elected to the Revolutionary Council of the Democratic Republic of Afghanistan (DRA) and appointed minister of social affairs. Other influential PDPA women in the Taraki government (April 1978–September 1979) included (no last name) Firouza, director of the Afghan Red Crescent Society (Red Cross); and Professor R. S. Siddiqui (who was especially outspoken in her criticism of "feudalistic patriarchal relations"). In the Amin government (September–December 1979), the following women headed schools and the women's organization, as well as sat on government subcommittees: Fawjiyah Shahsawari, Dr. Aziza, Shirin Afzal, Alamat Tolqun. These were the women who were behind the program for women's rights. Their intention was to expand literacy, especially for girls and women; encourage income-generating projects and employment for women; provide health and legal services for women; and eliminate those aspects of Muslim family law that discriminate against women—unilateral male repudiation, a father's exclusive rights to child custody, unequal inheritance, and male guardianship over women.

Patriarchal Resistance to Change

PDPA attempts to change marriage laws, expand literacy, and educate rural girls met with strong opposition. Fathers with unmarried daughters resented Decree No. 7 most because they could no longer expect to receive large brideprice payments, and because it represented a threat to male honor. According to Beattic, "By banning brideprice—and especially by declaring that women could marry whom they pleased—it threatened to undermine the strict control over women on which the maintenance of male honor depended."[37]

The right of women to divorce was one of the most significant measures introduced by the PDPA. Although the divorce law was never officially announced, owing to the outbreak of tribal Islamist opposition to the regime, the family courts (*mahakem-i famili*), mostly presided over by female judges, provided hearing sessions for discontented wives and sought to protect their rights to divorce and on related issues, such as alimony, child custody, and child support.

PDPA attempts to institute compulsory education—provided for in the Constitution of 1964 but ignored by the population—were opposed by traditionalists and by fathers keen to maintain control over their daughters. Believing that women should not appear at public gatherings, villagers often refused to attend classes after the first day. PDPA cadre viewed this attitude as retrograde and resorted to various forms of persuasion, including physical force, to change minds. Often PDPA cadre were either ousted from villages or murdered. In the summer of 1978 refugees began pouring into Pakistan, giving as their major reason the forceful implementation of the literacy program among women. In Kandahar, three literacy workers from the women's organization were killed as symbols of the unwanted revolution. Two men killed all the women in their families to save them from "dishonor."[38] An Islamist opposition began organizing and conducted several armed actions against the government in spring 1979.

Internal battles within the PDPA (especially between its two wings, Parcham and Khalq) exacerbated the government's difficulties. In September 1979 President Taraki was killed on orders of his deputy, Hafizullah Amin, a ruthless and ambitious man who imprisoned and executed hundreds of his own comrades in addition to further alienating the population.[39] The Pakistani regime of Zia ul-Haq was opposed to leftists next door, and supported the mujahideen armed uprising. In December 1979 the Soviet army intervened, beginning a long military engagement in the civil war on the side of the PDPA government. Amin was killed and succeeded by Babrak Karmal, who initiated what was called "the second phase" (*marhale-i dovvom*).

PDPA and DOAW attempts to extend literacy to rural girls have been widely criticized for heavy-handedness by most commentators on Afghanistan. Three points regarding this criticism are in order. First, literacy campaigns are common during or following popular revolutions and movements for national or social liberation: the Bolsheviks, Chinese, Cubans, Vietnamese, Angolans, Palestinians, Eritreans, and Nicaraguans had extensive literacy campaigns. Second, the PDPA's rationale for pursuing the rural literacy campaign with some zeal was that all previous reformers had made literacy a matter of choice; male guardians had chosen not to allow their females to be educated, hence 98 percent of Afghan women were illiterate. It was therefore decided that literacy was not a matter of (men's) choice but, rather, a matter of principle and law. Third, state coercion to raise the status of women had been employed elsewhere, notably Soviet Central Asia and Turkey in the 1920s, and other governments have issued decrees that have been resisted. The last point is not to condone the use of force but to point out that rights, reforms, and revolutions have been effected coercively or attained through struggle.

It should be noted that not everyone in the PDPA and the DOAW was in favor of the pace of the reforms. According to Soraya, many DOAW activists, including herself, thought they should be sought in a more measured fashion. As a result of her antagonism toward Hafizullah Amin, Soraya, like many in the Parcham wing, was imprisoned and even tortured. She and the others were released after the Soviet intervention, the death of Amin, and his replacement by Babrak Karmal.[40]

In 1980 the PDPA slowed down its reform program and announced its intention to eliminate illiteracy in the cities in seven years and in the provinces in ten. In an interview that year Anahita Ratebzad conceded errors, "in particular the compulsory education of women;" "the reactionary elements immediately made use of these mistakes to spread discontent among the population."[41] Despite the moderation (including concessions such as the restoration of Muslim family law),[42] the Peshawar-based opposition—supported by Pakistan, the United States, China, the Islamic Republic of Iran, and Saudi Arabia—intensified its efforts to destroy the Kabul regime. In contrast to other states, the Afghan state was unable to impose its will through an extensive administrative and military apparatus. As a result, the program for land redistribution and women's rights faltered. The efforts to raise women's status through legal innovations regarding marriage were stymied by patriarchal structures highly resistant to change, by a hostile international environment, and by an extremely destructive civil war.

There can be no doubt that the manner in which land reform and women's emancipation were implemented immediately after the Saur Revolution was seriously flawed. Some of the bold symbols of the revolution—red flags, the term *comrade*, pictures of Lenin, and the like—were also ill-advised, considering the extremely conservative and patriarchal social structure, and they contributed to the hostility. Nevertheless, the conflict in Afghanistan must be understood as contestation over two unalterably opposed political-cultural projects: development and reform on the one hand, tribal authority and patriarchal relations on the other.

The literature on Afghanistan has been exceedingly partisan, and much of it very pro-mujahideen, with a noticeable reluctance to discuss the positive aspects of the PDPA state's social program, notably its policy on women's rights. One political journalist, however, has written that "one genuine achievement of the revolution has been the emancipation of (mainly urban) women."

> There is no doubt that thousands of women are committed to the regime, as their prominent participation in Revolutionary Defense Group militias shows. Eyewitnesses stated that militant militiawomen played a key role in defending the besieged town of Urgun in 1983. Four of the seven militia commanders appointed to the Revolutionary Council in January 1986 were women."[43]

As one enthusiastic teenage girl said to me at a PDPA rally in Kabul in early 1989: "This revolution was made for women!"

The early PDPA emphasis on the woman question subsided in favor of a concerted effort at "national reconciliation," that began in January 1987. In the Constitution of November 1988, the result of a Loya Jirga, or traditional assembly, PDPA members and activists from the Women's Council tried to retain an article stipulating the equality of women with men; it was opposed by the non-PDPA members of the assembly. A compromise was reached in Article 38:

> Citizens of the Republic of Afghanistan—men and women—have equal rights and duties before the law, irrespective of national, racial, linguistic, tribal, educational and social status, religion, creed, political conviction, occupation, kinship, wealth, and residence. Designation of any illegal privilege of discrimination against rights and duties of citizens are forbidden.[44]

Women in Kabul and in Peshawar: A Comparison

During the 1980s in areas under government control, and especially in Kabul, women were present in the various ranks of the party and the government, with the exception of the Council of Ministers. The Loya Jirga included women delegates; in 1989 Parliament had seven female members. Women in prominent positions in 1989 included Massouma Esmaty Wardak, president of the Women's Council; Shafiqeh Razmandeh, vice-president of the Women's Council; Soraya, director of the Afghan Red Crescent Society; Zahereh Dadmal, director of the Kabul Women's Club; Dr. Soheila, chief surgeon of the Military Hospital, who also held the rank of general. The Central Committee of the PDPA had several women members, including Jamila Palwasha and Ruhafza (alternate member), a working-class grandmother and "model worker" at the Kabul Construction Plant (where she did electrical wiring).

In Kabul in January–February 1989, I saw women employees in all the government agencies and social organizations I visited. Ariana Airlines employed female as well as male flight attendants. A thirty-seven-year-old male employee of the Peace, Solidarity and Friendship Organization told me that he had a woman supervisor who was ten years his junior. There were women radio announcers, and the evening news on television (whether in Pushtu or Dari) was read by one male and one female, who was unveiled. Women technicians as well as reporters worked in radio and television, and for newspapers and magazines. Women laborers were present in the binding section of a printing house in Kabul; in the page-setting section of the Higher and Vocational Education press house; at the state-run CREPCA carpet company (where young women wove carpets and received wages); and at the Kabul Construction Plant (which specialized in housing and prefabricated materials). Like their male counterparts, these women were members of the Central Trade Union. I also saw one woman employee (and several women volunteer soldiers) at Pol-e Charkhi prison; she oversaw the six remaining female political prisoners, all charged with terrorist acts. I was told that there were women soldiers and officers in the regular armed forces, as well as in the militia and Women's Self Defense (Defense of the Revolution) Units. There were women in security, intelligence, and the police agencies; women involved in logistics in the Defense Ministry; women parachutists; and even women veterinarians — an occupation usually off-limits to women in Islamic countries. In 1989 all female members of the PDPA received military training and arms. These women were prominent at a party rally of some fifty thousand held in Kabul in early February 1989.

Above the primary level, schools were now segregated, and middle school and secondary school girls were taught by female teachers—a concession made to traditionalist elements. In offices and other workplaces, however, there was no segregation. Nor were buses divided into male and female sections.

During the 1980s a number of social organizations had considerable female participation and visibility. Apart from the PDPA itself, they included the Council of Trade Unions; the Democratic Youth Organization; the Peace, Solidarity and Friendship Organization; the Women's Council; and the Red Crescent Society. Two of these organizations were led by women: the president of the Afghan Red Crescent Society was Soraya, and the Afghan Women's Council (AWC; formerly the DOAW) was run by Massouma Esmaty Wardak and a staff of eight.[45] Wardak was not a PDPA member, but some of the staff were. A graduate of the Academy of Sciences, she had a degree in sociology and an interest in literature and history. Among her published works is a book on women in Afghan society: from the late eighteenth century to the late nineteenth.

In discussions with Wardak and Soraya, I learned AWC had become less political than in the past and more service-oriented. Typical of its work: literacy and vocational training in such fields as secretarial work, hairdressing, and sewing (workshops were located in its complex); organizing income-generating activities (mainly weaving rugs and carpets, and sewing); assisting mothers and widows of "martyrs of the Revolution" with pensions and coupons; and giving legal advice, mainly through a network of women lawyers. Some women had "outwork" arrangements with the AWC, as Wardak explained, "They prefer to work at home; they bring their work to us and we pay them." During two visits to the AWC I observed dozens of women (many of them poor and veiled) entering the grounds to attend a class or to seek help.

The AWC had a membership of 150,000 and branches in all provinces except Wardak and Katawaz. The branches organized traditional festivals and "peace camps," which provided medical care and distributed free garments and relief goods. The branches also helped women to earn money through various farm enterprises such as raising chickens and producing eggs and milk, and through sewing and craftwork. The work of the AWC was generously supported by the government.[47]

The principal objectives of the AWC were to raise women's social consciousness, to make them aware of their rights, particularly their right to literacy and work, and to improve their living conditions and professional skills. Equal pay with men and workplace child care were two important achievements. There was also an ongoing radio and television campaign against "the buying and selling of girls." In early 1989 the AWC was also trying to change the child-custody laws that favor the father and his agnates.

Like the AWC, the Kabul Women's Club was located on spacious grounds and held literacy classes daily, conducted vocational training, and housed workshops where women wove rugs and carpets, sewed uniforms, embroidered, and produced handicrafts. The work was entirely waged, and child care and transportation were provided. Courses on house management, health, hairdressing, and typing were offered free of charge. The Women's Club also worked with the Public Health Ministry on mother-and-child issues, such as prevention of diseases, vaccination of children, breast feeding, and family planning.[48]

In Kabul I asked many party members and workers of the AWC if women's rights would be sacrificed on the altar of national reconciliation. All were fervent believers in the party's duty to defend the gains made in women's rights, and in the ability of the women's organizations to stand up for women's rights to education and employment. Among women in the capital, there was considerable hostility toward the mujahideen, and I was told several times that "the women would not allow" a mujahideen takeover.

In the refugee camps in Peshawar, Pakistan, the situation of women and their opportunities were very different. Unlike liberation, resistance, and guerilla movements elsewhere, the Afghan mujahideen never encouraged the active participation of women. In Cuba, Algeria, Vietnam, China, Eritrea, Oman, Iran, Nicaragua, El Salvador, and Palestine, women were or are active in the front lines, in party politics, and in social services. It is noteworthy that the mujahideen had no female spokespersons. Indeed, women in Peshawar who became too visible or vocal were threatened and sometimes killed. The group responsible for most of the intimidation of women was the fundamentalist Hizb-e Islami, led by Gulbeddin Hekmatyar, who over the years received substantial military, political, and financial support from the United States, Pakistan, and Saudi Arabia.

The education in Peshawar was extremely biased against girls. In 1988 some 104,600 boys and 7,800 girls were enrolled in schools. For boys, there were 486 primary schools, 161 middle schools and 4 high schools; For girls, 76 primary schools, 2 middle schools, and no high schools.[49] A UNICEF study indicated that there were only 180 Afghan women with a high school education in the refugee camps.

The subordinate status of women was apparently decried by some in Peshawar. The Revolutionary Association of Women of Afghanistan (RAWA) was founded in 1977 (as a Maoist group) but was made prominent on February 4, 1987, when its founder, Mina Kishwar Kamal, was killed by Islamists in Quetta. RAWA staged a demonstration by women and children in Rawalpindi on December 27, 1988, the ninth anniversary of the Soviet military intervention in Afghanistan. The demonstrators distributed pamphlets attacking the KGB, Khad (the Afghan political police), and the Hizb-e Islami in the strongest terms. They claimed that the majority of Afghans stood for an independent and democratic Afghanistan, where social justice and freedom to women were guaranteed.[50] In a communiqué distributed that day RAWA deplored "the reactionary fanatics [who] are savagely suppressing our grieved people, specially [sic] the women." It continued:

> Killing the innocent men and women, raping, to marry forcefully young girls and widows, and hostility toward women literacy and education, are some customary cruelties committed by the fundamentalists who have made the life inside and outside the country bitter and suffocating. In their cheap opinion, the women's struggle for any right and freedom is regarded as infidelity which must be suppressed brutaly [*sic*].

The communiqué also decried the "anti-democratic and anti-woman" activities of the fundamentalists and warned of "fundamentalist fascism" replacing the Najibullah regime.

Following the withdrawal of Soviet troops in February 1989, there was some hope that a compromise could be reached between the government of President Najibullah and the mujahideen. To facilitate this, the government revised its ideological and programmatic orientation. Following its congress in spring 1990, the PDPA changed its name to the Hizb-e Watan, or the Homeland Party. Constitutional changes were also made, stressing Islam and nation and dropping altogether references to the equality of men and women. Clearly, a decision had been made that the emancipation of women would have to await peace, stability, reconstruction, and development. But by April 1992, when the new UN secretary-general, Boutros Boutros Ghali, and his envoy, Benon Sevan, failed to secure the cooperation of the Mujahideen, Pakistan, Iran, and the United States towards a cessation of hostilities, Najibullah agreed to give up power. This triggered demoralization and desertion in the Afghan military, dissension within the government, and the takeover of Kabul by mujahideen fighters. Once they came to power, mujahideen factions began to fight one another, but the men all agreed on the question of women. Thus the very first order of the new government was that all women should wear veils. One journalist wrote from Kabul in early May 1992:

> The most visible sign of change on the streets, apart from the guns, is the utter disappearance of women in western clothes. They used to be a com-

mon sight. Now women cover up from ankle to throat and hide their hair, or else use the burqa. Many women are frightened to leave their homes. At the telephone office, 80 percent of the male workers reported for duty on Saturday, and only 20 percent of the females.[51]

IV. Conclusions: Reflections on Feminist Nationalism

If we define *feminism* not in the Western ethnocentric sense but, rather, as "organized activity on behalf of women's rights and interests," and if we define *nationalism* as "organized activity to promote the advancement of the nation," then clearly the PDPA government had a feminist nationalist agenda, as did the government of King Amanullah in the 1920s. By no stretch of the imagination, however, can we consider the mujahideen to have had—or to have now—anything resembling a program for women's rights. To the contrary, their armed opposition to the PDPA government, as we have seen, was very much motivated by the reforms to improve the status of women. As in the 1920s, tribal-Islamist reaction to legal reforms undermined attempts to transform a deeply patriarchal society and to improve the status of women. Nor can we regard the mujahideen as nationalists, considering their tribal origins and the fragmentation of the mujahideen alliance into warring factions after 1992.

Why, then, was the Afghan government not supported in its endeavors by the international community? Why did feminists and women's organizations around the world not rally to the support of the program for the emancipation of women in Afghanistan? Why, to the contrary, was there so much international support for the mujahideen? One reason is that the Afghan government was caught in the continuing Cold War confrontation and competition between the United States and the Soviet Union. When it came to power in 1978, it soon came to be seen as a Soviet pawn, and the association tainted the government even before the military intervention of the Soviet army in December 1979. Related to this was the tendency, during the 1980s, to regard the mujahideen as valiant rebels, guerrillas fighting to liberate their country from an oppressive government and an imperialist superpower. It may also be that the international women's movement, being far less organized in the early to mid-1980s than it has been in the post-Nairobi period, and especially during the 1990s, lacked the capacity to put forward criticisms and recommendations. Women's organizations that were sympathetic to the reform program were either unable to provide any concrete support or were reluctant to be perceived as supporting the PDPA government.

Perhaps a very crucial reason for the absence of support for the women's rights and reform program was a widespread perception that this was somehow inappropriate in a developing Muslim context. It should be recalled that during the 1980s, debates raged around issues of universalism versus cultural relativism, women's rights and community rights, orientalism and neocolonialist discourses, the nature of Islamist movements, and the meaning of development. Feminists from around the world had not yet found common ground, and there existed a notion that there was a feminism for the West but different priorities for the women of the South. Thus, in the mid–1980s, Nancy Tapper could write: "Such proposed reforms, casting the issues of poverty and women's status into a basically First World perspective, may be seen as a radical improvement from the legislators' point of view, [but] this perspective has many critics in the Third World and elsewhere."[52]

Concepts of liberation and autonomy were viewed as legitimate for national movements but inappropriate when applied to gender relations, especially in Muslim countries. Veiling and seclusion were regarded as cultural artifacts not to be criticized. Kathleen Howard-Merriam wrote:

> The mujahideen leaders recognize women's importance to the jihad (holy war) with their exhortations to preserve women's honor through the continued practice of seclusion. The reinforcement of this tradition, most Westerners have failed to notice, serves to strengthen the men's will to resist. . . . Purdah provides the opportunity for preserving one's own identity and a certain stability in the face of external pressures. . . .[53]

In point of fact, such statements and positions were simplistic and suspect for at least three reasons. First, the government of Iran, next door to Afghanistan, was widely criticized for its imposition of veiling and other forms of social control over women, instituted during the early 1980s. "Universal" concepts of women's rights were applied to the Iranian case but not to the Afghan case. Second, the opponents of the PDPA government and the supporters of the mujahideen made no claim that the mujahideen brand of nationalism was compatible with feminism or with women's rights. The mujahideen's retrograde position on women was clear to all (suggesting that anti-communism rather than the mujahideen's social program motivated much of the international support). Third, there is much diversity in women's legal status and social positions in the Muslim world, ranging from extremely circumscribed (Afghanistan, the Gulf sheikhdoms, Saudi Arabia) to quite liberal (Tunisia, Turkey, Egypt), with a great deal of domestic variation along class lines (generally, the more educated the women, the more their lifestyles and attitudes mirror those of women in any other country).

In more recent years, feminists from around the world have come to converge on issues pertaining to women's rights and interests. Feminist networks link women's groups in developed and developing countries alike. It is no longer possible to speak of one feminism for the West and another for the developing world. Feminists everywhere are now agreed on the basic issues of education, income, and reproductive rights for women, no matter what the cultural context, and they are struggling for greater political representation and participation in economic decision making. Feminist movements have proliferated in the Muslim world—especially in Algeria, Egypt, Tunisia, Turkey, Malaysia, and Pakistan—and they have taken strong exception to forms of nationalism that link cultural and national identity to an exclusively domestic role for women or to certain forms of mandatory dress.

The case of Afghanistan illustrates, in particular, that movements for national liberation must be judged on their social programs, especially on women's rights.

Notes

1. This chapter draws on my previously published work, especially chapter 7 in *Modernizing Women: Gender and Social Change in the Middle East* (Boulder: Lynne Rienner, 1993); and "Reform, Revolution and Reaction: The Trajectory of the Woman Question in Afghanistan," in *Gender and National Identity: Women and Politics in Muslim Societies* ed. V. M. Moghadam (London: Zed Books, 1994).

2. Louis Dupree, *Afghanistan* (Princeton: Princeton University Press, 1980); Olivier Roy, *Islam and Resistance in Afghanistan*, 2d ed. (Cambridge: Cambridge University Press, 1990).

3. Vartan Gregorian, *The Emergence of Modern Afghanistan* (Stanford: Stanford University Press, 1969); Thomas Hammond, *Red Flag Over Afghanistan* (Boulder: Westview Press, 1984), p. 5; Mark Urban, *War in Afghanistan* (New York: St. Martin's Press, 1988), p. 204.

4. Gregory Massell, *The Surrogate Proletariat: Moslem Women and Revolutionary Strategies in Soviet Central Asia, 1919–1929* (Princeton: Princeton University Press, 1974), p. 9.

5. On Pushtunwali and Islam, see Roy, *Islam and Resistance in Afghanistan*, pp. 34–37; John C. Griffiths, *Afghanistan* (Boulder: Westview Press, 1981), pp. 111–12; Inger Boesen, "Conflicts of Solidarity in Pukhtun Women's Lives," in *Women in Islamic Society* ed. Bo Utas, (Copenhagen: Scandinavian Institute of Asian Studies, 1983).

6. On the brideprice and property rights, see Nancy Tapper, "Causes and Consequences of the Abolition of Brideprice in Afghanistan," in *Revolutions and Rebellions in Afghanistan* ed. M. Nazif Shahrani and Robert L. Canfield (Berkeley: Institute of International Studies, 1984); and *Bartered Brides: Politics, Gender and Marriage in Our Afghan Tribal Society* (Cambridge: Cambridge University Press, 1991). A comprehensive study is in Mohammad Hashim Kamali, *Law in Afghanistan: A Study of the Constitutions, Matrimonial Law and the Judiciary* (Leiden: E. J. Brill, 1985). See also Raja Anwar, *The Tragedy of Afghanistan* (London: Verso, 1988), esp. chap. 11, "The Contradictions of Afghan Society."

7. Haleh Afshar, "The Position of Women in an Iranian Village," in *Women, Work and Ideology in the Third World*, ed. H. Afshar (London: Tavistock, 1985), esp. pp. 75–76; Günseli Berik, *Women Carpet Weavers in Rural Turkey: Patterns of Employment, Earnings, and Status* (Geneva: ILO, 1987), esp. chap. 4; Deniz Kandiyoti, "Rural Transformation in Turkey and Its Implications for Women's Status," in UNESCO, *Women on the Move* (Paris; UNESCO, 1984), pp. 17–30.

8. John Caldwell, *A Theory of Fertility Decline* (New York: Academic Press, 1982); Deniz Kandiyoti, "Bargaining with Patriarchy," *Gender and Society* 2, no. 3 (September 1988): 274–290.

9. On *fitna*, see Fatna Sabbah, *Woman in the Muslim Unconscious* (New York: Pergamon Press, 1984); and Mai Ghoussoub, "Feminism—or the Eternal Masculine—in the Arab World," *New Left Review* 161 (January/February 1987): 3–13. See also Naila Kabeer, "Subordination and Struggle: Women in Bangladesh," *New Left Review* 168 (March/April 1988): 95.

10. See Hanna Papanek, "To Each Less Than She Needs, From Each More Than She Can Do: Allocations, Entitlements, and Values," in *Persistent Inequalities*, ed. Irene Tinker (New York: Oxford University Press, 1990). See also Valentine M. Moghadam, "Patriarchy and the Politics of Gender in Modernising Societies: Iran, Pakistan and Afghanistan," *International Sociology* 7, no. 1 (March 1992): 35–53.

11. Tapper, "The Abolition of Brideprice in Afghanistan," p. 293. See also Tapper, *Bartered Brides*, pp. 45, 104, 142.

12. Griffiths, *Afghanistan*, p. 78.

13. Veronica Doubleday, *Three Women of Herat* (Austin: University of Texas Press, 1988), p. 149.

14. This was also confirmed to me in interviews with Dr. Saidali Jalali and Dr.

Azizullah Saidi, Indira Gandhi Hospital, Kabul, February 11, 1989. For data on health and other social indicators, see Moghadam, *Modernizing Women*, chap. 7.

15. Boesen "Conflicts of Solidarity"; Tapper, "Abolition of the Brideprice;" Doubleday, *Three Women of Herat*; Simone Bailleau Lajoinie, *Conditions des femmes en Afghanistan* (Paris: Notre Temps/Monde, 1980).

16. Massell, *The Surrogate Proletariat*, pp. 160–163; Tapper, *Bartered Brides*, esp. chaps. 7, 8, 9.

17. For a thorough discussion of state capabilities, see Joel Migdal, *Strong Societies and Weak States: State-Society Relations and State Capabilities in the Third World* (Princeton: Princeton University Press, 1988). On the weak Afghan state, see Urban, *War in Afghanistan*, p. 4.

18. See in particular, Gregorian, *The Emergence of Modern Afghanistan*. See also Griffiths, *Afghanistan*; Hammond, *Red Flag Over Afghanistan*; Henry Bradsher, *Afghanistan and the Soviet Union* (Durham: Duke University Press, 1985); Urban, *War in Afghanistan*.

19. Urban, *War in Afghanistan*, p. 204.

20. Ibid., p. 138. See also Lajoinie, *Conditions des femmes en Afghanistan*, p. 61. This is known as the levirate.

21. Gregorian, The *Emergence of Modern Afghanistan*, p. 139.

22. Ibid., p. 172.

23. Ibid., p. 198.

24. Ibid., p. 241.

25. Ibid., p. 244.

26. Ibid., p. 244.

27. See Massell, *The Surrogate Proletariat*, p. 219.

28. Gregorian, *The Emergence of Modern Afghanistan*, p. 264.

29. Kamali, *Law in Afghanistan*, pp. 86–87.

30. Interview with Soraya, DOAW founding member and past president, Kabul, February 6, 1989, and Helsinki, October 8, 1990. Soraya identified three of the four women parliamentarians: Anahita Ratebzad, Massouma Esmaty Wardak, and Mrs. Saljugi.

31. This paragraph draws from Nancy Hatch Dupree, "Revolutionary Rhetoric and Afghan Women," in Shahrani and Canfield, *Revolutions and Rebellions in Afghanistan*.

32. Hugh Beattie, "Effects of the Saur Revolution in Nahrin," in Shahrani and Canfield, *Revolutions and Rebellions in Afghanistan,* p. 186.

33. Quoted in Tapper, "Abolition of Brideprice in Afghanistan," p. 294.

34. Beattie, "Effects of the Saur Revolution in Nahrin."

35. Suzanne Jolicoeur Katsikas, *The Arc of Socialist Revolutions: Angola to Afghanistan* (Cambridge, MA: Schenkman, 1982), p. 231.

36. Fred Halliday, "Revolution in Afghanistan," *New Left Review* 112 (November/December 1978): 3.

37. Beattie, "Effects of the Saur Revolution in Nahrin," p. 191.

38. See Dupree, *Afghanistan*.

39. See Anwar, *The Tragedy of Afghanistan*, esp. chaps. 14, 15.

40. Interview with Soraya, Kabul, February 6, 1989.

41. Quoted in Dupree, *Afghanistan*, p. 330.

42. The formal reinstatement of Muslim Family Law did not apply to party members. Interview with a PDPA official, New York, October 28, 1986.

43. Urban, *War in Afghanistan*, p. 209.

44. Interview with Farid Mazdak, PDPA official, Kabul, February 9, 1989.

45. In 1990 Mrs Wardak was made minister of education, which she remained until the collapse of the government in 1992.

46. Interview with Massouma Esmaty Wardak, Kabul, February 1, 1989.

47. Interview with Massouma Esmaty Wardak, Kabul, January 24, 1989.

48. Interview with Zahereh Dadmal, Kabul, February 8, 1989.

49. *New York Times*, April 2, 1988, p. A2.

50. Rahimullah Yusufzai, "Afghanistan: Withdrawal Symptoms," *Herald*, January 1989.

51. Derek Brown, "New Afghanistan Carries on Grisly Game of the Old," *Guardian* (U.K.), May 4, 1992, p. 7.

52. Nancy Tapper, "The Abolition of Brideprice in Afghanistan," p. 291.

53. Kathleen Howard-Merriam, "Afghan Women and Their Struggle for Survival," in *The Afghan Conflict: The Politics of Survival*, ed. Grant Farr and John Merriam (Boulder: Westview Press, 1987), p. 114.

Shifting Sands:
The Feminist-Nationalist Connection in the Palestinian Movement

Sherna Berger Gluck

Feminist suspicion of nationalism has been fueled both by the abysmal European record and by the failure of national liberation movements in the Third World to live up to their promises to women. Indeed, women's experience in the postcolonial Algerian state has become emblematic of the way in which women's gender interests are subverted, if not completely submerged, following independence.[1] Almost thirty years later, and in the context of worldwide women's movements, it initially appeared that Palestine would offer a different model.[2] And during the height of the *intifada*, the Palestinian uprising against Israeli occupation, women activists regularly echoed the refrain "We will not be another Algeria!"

Six years later, as Palestinians began to position themselves for state formation, these same women are considerably less confident, even as they have mobilized to forward a women's agenda. And although the dialogue within the women's movement signals a new level of feminist consciousness, the response from the male leadership of the national movement more closely mirrors old-style nationalist politics. Nevertheless, the emergence of feminist nationalism has changed both the discourse of Palestinian politics and the expectations of large numbers of women.

Tracing the evolution of these recent changes in the seventy-year-long history of the Palestinian national movement helps us to understand better the conditions that promote or hinder the development of feminist nationalism. It is a history that begins with the collapse of the Ottoman Empire; builds strength during the British Mandate; and matures as an anticolonial liberation movement with the loss of the Palestinian homeland after the creation of Israel—especially after the founding of the Palestine Liberation Organization (PLO) in 1964. It has flowered in very different contexts: in the territory remaining of historic Palestine, that is, the West Bank, Gaza, and East Jerusalem; and in the Diaspora, particularly Lebanon, where it established a quasi-autonomous governing authority over the large Palestinian refugee population. As the context changed and in different historical moments, the nature of women's involvement in the nationalist movement varied and so did the development of a feminist agenda.[3]

The Emergence of Palestinian National Consciousness

Until the revolt of the Young Turks in 1908, Palestine, like the other Arab regions in the Ottoman Empire, enjoyed political and cultural autonomy, and local notables served as the governing arm.[4] The Arab consciousness of these notables, that is, their sense of being a distinct ethnic and cultural group based on a shared language and belief in a common origin, was affronted by the effort to impose the Turkish language and culture. Joining forces with the opposition in other parts of the region, they began to press for Arab autonomy within the framework of the Ottoman Empire.[5]

During this same period, following the second "aliyah" (the immigration of Jews to Palestine), the Jewish population of Palestine more than tripled, reaching a new height of more than 80,000. The Palestinian Arabs had not felt threatened by the largely apolitical religious Jews who had lived in their midst for centuries, but they were troubled by these new political immigrants. The peasants, on the one hand, were losing land and access to grazing; the urban elite, on the other hand, was threatened by the possibility of Jewish economic competition. The new Ottoman rulers were not only indifferent to Arab protestations but believed that it was in their own interest to cooperate with the Zionists. As a result, they abolished immigration restrictions of Jews to Palestine and permitted land sales.[6]

Following the defeat of the Ottoman Turks in World War I and the European dismemberment of Greater Syria, the British were granted mandatory power over Palestine. Their support of Zionist aspirations, as codified in the Balfour Declaration, laid the foundation for the emergence of a geographically defined Palestinian nationalism.

For the next thirty years, during the British Mandate of Palestine and until the UN partition plan of 1947, Palestinian nationalists campaigned against continued Jewish immigration. With the exception of the revolt of 1936–1939, the movement remained largely in the hands of the old notable families. After the creation of the state of Israel in 1948, the subsequent Arab-Israeli war, and the exodus of three-quarters of a million Palestinians from the territory taken by the Israelis, the nationalist movement became relatively quiescent. Coping with the shock of their loss and bridled by the Egyptians (who had authority over the Gaza Strip) on the one hand and the Jordanians (who governed the West Bank, including East Jerusalem) on the other hand, Palestinians seemed unable to develop a political agenda that dealt with their new situation.

It was not until the founding of the PLO in 1964 that the national movement was revived. And although small-scale guerilla attacks were launched against Israel as early as 1965, it was the 1967 war and the Israeli occupation of what remained of historic Palestine that gave the Palestinian nationalist movement its real impetus.

The old elite families continued to dominate Palestinian politics in the West Bank, but new nationalist leaders and new political parties (usually referred to as factions) emerged in the Diaspora. From 1970, following the expulsion of the PLO from Jordan, until 1982, when Israel invaded Lebanon, this new generation consolidated its leadership over the nationalist movement. It established political and social bureaucracies to run the affairs of the Palestinians in the refugee camps in Lebanon.

After the expulsion of the PLO from Lebanon, few outlets remained for popular expression of nationalist aspirations. Instead, the nationalist movement in the Diaspora turned its attention to the diplomatic-political arena. By then the internal political climate in the Occupied Palestinian Territories (OPT), particularly in the West Bank, had been transformed. A new local leadership had emerged following municipal elections in 1976, and a new generation of activists became involved in grassroots organizing. Women were a vital part of this process, and in this context they also formed the first of their own women's committees, planting the seed for the feminist nationalism that blossomed ten years later during the *intifada*.

Nationalism, Women's Activism,
and Gendered Boundaries

Activism on behalf of national aspirations was not new to Palestinian women. Historical accounts are too sketchy to assess the extent of their participation in the very earliest spontaneous peasant resistance to Zionist settlement. There are hints, however, that they did participate in an armed clash between Palestinian peasants and Jewish settlers in Affula in 1911.[7]

Starting in 1917, urban women joined the demonstrations against the Balfour Declaration, and in 1920 they were included in a delegation that met with the British high commissioner. One year later, a group of educated, upper-class urban women—most of whom were tied to the male notables who led the nationalist movement—founded the Palestine Women's Union.[8] Significantly, although clan rivalries marked the politics of the men, the women seemed to transcend these differences.

These elite urban women also began to cross traditional gendered boundaries as they moved beyond the charitable work in which women of their class engaged. They traveled to villages in groups of five and six to organize women.[9] And in a bold move, they claimed male public and religious space by holding a demonstration and making speeches at both the major Muslim and Christian holy sites in Jerusalem (Al Aqsa Mosque and the Church of the Holy Sepulchre).[10] Cloaked in the rhetoric of nationalism, their actions subverted, even if they did not openly challenge, the highly gender-segregated structure of the society that was prevalent among their class. In contrast to their contemporaries in Egypt, the Palestinian women made no explicit linkage between their nationalist activism and their own subordinate position.

For the next two decades, these elite urban women mainly pursued their charitable work, although they did provide assistance to the peasants and launched a boycott of Zionist products during the 1936–1939 revolt.[11] They also used their connections to garner support against Zionism from women in other Arab countries. When violence escalated in 1947 following passage of the UN resolution partitioning Palestine, some of these women also joined revolutionary cells and provided the guerrillas with food and water.[12] Later, in 1948, when full-scale war broke out, they played a crucial support role.

The defeat of the Arab forces and the displacement of 800,000 from their land ushered in a very different era. For women, it meant a retreat from direct struggle and the bolder activities in which they had earlier engaged and a return to social and charitable work.[13] Although women's social world had begun to expand in the 1920s and 1930s, meaningful transformations in gender ideology had not taken root. Not only did women remain relegated to their roles in the home but the traditional concept of honor—which was defined by the virtue of women—still prevailed. As a result, the Israeli military succeeded in driving out large numbers of Palestinians from the countryside by playing on the fear of rape.[14]

Faced with the material loss of their homes and possessions and the psychological devastation resulting from the loss of their homeland, refugee women had to devote all their energies to the sheer survival of their families. For those not uprooted, it meant mobilizing all their resources to meet the needs of the ragged, hungry refugees and the wounded fighters streaming into the West Bank and Gaza. Their efforts set the stage for the formation of new charitable organizations, the precursors of many of the institutions that were established in the West Bank in the 1960s. While the older exiled elite women resumed their charitable organizational work in Jordan and Lebanon, their younger counterparts among the middle-class and in refugee camps began to join the political parties that were being formed.[15]

The founding of the PLO in 1964 was a turning point in the nationalist movement, and a new era of women's activism was ushered in. The original Palestinian Women's Union participated in the founding meeting of the Palestinian National Council in East Jerusalem in 1964 and formed branches of the union throughout the West Bank. Operating under the cover of charitable organizations, they organized literacy, sewing, first-aid, and nursing courses, as well as founding orphan homes, hospitals, and schools.[16] The institution-building of these women became the backbone of the campaign of *sumud* (steadfastness) that characterized the period. Some women also began to join political parties and to participate in marches, demonstration and the distribution of leaflets, particularly after the 1967 Israeli invasion and subsequent occupation of the West Bank, including East Jerusalem, and Gaza.

There were no dramatic shifts in the kinds of organizing around and consciousness of gender issues among women in Occupied Palestine until well into the 1970s, but a new and different dynamism marked the experiences of women in the Diaspora. The period of PLO operation in Jordan has been characterized as a "revolutionary tide," and women were part of this tide, joining military operations and becoming full-time cadres.[17] These women, like the earliest nationalist activists, were crossing gendered boundaries, and although there was a spate of statements calling for women's equal participation in the revolution, no real attention was paid to women's issues.

Following the expulsion of the PLO from Jordan in 1970 and during the Lebanon period that followed (1972–1982), women were largely displaced from the armed struggle. Nevertheless, the intense institution-building and internal consolidation of the Resistance movement created opportunities for women. They became members and, occasionally, officials in various organizations as well as employees in the Resistance/PLO offices.[18]

Tremendous efforts were made to mobilize women in the refugee camps in Lebanon, but more attention was paid to defense training, consciousness-raising on nationalist issues, and maternal health projects than to programs that would develop women themselves.[19] Without such programs, the very condition of exile only exacerbated an emphasis on women's domestic and reproductive roles. No longer able to work on the land, the displaced peasant women had few roles outside the home. Furthermore, removed from familiar kin networks, women refugees and exiles in Muslim cultures historically have faced increased restrictions on their movements.[20] This is captured quite poignantly in the words of a Palestinian woman who had been an activist as a teenager in the 1936–1939 revolt and before exile:

> The Palestinian used to be much more advanced in his own country and women were more independent and freer . . . but after 1948 this changed: in the camps the Palestinian became ultra-strict, even fanatic about the "honour" of his women. Perhaps this was because he had lost everything that gave his life meaning and "honour" was the only possession remaining to him.[21]

Additionally, the task of preserving and reproducing both the culture and the people falls to women. After the massacres in the refugee camps in 1975–1976 and again in 1982, the burden of bearing more children became enormous. As Hamida Kazi points out, "in the absence of any state or government of their own, the family assumes a strong institutional character and women find themselves as the bearers of Palestinian culture which only they can keep alive wherever they may be."[22]

In the face of these pressures, the general Union of Palestinian Women (GUPW) had neither the vision nor the will to challenge the prevailing gender ideology of the nationalist movement. Formed in 1965 as a result of a call by one of the original founders of the Palestinian Arab Women's Union, the GUPW succeeded in unifying the work of Palestinian women in small organizations scattered throughout various Arab countries. Its decision to seek recognition as the *official*, legitimate representative of Palestinian women rather than retain autonomy doomed any potential it might have had as a feminist force. In the late 1960s, on orders from their political superiors, the women aligned with Arafat's Fateh faction took over the organization, removing the president and incorporating the operation of all charitable organizations under its umbrella.[23]

In contrast to the leftist factions in the PLO, which at least acknowledged "the woman question," the mainstream Fateh faction had no articulated ideology on women's liberation. Furthermore, as Rosemary Sayigh has pointed out, the leaders of the GUPW related more to the leaders of their own factions than to one another, making cooperation among women cadres rare. The single demand on which they could agree was to have their chair placed on the Central Executive Committee of the Resistance movement. Even this nod to women's equal participation never materialized.[24]

It is difficult to determine the extent to which the development of more autonomous women's groups in the West Bank placed pressure on the GUPW in Lebanon. In any event, in the 1980s a new generation of activists in the GUPW began to raise feminist issues, including concern about the conditions of working women, reform of family law, change of gender relations within the movement, and the need for better primary health care.[25] These discussions culminated in a 1982 women's symposium. Whatever promise these developments might have held for radicalizing the GUPW and making it more responsive to women's needs, all possibility was crushed with the collapse of the Resistance movement following the 1982 Israeli invasion of Lebanon. Instead, the GUPW became one more arm of the PLO bureaucracy in Tunis and continued to toe the narrow nationalist platform.[26]

The Evolution of Feminist Nationalism

Removed from the bureaucratized structure of the PLO in Lebanon and fueled by a new generation of activists, a different kind of women's movement, with a very different consciousness, was spawned in the Occupied Palestine Territories. As young women joined the mixed-gender voluntary work groups that were fanning out to towns, villages, and refugee camps, they found that they had to contend with both the opposition of their families and the ingrained sexism of the young men in the work groups.[27] Paralleling the course taken by women engaged in other social movements, the young women in the work groups were led by their experiences to focus on their own oppression and a need to create their own women's liberation groups:

> The women in the group started meeting after our voluntary work and hotly discussed works on women's issues and the conditions of the Palestinian women. The charitable organizations were active but we were not satisfied with their kind of work. . . . Our criticisms were that the number of women they were dealing with was too small, that they were reinforcing through their work the traditional role of women instead of working towards women's liberation, and that they were dealing mostly with city women.[28]

In addition to this emergent generation of university graduates, there were slightly older, politically active professional women, like Zahera Kamal, who were also frustrated by the narrow scope of the women's charitable organizations. It was only natural that they would move from the leftist discussion groups where "the woman question" was being debated to joining forces with other women to found the first women's committee on March 8, 1978.[29] As Kamal had explained earlier in a 1985 newspaper interview:

> We wanted to change the situation whereby women are prevented from studying, working, developing their consciousness and taking part in the national struggle of our people. . . . [W]e are not prepared to relegate to the sidelines issues related to improving the status of us women; we consider it to be at the heart of our activities, for only thus can women gain a foothold in the struggle for national and social liberation.[30]

Ironically, the group initially had to invite men to give lectures on Palestinian women.

The shifting discourse of the Left factions, the growing number of educated women, the emergence of a class of women intellectuals and professionals, the increase (to 17 percent) of women wage earners, and the new emphasis on grassroots organizing all combined to make this the right moment to build a new women's movement that simultaneously addressed the national and social oppression of women. The changes inside the OPT provided fertile ground for the development of this movement, and the growth of feminism internationally gave it added strength. Many of the Palestinian women returning in the late 1970s from studies abroad had participated in feminist consciousness-raising groups.[31]

What initially differentiated the newly formed Women's Work Committee from the official PLO organ, the GUPW, was its apparent independence from any single nationalist faction and especially its commitment to grassroots organizing.[32] In reality, the new group was organized primarily to recruit women to the nationalist movement, but it tended to develop a dynamic of its own and opened up a free space where mainly urban, college-educated women began to explore their own gender oppression.[33] But as they began to reach out to women in villages and refugee camps, the urban women came face-to-face with the miserable conditions under which these women lived, and they developed programs to address their needs directly, including health projects, child-care centers, and sewing workshops.

Mirroring the way that elite women in the 1920s transcended clan and family-based political affiliations, the women initially worked cooperatively in a single committee. However, this fragile unity had dissolved by 1980 as debates erupted over priorities and the number of representatives. In 1981 women aligned with the Communist Party broke off to form the Social Service Committee in Jerusalem (the precursor of their Union of Working Women's Committees), announcing that their first priority was "to raise consciousness of working women to their complex of oppressions: a traditional patriarchal society, exploitation in the workplace, and the special differences of an occupied people."[34]

The following year the Palestinian Women's Committee (what became the Union of Palestinian Women's Committees, UPWC) was formed by women aligned with the Popular Front for the Liberation of Palestine (PFLP), and in 1983 the Fateh women formed the Women's Social Work Committee (WSWC). The women from the Democratic Front for the Liberation of Palestine (DFLP) maintained the original committee—they had been in the forefront of its founding—eventually changing its name to the Federation of Women's Action Committees.[35]

The breakup of the original group into four separate women's committees had to do more with factional disputes than with feminist politics. The UPWC and WSWC were accused of having "invisible constituencies," and when the spokesperson for the UPWC was asked about its program, she was unable to elaborate major differences between the new group and the original committee.[36] Indeed, because the three committees aligned with the Left all focused on unions and nurseries in urban areas and cooperative projects with village women, they often ended up duplicating one another's programs. In contrast, the Fateh-aligned group had no distinct ideology or program concerning women and did little more than traditional charitable work until after the start of the *intifada*.

The multiplication of women's committees sowed confusion and was also a source of frustration for women with a feminist consciousness, as one of them commented, "The Palestinian national movement, which is basically a men's movement, is divided along ideological and sectarian lines, but the women's movement must be united because of the very weak position of women under occupation."[37] Nevertheless, the committees succeeded in attracting several thousand women to their annual International Women's Day events, occasions generally used to forward the political line of the faction with which each was aligned. By March 1987, in their first unified celebration of International Women's Day, all four committees expressed concern about the "class, social, personal and political oppression of Palestinian women."[38]

This shared rhetoric masks real differences in their thinking, however. Although most feminist women outside the organized women's committees, particularly professionals and academicians, were consistently adamant about the need to integrate women's liberation fully into the national liberation movement, the women's committees had been more equivocal. Their positions ranged from the insistence of two of the Left groups that there must be a simultaneous struggle to an argument by the third that the nationalist struggle must be given priority at certain times. On the other hand, the mainstream Fateh-aligned group, at best, adhered to the line that women's liberation will follow national liberation. As we will see, however, these positions have been in flux.[39] Additionally, the public discourse promulgated by the committees does not always accurately reflect either their feminist consciousness or the subversive feminist intent of some of their programs. For instance, by 1987 several of the groups had already established child-care centers, sewing workshops, literacy classes, and even economic production cooperatives that were explicitly designed to "build the basis of women's emancipation."[40]

By the time the third International Women's Conference was held in Nairobi in 1985, the kind of nationalist activism that had been the hallmark of the old charitable-society women's movement had been supplanted. The old generation had been the mainstays of the Preparatory Committee for the 1975 International Women's Year Conference (formed jointly with Jordanian women), but by the end of the 1985 conference in

Nairobi marking the end of the UN Decade for Women, it was the leaders of the women's committees and nonaligned feminists who were in the forefront. Their international connections were strengthened there and became increasingly important, particularly after the start of the *intifada*.

The Intifada, Free Spaces, and Changing Consciousness

The foundation for feminist discourse had been laid even before the beginning of the popular uprising that began on December 9, 1987, in Gaza.[41] But the *intifada,* with its fluidity and creativity, provided a new free space in Palestinian society where boundaries were crossed and social relations were transformed.

Urban women across group affiliations came together in neighborhood committees to distribute food and supplies; to organize classes for the children whose education was disrupted by the Israeli closure of the schools; and to participate in first-aid training. In the villages and refugee camps, many women organized canning projects and *intifada* gardens in order to facilitate the boycott of Israeli goods. Many of these activities simply mirrored women's traditional role as nurturers and were often framed within the discourse of domesticity, for example, protecting their own and others' children. Nevertheless, the blurring of the distinction between domestic and political responsibilities had a transformative potential for many of the married women who came together in public spaces to engage in actions that carried political weight.

As young men and women of the new generation joined together freely in political activities, many cultural practices were subverted, as they recounted with great regularity:

> Before the *intifada,* no girl was allowed to walk in the streets alone. She had to be either with her father, either with her brother. . . . Now I come back to home maybe after 10 P.M. . . . If they allow us to do something, it's suddenly not just allowed, we do it normally.[42]

Not only did the unheard of become normal but many of the these young, grassroots-activist women began to envision a future in which they would have more choices. All the young single committee members with whom I spoke were definite about wanting to have small, carefully planned families. They intended to continue working outside the home after marriage and to remain involved in committee activities, relying on child-care centers, and some even began to question the assumption that they would marry at all. Many took it for granted that their husbands would share household work with them. Several who were already married had succeeded in establishing this redistribution of domestic labor, mentioning, however, that it was possible only because they did not live with their in-laws.[43]

Just as the younger women were convinced that they would marry the man of their choice, so too the women of the previous generation believed that their own forced marriages were a thing of the past. In talking about their lives, these older, married women revealed how the *intifada* activities had created a free space for them, too. The small-scale cooperative projects in which they engaged ranged from the production of *zaatar* (a mixure of dried wild thyme, sesame seeds, and salt) and in a *taboun* baked bread (a traditional covered outdoor oven; dough is placed directly on hot coals) to sewing or knitting garment, to politicized conventional domestic tasks. And the child-care centers established in their villages relieved them of domestic responsibilities for at least part of the day. Their participation in women's groups legitimized independent nonkinship affiliations outside the home. These new relationships, in turn, had repercussions for family dynamics, as attested by a young mother of four, "There was opposition before when I went out. So, in the old days, I went out without telling him. Now I tell him and he tells me to go. There is an openness now."[44] When committee activities were coupled with discussions of the writing of Arab feminists like Nawaal Sadawi and Fatima Mernissi, these village women were also given the tools to name their own oppression.[45]

Women who engaged in the range of *intifada* activities felt that they had a stake in a future Palestinian state, and they assumed that their roles would continue. The younger ones saw themselves, or at least members of their generation, as active participants in a future government, even as members of parliament.[46] Their slightly older cohort who were already married and had children envisioned a state that would provide services to lighten their load, as one young mother stated:

> They'll take more care of women and open more kindergartens and nurseries. . . . Women will have more time when they have all this help from the state . . . and my husband will start paying more attention to his children and his house.[47]

The changes in consciousness that grassroots Palestinian women activists experienced might have mirrored those of the women in Algeria and elsewhere. What is different about the Palestinian case is the presence of an organized women's movement that increasingly was willing to challenge patriarchal values and authority. For instance, committee activists frequently encountered male resistance as they recruited women to engage in activities outside the home, particularly those that provided women the basis for more autonomy, like health-information classes, economic projects, and even child-care centers. They responded to the refusal of men to allow their wives or daughters to participate in the committee or its projects in different ways: one group used the mechanism of direct intervention with the family; another tried to bolster the confidence of the women to confront the family herself; failing that, the committee leaders used their political networks and recruited their male political associates to talk to the men in the women's families.[48]

At times the contest between committee leaders and village elders was more directly confrontational. For example, in one village the men objected to a family planning program that one of the committees had established, and they demanded that all the committee's programs there be dismantled because they were "teaching the women to disobey." The national leader of the committee stood her ground, telling the men: "It is the women's decision. We are here to hear from the women. If they don't want us to continue, it's okay. But if there is any woman who wants it, we will stay. It's not your decision."[49] Using her own national standing, the committee leader not only challenged the village elders but empowered the women. Although this calculated act succeeded, the attacks on women's programs were not always successfully withstood.

The reach of the committees was broad, as evidenced by studies in both Shatti Refugee Camp in Gaza and Jalazon Camp in the West Bank. Almost half of the women aged sixteen to thirty-five in Shatti Camp were aware of the committees, and among this age group, 30 percent supported their activities.[50] Similarly, the 1991 study of women in Jalazon Camp found that 39 percent of the unmarried women were participating in the women's committees during the fourth year of the *intifada*—even as the earlier safe cover of the committees as a social group was being lifted.[51]

These participation rates of young women are high and the changes in consciousness that many activists seem to have experienced are significant, especially among younger unmarried women. For instance, although most of the homemakers studied in Jalazon Camp were content with the gendered division of labor in the household, the majority of un-married women perceived it to be unfair and rejected it—at least until marriage when, they feared, they might be "forced to accept reality" in the households of in-laws.

Despite these findings and the evidence from the oral histories that I conducted with young activists, it is doubtful that gender ideology was transformed or that changes in social practices kept pace with changes in consciousness. Furthermore, even if individual consciousness is trans-formed, it cannot lead to meaningful social change without broader insti-tutional restructuring. The first step in this process of challenging the patriarchal structure of Palestinian society was taken by virtue of the activ-ities and programs of the women's committees. And as the women's move-ment flowered, it introduced gender discourse into the national movement and began to define gender interests in increasingly feminist terms.

Changing Gender Discourse and Interests

In the earlier days of the *intifada,* despite the programs they sponsored to promote women's independence, most of the women's committee lead-ers eschewed the feminist label. In 1988 interviews with leaders of the four committees, only one described her group in unequivocal feminist terms.[52] The reluctance of the others was more a reflection of their own ambivalence than a clear-cut hostility to feminism, and often a rejection of their *perceived* understanding of feminism as an ideology that promoted only women's interests—and was even "man-hating." Their ambivalence is captured in the comment made by the leader of the most socially con-servative women's committee, the Fateh-aligned Social Work Committee: "No, no we are not feminist. We are for women, and we are for helping them to be independent—independent from men—but, no, we are not a feminist group."[33] Regardless of the stance they espoused, allegiance to their own political factions hindered the women's committees from uni-fying around a single women's agenda, even after they tried to work to-gether in the framework of the Women's Higher Council (WHC).

The WHC was founded in March 1988 at the behest of the PLO bu-reaucracy in Tunisia.[54] Although the original call contained no real evi-dence of a commitment to women's issues, women transformed the process by, among other things, incorporating independent feminists into the ranks of the WHC. For the independent feminists, the council finally provided an arena for participation without having to align themselves with one of the political factions. On the other hand, activists from the semiautonomous women's committees now found themselves under more pressure to pursue the feminist aims to which many subscribed personally.[55] Even though the WHC remained plagued by the same power brokering that marks the broader arena of Palestinian politics, it did open up another one of those free spaces where women waged an internal debate over what their gender interests were. At times, this even brought them face-to-face with the need to challenge sacrosanct cultural values, including the concept of honor.[56]

Young women arrested by the Israelis or placed in detention were frequently confronted with an array of sexual acts that were designed both to shame them and to inflame the men in their family. Israeli soldiers, jailors, and interrogators regularly exposed themselves, forced the women to disrobe, and sexually assaulted them in acts ranging from fondling their breasts to rape. After their release from jail or prison, the women frequently were punished by the men in the family for having "dishonored" *them*. The WHC was not able to devise a strategy that dealt effectively with this issue, but simply by introducing sexual harassment as part of the public discourse it paved the way for a broader feminist discussion of violence against women.

Women's groups were not able to formulate a unified women's agenda during this period, but they did come together when women's freedom of movement was threatened, for instance in 1989 during the HAMAS campaign to impose modest dress on women. Their unified opposition pressured the Unified National Leadership of the Uprising (UNLU) the underground governing authority, to issue a communiqué condemning the harassment of women.[57] By the time the HAMAS campaign for women's modest dress reemerged one year later, the feminist voice of the women's movement had been strengthened through the establishment of several independent women's centers and women's studies committees.[58]

Driven by a scholarship dedicated to social action and change, these centers began to sponsor forums that, among other things, examined the cultural oppression of women. The Conference on Women's Social Issues mounted in December 1990 by the Women's Studies Committee of Bisan Research Centre, and a June 1991 workshop on wife battering sponsored by the Women's Studies Centre paved the way for a new gender discourse and the promotion of a feminist analysis.[50] In both cases, the organizers faced the admonition of national leaders that "now is not the time" to

raise gender issues that were potentially divisive. And although both forums were held, the Bisan Centre organizers did drop their initial plan to
focus on the *hijab* (the veil or modest head covering). They also tried to
dispel fears that their feminism was detracting from the nationalist movement by using the language of ambiguity.[60] Ironically, by broadening the
focus of the conference, the wide-ranging discussion that took place, especially the comments from the floor, represented an even greater challenge to patriarchal values.[61]

Just as the commitment to feminism was gathering strength in the
women's committees, in the face of the Gulf War, all activity came to a
standstill. Subsequently, beginning in the spring of 1991, with the start of
the shuttle diplomacy of U.S. Secretary of State James Baker, several of
the committees shifted their emphasis from developing programs for
women to wooing women to the political analysis of the peace process
forwarded by their political faction. These debates continue to dominate
Palestinian political life and, as we shall see, until 1994 detracted from the
ability of the women's movement to develop a unified agenda and forward their vision of feminist nationalism.

On the other hand, the women's studies centers and research groups—
including the nascent women's studies program at Birzeit University—
showed an increasing readiness to concentrate on culturally sensitive
issues, including violence against women.[63] This, in turn, has emboldened
the women's committee, which for instance, issued a joint public statement in December 1993 condemning violence against women not only
in the streets and in the home, but in the ranks of the nationalist factions.[63] Subsequently, one of the women's committees established a hot
line to handle calls about violence against women; the leader of another
committee intervened directly in several cases of forced marriage in Ramallah; and feminist activists have begun to discuss the need to establish
a women's shelter.[64] Women's subordination in the family has been challenged further by the raising of issues like marital rape (which emerged
from one of the forced-marriage incidents during the summer of 1994).

It is clear that the Palestinian women's movement has expanded its scope
and its vision, and has introduced gender into the public discourse. A host
of projects and training programs designed to "empower women through
gender awareness" were initiated in both the West Bank and Gaza.[65] Even
though this new, less threatening language might be donor driven, that is,
reflect the agenda of granting international NGOs, it has had the effect of
providing much wider exposure and acceptance of feminist issues.

While struggling to define its own version of feminism, the Palestinian women's movement has also clearly allied itself with the international movements of women.[66] And although too much credit should not be given to the influence of the international feminist movement in helping the Palestinian women's movement to develop a feminist agenda, its role must be acknowledged. The close ties forged since the beginning of the *intifada* with Italian feminist groups, in particular, and with individual feminists from the United States and Europe often created another space for a dialogue on feminism. Furthermore, both the direct contact with Third World feminists at international conferences and the study of their writings has helped to promote a Palestinian feminism that integrates their identities as women and as Palestinians—a Palestinian feminist nationalism. As we shall see, these international connections have become increasingly important as women begin more serious planning for a future state.

Women and State Formation

Although the emergent national leadership in the prefigurative state in the Occupied Territories had begun to incorporate women's interests into its political discourse, the PLO leadership in Tunis had remained untouched by the women's movement. And as the reins of authority were transferred from the activists on the ground to the overwhelmingly male politicians,[67] women began to see their gains threatened.

When only four women were among the more than three hundred appointees to the technical committees formed after the Madrid conference, the "loyalist" leadership of the women's movement, that is, those who supported the Oslo Accord, mobilized to form the Women's Affairs Technical Committee.[68] In addition to demanding the appointment of more women, they argued that gender awareness should govern the work of all committees. Their representation on the committees did increase, particularly on the media committee.

Women mobilized again when the first draft of the Basic Law, the temporary constitution for the interim period, was issued in December 1993 with less than full and unequivocal equality. Following criticism from the women's movement and other democratic forces, the third draft was greatly improved, although the UN Convention to End Discrimination Against Women (CEDAW) is still noticeably absent from the list of UN conventions acknowledged[69]

Small gains like these have done little to allay the concerns of women, even of longtime Fateh loyalists. One of the leaders of the Women's Social Work Committee who, by 1994, was unequivocal in embracing feminism, averred: "If we don't catch our opportunity [that is, take advantage of the situation] now, it may be another twenty years, twenty-five years before we are going to accomplish anything for women."[30] Acting on this sense of urgency, she was part of a delegation of women's movement leaders who met with Arafat shortly after his return to Gaza in the summer of 1994. The women wanted to ensure that women's interests would be incorporated into all ministries and not merely assigned to a special ministry. So they proposed that a "Women's Secretariat Office" be attached to the presidency to serve as an oversight group.[71] Intisar Wazir (best known as Umm Jihad, the widow of Abu Jihad), the only woman appointed to head a ministry (Ministry of Social Affairs) in the Palestinian Authority (PA), joined Arafat at the meeting. Although both she and Arafat seemed generally supportive of the women's proposal, no definitive answer was given. Several weeks later Arafat alluded to the idea in a conversation with French journalists in Paris, but nothing has come of the idea and subsequent developments do not bode well for this kind of accommodation to women's interests.

Many of these "loyalist" women leaders are critical of the agreements signed with Israel *after* the Oslo Accord and of the way that Arafat has ignored the democratic forces that had flowered in the OPT during the *intifada*. In fact, it might be more appropriate to label them pragmatist-loyalists. But in contrast to the "secular oppositionists," their strategy is to try to maneuver within the extant political context and to engage directly with the Palestinian Authority—a stance aptly described by one of their numbers as a "foot in/foot out strategy."[72]

Because the Women's Affairs Technical Committee (now referred to simply as the Women's Affairs Committee) was viewed as a quasi-governmental body, the oppositionist women refused to join it. Nevertheless, the two camps reached a modus vivendi, coming together in the ad hoc Women's Document Committee to draft the Women's Charter, also referred to as the Women's Bill of Rights.[73] In turn, at the urging of one of the oppositionist women's movement leaders, the GUPW in the OPT, which is still dominated by the old-line, charitable society women, was pulled into the process. The idea was to gain greater legitimacy for the document and build a broader base. These socially conservative women of the previous generation had been largely marginalized from the women's movement during the *intifada,* and they were often the ones who pressured the emergent feminist nationalists not to pursue culturally sensitive issues. Yet, after some hesitation, and with few changes, they endorsed the charter and issued it in their name.

An unequivocal feminist document, the charter derives its authority from various UN conventions and documents, including the Convention to End Discrimination against Women (CEDAW). The intent of the framers is to push for the principles enunciated in the charter to be "incorporated into the constitution and the legislation of the future Palestinian state."[74] To accommodate the differing political strategies of the pragmatist-loyalists and secular oppositionists, it was agreed that each institution or women's committee was free to use the document however it chose, but that the document was to be presented formally to the PLO—not the Palestinian Authority—for use in a future independent state. Because of this understanding, a crisis erupted when Minister of Social Affairs Intisar Wazir of the Palestinian Authority appeared at the press conference where the charter was unveiled.

In line with their belief that the structure of the interim authority presages how a future state will operate, the pragmatists began to develop a strategy for elections well in advance of their being formally called. Several members of the Women's Affairs Committee went to observe the Jordanian and the South African elections and met with women candidates and activists in both countries.[75] Despite their ideological reservations about a quota system—"after all, women are not a minority" they returned convinced that a 30 percent quota for women was necessary, at least initially, to ensure their representations.[76]

The feminist pragmatists subsequently raised this demand as formal preparations for the elections were being made in late fall, 1995, and were supported by independent, democratic figures like Haidar Abdul Shafi, the leader of the Palestinian delegation to the Madrid conference. And even though five of the original eighty-three seats in the legislative body to be elected were reserved for Christians and one for the Samaritan sect of Jews who live in Nablus, the idea of a quota for women was completely rejected. A member of the Elections Commission, the body charged with drafting the Palestinian Election Laws, justified the decision by saying: "We have given women equality. For the first time in the elections in the West Bank they have the same rights as men: they can vote, they can run as candidates for the Council and even for President. That is the most we can do."[77]

Like Arafat's earlier comment that he could accept the principles of the Women's Charter if they did not conflict with S*haria* (Islamic) law, this nonresponsiveness to the women's demands is another indication of Arafat's growing readiness to accommodate the political Islamists, and HAMAS in particular.[78] On the other hand, it seems that the disaffection of even loyalist women has forced some concessions from Arafat's Fateh faction, which announced that the list of candidates from each of the sixteen districts should include at least one woman, "whether that woman is Fateh or independent."[79] Ironically, HAMAS, in obtaining a license for the National Salvation Party, listed two women among the leadership, the first time women have taken a public role in the Islamic movement.[80]

Déjà Vu?

Although the women's movement did manage to forge functional unity around the Women's Charter, as the Palestinian movement moves into a new stage, old factional political splits once again are driving a wedge between groups of women. Some of the oppositionists have been retreating from their feminist nationalism, accusing the women's movement of moving "from political activity into developing a feminist agenda independent of national liberation activity."[81] They have taken on prominent roles in the GUPW, and although they have introduced some feminist issues into the work of that organization, they have essentially reempowered the older generation of women activists and the political line that privileges national liberation issues.[82] This was quite evident at the NGO Forum on Women in China, September 1995, where half the Palestinian workshops were led by women from the GUPW and the old-line charitable societies who focused mainly on continued Israeli occupation.

The feminist nationalism that slowly evolved over the past decade can probably survive this latest political storm, however, and it will continue to be an important force in the democratic civil society that is the legacy of the *intifada*. More problematic than the ebb and flow of feminist unity is the shift away from popular organizing. Ironically, as intellectuals and urban activists were mobilizing to infuse feminist issues into the national debate, the potential for change among village women was being undermined. The free spaces that the women's committees had earlier created for village and camp women began to contract following the Gulf War.

Although the economic devastation resulting from the war was partially to blame, so was the confusion over the direction of the *intifada* and the prospect of negotiations. Some of the committees were still holding discussions of women's issues, but the political networks among village and camp women were disintegrating.[83]

By the summer of 1994, ties to the grassroots, if not broken, had become tenuous, and there was sparse evidence that the various projects designed to "train the trainers" either had reached village women or had any impact on them. Instead, at the village level, many of the cooperative projects had dried up or had become privatized; most of the women's committee centers as well as the kindergartens they ran had closed down; village literacy programs had been curtailed; and committee meetings were rarely held. One thirty-five-year-old mother of four in Kufr Nameh, who earlier had been so proud of her accomplishment in learning to read and write, lamented that without follow-up she was unable to maintain her literacy skills. The bread-making cooperative that she had initiated a few years earlier had been appropriated by one of the members as her private business.[84] And to make matters worse, she complained, the committee was emphasizing projects and programs that women could pursue in their own individual households.[85] In other words, women's lives were becoming reprivatized and in the process, old patterns were reemerging.

The young former activists in the villages and camps who had gotten married by 1994 and who were either already mothers or expecting their first child complained to me that there were no options for them outside the home anymore.[86] It seemed that only the former grassroots activists who remained single had had any luck in fashioning futures along the lines of their changed expectations.[87]

Conclusion

As the historical record demonstrates, the kinds of changes in consciousness that so many of these grassroots activists earlier experienced remain personal, at best, unless they are accompanied by institutional mechanisms. On the other hand, the mere enactment of laws redefining women's status seldom provides a basis for permanent change unless accompanied by a shift in consciousness. Indeed, women themselves often resist the legal challenges to oppressive cultural practices.[88]

121

Of graver consequence for women's future is the fact that the leadership of the nascent Palestinian state never developed a vision that acknowledged women's diverse roles. Instead, the record and rhetoric of the majority Fateh stream, particularly since 1982, has reflected a belief in women's primary role as the mainstay of the family and the vessel of Palestinian culture. This "woman-in-the-family" line is very similar to the one promoted by HAMAS, the largest of the opposition groups.[89] In contrast to Algeria, however, where there were few competing groups organized to contest this ideology, there is a strong women's movement in Palestine that is part of both an active civil society nourished by the *intifada* and of global women's movements. Their efforts have succeeded in introducing gender into political discourse. Moreover, as they share common apprehensions about the new period, they continue to debate the meaning and direction of their feminist–nationalist vision.[90]

Ultimately, the fate of Palestinian women is bound up with the direction of both the continued external struggle with the Israelis over the establishment of an independent state and the internal struggle for a pluralist, democratic society, including economic development that does not merely reproduce class and gender hierarchies. Even as the women's movement concentrates on building institutions and developing legal mechanisms for a future state, it is critical that it broaden its base and develop programs at the local level that speak to the daily lives of ordinary women. At the same time, it is important that it pay attention and be responsive to the competing Islamic discourse—and especially, to engage in dialogue with the small but increasing number of Islamic women who are attempting to define their own feminist vision.[91]

Notes

1. For the best discussions of Algeria, see Marie-Aimee Helie-Lucas "Women, Nationalism and Religion in the Algerian Liberation Struggle," in *Opening the Gates: A Century of Arab Feminist Writing*, ed. M. Badran and M. Cooke (Bloomington: Indiana University Press, 1990); "Women's Struggles and Strategies in the Rise of Fundamentalism in the Muslim World: From Entryism to Internationalism," in *Women in the Middle East: Perceptions, Realities and Struggles for Liberation*, ed. Haleh Afshar (New York: St. Martin's Press, 1993), and Bouthaina Shaaban, *Both Right and Left Handed: Arab Women Talk About Their Lives* (London:

Women's Press, 1989), pp. 182–235; and most particularly, Marnia Lazreg, *The Eloquence of Silence: Algerian Women in Question* (New York: Routledge, 1994).

2. Sherna Berger Gluck, " 'We Will Not Be Another Algeria': Women's Mass Organizations, Changing Consciousness and the Potential for Women's Liberation in a Future Palestinian State," *International Annual of Oral History,* 1990; also, Gluck, *An American Feminist in Palestine: The Intifada Years* (Philadelphia: Temple University Press, 1994).

3. I am drawing primarily on my own field research for the analysis of the women's movement in the Occupied Palestinian Territories (OPT) from 1978 to 1994. For the discussion of the Diaspora, particularly Lebanon, I have relied on Julie Peteet, *Gender in Crisis* (New York: Columbia University Press, 1991); Rosemary Sayigh, "Palestinian Women and Politics in Lebanon," in *Arab Women: Old Boundaries, New Frontiers,* ed. Judith Tucker (Bloomington: Indiana University Press, 1993); and Judith Tucker, introduction to Orayb Najjar, *Portraits of Palestinian Women* (Salt Lake: University of Utah Press, 1992).

4. The Young Turks were a group of junior army officers who staged a revolt in 1908, exiling Abdulhamid and naming his brother as the new sultan.

5. Muhammad Muslih, *The Origins of Palestinian Nationalism* (New York: Columbia University Press, 1988), pp. 61–62.

6. Ibid. pp. 70–72.

7. Usama Khalid alludes to women's participation in her historical survey: "A Palestinian History of Woman's Struggle," *Al Fajr,* pt. 1, March 8, 1985, and pt. 2, March 15, 1985. (Originally published in Arabic in *Al Hadaf,* 1981.)

8. Although the union was actually founded in 1921, it was not until 1929 when it organized the first Palestine Arab Women's Congress with two hundred to three hundred delegates that it was consolidated as a formal organization, which accounts for the discrepancy in founding dates in different accounts.

9. Peteet, *Gender in Crisis*, p. 48.

10. Ibid., p. 52.

11. Peteet, *Gender in Crisis*, p. 53.

12. Khalid, "A Palestinian History of Woman's Struggle"; Peteet, *Gender in Crisis*, p. 58; and Sayigh, introduction to Najjar, *Portraits of Palestinian Women*, p. 5.

13. Usama Khalid attributes this retreat to the bourgeois character of the leadership, but this explanation both ignores the earlier role of bourgeois women and overlooks the specific implications for women of being forced into exile.

14. Although it is not clear how widespread rape was, there is evidence from a host of sources, including Israeli military intelligence, that threats of rape and sexual harassment were part of the Israeli arsenal against the civilian population.

15. Peteet, *Gender in Crisis*, p. 60; also Sayigh, introduction to Najjar, *Portraits of Palestinian Women*, p. 6.

16. Khalid, "A Palestinian History of Woman's Struggle."

17. Sayigh, "Palestinian Women and Politics in Lebanon," pp. 176–177; Sayigh, introduction to Najjar, *Portraits of Palestinian Woman*, p. 8.

18. Sayigh, "Palestinian Women and Politics in Lebanon," p. 176.

19. Sayigh, introduction to Najjar, *Portraits of Palestinian Women*, p. 2. For an excellent study of women's organizing in Lebanon during this period, see Peteet, *Gender in Crisis*.

20. This experience has been reproduced in other conditions in the Muslim world, e.g., Afghani women refugees who had gone without veils in their home communities were forced to veil in the refugee camps of Pakistan, where they were surrounded by strangers.

21. Soraya Antonius, "Fighting on Two Fronts: Conversations with Palestinian Women," in *Third World, Second Sex*, ed. Miranda Davies (London: Zed, 1983, p. 72).

22. Khamsin Collective, "Palestinian Women and the National Liberation Movement: A Social Perspective," *Women in the Middle East* (London: Zed, 1987).

23. Peteet, *Gender in Crisis*, pp. 63–65.

24. Sayigh, "Palestinian Women and Politics in Lebanon," p. 180.

25. Ibid., p. 196.

26. As reported in *Al-Quds,* November 29, 1993 (reprinted in English in *Palestine Report,* December 6, 1993, p. 8), the secretary of the GUPW in a trip to the Occupied Territories commented that the future role of Palestinian women would be "to complement and blend with the responsibilities of men."

27. This discussion of the work of the voluntary committees and its role in stimulating the formation of the first women's committee is based on interviews with Rita Giacaman and Zahira Kamal and on the account of Amni Rimawi's personal experience in Ebba Augusin, *Palestinian Women: Identity and Experience* (London: Zed, 1993), pp. 77–80.

28. Ibid., p. 79.

29. Interview with Zahera Kamal, Jerusalem, January 1989.

30. *Al Fajr*, March 29, 1985, pp. 10, 15.

31. Interviews with Rita Giacaman (Ramallah, January 1989, and Topanga, 1989), and Rana Nashashibi (Jerusalem, January 1989).

32. Although several of the founders of the group became the leaders of what eventually became the Women's Action Committee (the women's committee aligned with the Democratic Front for the Liberation of Palestine), the original committee drew women from many different affiliations and from among those who had no political affiliation.

33. This observation is based on interviews and conversations with Rita Giacaman, Zahira Kamal, and Assia Habash as well as the reflections of Amni Rimawi (Augustin, *Palestinian Women*). Although earlier literature has suggested that the first committee was formed mainly because of felt feminist needs of the women organizers, one of the founders now offers a more candid account. See

Fadwa Al-Labadi, "Memories of a Palestinian's Daughter," (Masters thesis, University of Kent, 1993).

34. Daoud Kuttab," Growing Pains of the Palestinian Women's Movements," *Al Fajr,* March 11, 1983, p. 16.

35. In 1993 when the DFLP split into two factions, one of which became FIDA, the WAC also split, although each retained the name.

36. Kuttab, "Growing Pains of the Palestinian Women's Movement," p. 16.

37. Quoted, ibid.

38. As gleaned from the reports in *Al Fajr* of each of the celebrations.

39. These observations are based on an examination of the programs, platforms, and newsletters of each of the groups, as well as personal interviews both with the leadership of the committees and with nonaligned women conducted intermittently over a period of almost six years, between January 1989 and July 1994.

40. From undated leaflet issued by the UPWC.

41. The following discussion is based on interviews conducted with grass-roots activists in several different villages and refugee camps in the West Bank and Gaza over a period of more than five years.

42. Interview with Khawla, Qadura refugee camp, June 1989.

43. Several young married male activists also made this point in informal conversations in the summer of 1989.

44. Nawaal, Kufr Nameh, January 1990; original in Arabic.

45. The UPWC established a program where the works of these authors were discussed, and committee members both in Jabalya Refugee Camp (Gaza) and in the West Bank village of Kufr Nameh alluded to these discussions. The WAC drafted its own literature for study.

46. Group interviews with young committee members of UPWC, UWWC, and WSWC in Kufr Nameh; WAC members in Issawiyeh; and also with older committee members, Umm Khaldoun, Kufr Nameh, June 1991, and Zam Zam, Issawiyeh, June 1989.

47. See note 44, above.

48. Based on interviews with Aida Issawi of Issawiyeh (affiliated with WAC), and with Kahwla of Qadura Camp, Ramallah (affiliated with UPWC).

49. Interview with Zahera Kamal, Beit Hanina, January 1989.

50. Erica Lang and Itimad Mohanna, *A Study of Women and Work in Shatti Refugee Camp of the Gaza Strip,* (Jerusalem: Arab Thought Forum, n.d. [1992?]), p. 167.

51. Majdi Malki, "Some Social Effects of the Intifada in Jalazon Camp," reprinted in *News from Within* 11 (September 1995). The conclusions that Malki draws from the data are different from mine, however. For instance, she attaches a negative meaning to the 39 percent participation rate because it represents a decline during the *intifada,* when their "innocent" cover was blown. I view these as

very high participation rates, particularly when compared to the extent of women's involvement in other countries, including during national liberation struggles.

52. Interview with Zahira Kamal of the Women's Action Committee, January 1989. Indeed, in its literature, the WAC identified itself as a socialist-feminist group.

53. Interview with Nahla Qura of the Women's Social Work Committee, January 1990.

54. The four main sectors (women's, health, and agricultural committes, and trade unions) were all called on to develop greater coordination and cooperation. The women's committees were the only sector able to act on the call immediately.

55. In their interviews, the leaders of the women's committees often revealed a considerably greater commitment to women's autonomy than was promulgated in the official ideology of their political faction.

56. Interview with Assia Habash, Jerusalem, Summer 1989.

57. The communiqué issued August 1989 reads: "Nobody has the right to accost women and girls on the street on the basis of their dress or absence of the 'head veil' [*hijab*]."

58. The first of these, the Women's Studies Centre was founded initially in 1989 as a research project of the Women's Action Committee. It has since opened up as an independent operation and has been conducting research, sponsoring workshops, and training women in research skills. The Women's Studies Committee of the Bisan Research and Development Centre in Ramallah was the next to start, in 1990. Although the Women's Affairs Centre Nablus was one of the earliest centers (1989), it did not have the kind of outreach, at least initially, that the other two did. A branch of the Women's Affair Centre in Gaza, which is now independent, has a programmatic focus that is more like the other two West Bank centers.

59. Although proceedings of the first of these conferences were published, the information on the WSC workshop is based on conversations with the centre's director and with some of the participants.

60. The conference proceedings are introduced with the following equivocating statement: "Palestinian women have chosen not to discuss some of the social and women's issues that might distract us from the main struggle against Israeli occupation. However, this choice—which we made of our free will and responsibility—must not prevent the discussion of important issues concerning social and women's problems, especially those which may constitute an obstacle to the development of Palestinian women's role in the struggle and politics."

61. Based on conversation with Eileen Kuttab, one of the key organizers of the conference.

62. For example, the Women's Unit of the Bisan Research Centre undertook

an extensive study of violence against women that, among other things, opened up a discussion on the problem of incest.

63. *Palestine Report,* December 12, 1993 (originally published in Arabic in *Al-Quds).* In addition, the group called on the PLO to make a declaration "affirming the right of women to a dignified life, employment and freedom of thought and to prohibit all kinds of violence against women."

64. This information is based on interviews conducted with Amal Kreish of the UWWC and Maha Nassar of the UPWC, July 1994. In September 1994, at the conference Women, Justice and Law (sponsored by the Al-Haq Project on Women's Empowerment through Law) a recommendation was made for the establishment of battered women's shelters.

65. These include seminars and courses at the Gaza Women's Affairs Centre, as well as workshops and colloquia sponsored by the Women's Advisory Center on Law, and the Al Haq project on women and the law, and programs established by the subcommittee on training of the Women's Affairs Technical Committee.

66. This is most clearly embodied in one of the justifications given for the December 1993 Conference on Women's Social Issues: "To [neglect] this discussion would threaten the achievements made by women during their long struggle. In addition this would cut Palestinian women off from the intellectual and cultural connectedness with women in the rest of the world, who are struggling for freedom, democracy and equality," p. 23.

67. Following the establishment of the National Authority in Gaza and Jericho in the summer of 1994, many feminists began to refer to the authority, run these bureaucrats and leaders, as "the government of the Abus." This denotes that most went by their noms de guerre—e g , Yasir Arafat is known as Abu Ammar and also a generational and social differentiation. Traditionally, men and women were referred to as the mothers (Umm) and fathers (Abu) of their eldest son.

68. The accounts of the formation of this committee are based on interviews conducted in July 1994 with three of the founding members: Amal Kreish, Zahera Kamal, and Nahla Qura.

69. Naseer Aruri and John Carrol document the reactions to the Basic Law and the process of revision in "A New Palestinian Charter," *Journal of Palestine Studies* 23 (1994): 5–17. They do not, however, describe the women's criticisms specifically. For these I have relied on interviews with the three women most closely involved with the Women's Affairs Committee and on a report of the meeting that seventy women had with the author of the Basic Law, Anis Qassem, *Palestine Report,* February 14, 1994, p. 3.

70. Interview with Nahla Qura, Jerusalem, July 1994.

71. In separate interviews, two of the women who attended described this meeting.

72. Islah Jad, quoted in Rita Giacaman and Penny Johnson "Searching for Strategies: The Palestinian Women's Movement in the New Era," *Middle East Report,* January–February 1994.

73. Interviews with Amal Kreish, Zahira Kamal, Nahla Qura, Maha Nassa, and Eileen Kuttab, July 1994. These women all referred to the document as a women's charter. When it was formally issued on August 3, 1994, it was entitled "Principles of Women's Legal Status."

74. The full text of the document can be found in *Palestine Report,* August 7, 1994, pp. 10–11.

75. The information about these trips is based primarily on the interview with Nahla Qura, Jerusalem, July 1994.

76. Based on interviews conducted in Jerusalem with Nahla Qura and Zahera Kamal, July 1994.

77. Ali Safarini, in an interview published in *Palestine Report,* November 17, 1995.

78. In what appears to be another accommodation, after the Christians were guaranteed five seats, an additional five seats were added to the legislative council from the Gaza district.

79. *Palestine Report,* December 15, 1995, p. 5.

80. As reported in *Palestine Report,* December 8, 1995.

81. Statement made by Suha Barghouti (PFLP) at the Roundtable on the Palestinian Women's Movement organized by the Women's Studies Program of Birzeit University, March 29, 1995. In *News from Within* 11 (April 1995): 5.

82. In fact, Samiha Khalil, the leader of the charitable society movement and the president of the GUPW in the OPT, placed her name in nomination for "rais" against Yasir Arafat. Rather than being a statement about women, it is a political statement about Arafat and the PA.

83. For a fuller discussion, see Gluck, *An American Feminist in Palestine.*

84. The sewing workshop run by another committee had similarly been appropriated and privatized by one of the local committee leaders.

85. Interview with Zahra, Kufr Nameh, July 1994.

86. Interviews with Hiem and Fedwa in Kufr Nameh, and with Basma, in Issawiyeh July 1994.

87. Interviews conducted with Amera, Gaza City, July 1994, and with Muna, Kufr Nameh, July 1994.

88. This is most poignantly revealed in Stephanie Urdang, *And Still They Dance: Women, War and the Struggle for Change in Mozambique* (New York: Monthly Review Press, 1989).

89. For instance, a longtime, women's activist was ousted as the director of the Hebron Society for the Planning and Protection of the Family after being warned by the PA's Ministry of Social Affairs to "concentrate on women's health issues and to strengthen programs that reinforce women's traditional roles as wives

and mothers." *News from Within*, (September 1995):13. For a fuller description of this category and its opposite, the "woman emancipation line," see Valentine M. Moghadam, *Modernizing Women: Gender and Social Change in the Middle East* (Boulder: Lynne Rienneri, 1993), pp. 69–74.

90. The proceedings of the roundtable on the Palestinian women's movement (see note 81, above) and the later commentary on it by the Women's Studies Program of Birzeit, *News from Within* 11 (July 1995), throws particularly interesting light on this ongoing quest.

91. Although there is not the kind of Islamic feminist movement emerging that we see in Egypt, and even in Iran, there are definitely signs of individual Islamic feminists, as reported to me by someone who attended one of the Women and the Law workshops held by Al Haq in Hebron in the summer of 1994.

Gender and Nation–Building in South Africa

Zengie A. Mangaliso

On April 26. 1994, South Africa made a shift from a minority government led by the Nationalist Party (NP) to a new government elected by the majority of the people and led by the African Nationalist Congress (ANC). The electoral process, which for the first time included majority-age members of all racial groups, symbolized political fulfillment and first-class citizenship for all South Africans. In the new and transitional constitution the government stipulates categorically its commitment to equality for all South Africans. The preamble outlines their entitlement to a "democratic constitutional state in which there is equality between men and women and people of all races so that all citizens shall be able to exercise their fundamental rights and freedoms."[1] Chapter 3, the Bill of Rights in the interim constitution, lists equality as the primary and fundamental right, and protection before the law, clearly stipulating that no person shall be discriminated against directly or indirectly on various grounds including sex and gender.[2]

The constitutional reference to equality raises several fundamental questions. How does a society that is still rooted in old gender traditions transform itself into a modern democracy that recognizes equality between men and women? As an agent of socialization and of resources that different interest groups compete for, the government plays what role in facilitating or even obstructing the shift toward gender equality? This chapter attempts to address the questions.

We begin with a brief history of women's involvement in social movements. A discussion of the positions taken by the various political parties as they competed for representation in government follows. We end with a discussion of how the gap can be closed between what appears to be government rhetoric on gender equality, and women's reality.

Gender and Nation-Building

It is axiomatic that universally women have gained the right to participate in the electoral process, to cast their ballots as does the rest of the citizenry, and then have found their participation in public institutions to be limited, thus curtailing their efforts in nation-building. This is ironical in the sense that women will have joined the various political movements and will have participated in guerilla movements aimed at deposing the enemy. At independence, women in most parts of the world have been excluded from the nation-building process and have been reminded that their rightful place and contribution are within the home. This trend, which is almost universal, raises questions about the South African situation. Again, for South Africa, the most pressing question is whether the intent and language of the constitution can become reality.

When one looks at the South African society, one sees its mosaic character. It is a society of several races and ethnicities that have been kept separate and unequal through apartheid. In reality, South Africa incorporates the Afrikaners, the English, and other smaller European groups who are considered part of the white group, a group that has been largely privileged under apartheid. South Africa also incorporates Coloreds, Indians, and Africans who are part of the black group that has been largely disadvantaged under apartheid. For simplicity, it can be asserted that apartheid in South Africa has produced two nations, a white South Africa and a black South Africa, each with its own historical and political experiences, its own sense of nationalism, and its own gender experiences.

As can be expected, what nationalism has meant for the white group, in particular the Afrikaner group that has been in power for more than forty years, is different from the nationalism articulated by disadvantaged black groups. Further, although similarities between the two groups could be drawn based on in-group hierarchical gender arrangements, gender experiences have also been different.

The origins of Afrikaner nationalism can be traced to the Afrikaners' defeat by the British in the Anglo-Boer War of 1899–1902.[3] The remnants of the scattered Boer communities had to forge a new identity in order to survive in the emergent British-driven, capitalist system. Originally, the Afrikaners had no monolithic identity and no single unifying language. They had to create a new community of the *volk*, with new and unifying traditions, highlighting their strong Calvinistic religion, and they also had to create a single written language.[4] In 1918 Afrikaans emerged as a legally recognized Boer language, reflecting the traces of the Dutch, French, and German origins of the Afrikaners. It can be argued that from the outset the Afrikaner identity had a clear class component. It was born primarily as a strategy of mobilization in order to overpower the British on the political and economic front, and to transform the South African system such that it would fit the Afrikaner ethos.[5]

Afrikaner nationalism has had a clear gender focus. A small elite group of Afrikaner men established in 1918 a secret society called the Afrikaner Broederbond (Afrikaner Brotherhood) whose strategy was to uplift the previously politically and economically downtrodden Afrikaner. The Broederbond became the custodian of Afrikaner nationalism, in that it strove to preserve Afrikaner values of cultural and racial superiority. It was synonymous with Afrikaner male economic and political interests. It is clear from its name that Afrikaner women were excluded from the society. Even though Afrikaner women had supported Afrikaner men during the war, as the men ascended to power, the women were assigned to motherhood, self-sacrifice, and stoicism.[6]

It was a position with contradictory outcomes. Denied formal political and economic power, Afrikaner women, however, shared the benefits of power accrued to Afrikaner men. In the process, they became complicitous in the operation of apartheid and the oppression of black people, including black women.[7]

It can be argued that African nationalism emerged as a response to the oppressive nature of apartheid. The African Nationalist Congress (ANC), founded in 1912 and ostensibly the first political organization established to challenge apartheid, in the preamble to its Freedom Charter called for national unity, asserting that "South Africa belongs to all who live in it black and white" and highlighting that all South Africans deserve to be treated as equals. The initial position of the ANC was not to take over political and economic power but to extend that power to blacks. Drawn from the urban intelligentsia and mostly mission-educated, the early members of the ANC demanded full civic participation in the society rather than a radical alteration of the existing power structures. The ANC turned to guerilla warfare when its demand went unheeded for decades and when it was instead met by violence from the apartheid government.

The language of the ANC was inclusive of people of color, and called for national unity, but its leadership was solidly male and hierarchical. This contradiction prompted the establishment of the Federation of South African Women (FSAW), a group within the ANC whose intent was to draw the attention of its members to the discrepancy between the language of the Freedom Charter and the experiences of women within the movement. It is important to note that even within African nationalism, the concept of motherhood was and still is prominent. Winnie Mandela has been hailed for her contributions to the struggle against apartheid as the "Mother of the Nation;" Miriam Makeba, the South African activist singer, has been addressed in most of Africa as "Ma Africa."[8]

The Pan Africanist Congress (PAC), an organization that broke off from the ANC because of the dispute over the inclusive language of the Freedom Charter, expressed stronger nationalist sentiments. The PAC vehemently opposed, and still opposes the language of the Freedom Charter. It argued that by proclaiming that South Africa belongs to all who live in it, the ANC is denying a historical fact and reality: South Africa belongs to the indigenous people, and their land was auctioned for sale to all who live in it. The PAC emphasized its commitment to the overthrow of the apartheid government and the restoration of the land to its rightful owners. The PAC's stance on African land ownership is expressed in its maxim: "Izwe Lethu" (The land is ours).[9] To this writer's knowledge, the PAC has been quiet on the issue of gender; however, it can be asserted that like most political movements, its hierarchy is gendered. It is axiomatic that most political movements whose primary goal is to take over ownership of government and land are dominated by males in all societies.

The primary question at this point is—considering that South Africa incorporates groups with divergent histories and gender experiences—what sort of national identity is needed in order to create a transformed and united nation? The process of creating a single nation has begun with the formation of the government of national unity, which is inclusive of most political parties, including parties whose numbers are former enemies. Purging the old national flag that represented the Afrikaner identity and replacing it with a flag that is representative of all South Africans, is another step toward developing a new sense of South African nationalism. Singing "Nkosi Sikelela i Afrika," adopted by the ANC as the national song, followed by the Afrikaner national song "Die Stem Van Suid Afrika" is yet another measure taken toward political inclusiveness. And, doing away with holidays and statues that are reminders of historical conflicts is one more attempt by the new government to create a united South Africa. The process of building such a nation and a new national identity is obviously a challenge, under constant negotiation and renegotiation. Different groups have their own notions of what a new South Africa should be like, and vociferously express their opinions. One group comprises some Afrikaners who prefer a homeland of their own where they can live separately and preserve their language, traditions, and identity. Another group is headed by Chief Mangosuthu Buthelezi, leader of the Inkatha Freedom Party (IFP), who is advocating the secession and self-determination of KwaZulu Natal, where a large proportion of the Zulus reside.

Gender equality within South Africa deserves special mention. In Western countries issues of gender equality are generally articulated by various women's groups and are largely informed by feminism. Western feminism within the South African context, and especially as it relates to the experiences of black women, has largely been viewed with skepticism. Black women assert that they have always dealt with issues of women's emancipation in their families, communities, and political movements without being aware of the existence of the term *feminism*. Also, the central tenet of feminist thought, which asserts that all women are oppressed becomes contentious. The assertion implies that women share a common lot, that factors like race and social class do not create a diversity of experience that requires different strategies to challenge inequality in society. For black women in South Africa, issues of racial inequality are still primary and cannot be overlooked in the sense that they affect a larger collective. This sentiment has been succinctly expressed by women in the liberation movement in the following statement:

> In South Africa, the prime issue is apartheid and national liberation. So to argue that African women should concentrate on and form an isolated feminist movement, focusing on issues of women in their narrowest sense, implies African women must fight so that they can be equally oppressed with African men.[10]

This is not to argue that issues of gender inequality are an irrelevance. On May 2, 1990, the National Executive of the ANC, for instance, issued the historic Statement on the Emancipation of Women, in which it was acknowledged that women's emancipation is not a by-product of national liberation and needs to be addressed within the democratic movement. This reflects the conflictual situation that black women in South Africa are faced with: they have to figure out under what circumstances to advance the race issue, and under what circumstances to advance the gender issue. For white women in South Africa, their unequal position as women in society has been compensated for by their being members of a privileged racial group.

Historical Considerations—Women's Struggles

Women in South Africa have been involved in every aspect of the struggle for freedom against apartheid. Some specific events that women have participated in can be highlighted. As early as 1913 (when African men were already mandated to carry passes), women successfully mobilized against the extension and implementation of pass laws, which were rescinded until 1950, when they were reinstated and forcefully implemented. It is worth noting that the effort drew support from women of various race groups.

Women have also been involved in various revolts and boycotts, including consumer boycotts. The revolts of rural women against the culling of cattle in Natal and their participation in the potato and bus boycotts to challenge certain unfair labor practices, which took place in the 1950s, are well documented.[11] Unfair labor laws eventuated in resistance movements, some of which were led by prominent women; Lillian Ngoyi is well known for her effective and brave leadership of the labor unions in the 1950s. Beginning in 1973, women increasingly participated in consumer and rent boycotts, many of which were sparked by real declines in standards of living. Because women have always had the responsibility of managing households, struggles against the escalating cost of living have had great appeal for them.[12] In the 1980s and 1990s women became active in the Congress of South African Trade Unions (COSATU) as it fought unfair practices in the workplace enabled by apartheid laws. Within the organization they addressed issues affecting them as women, such as night shifts, maternity leave and the implications of such leave, and sexual harassment in the workplace.

Aside from such involvement, the onslaught of the apartheid system on black families prompted women to join guerilla forces such as the Umkhonto Wesizwe (Spear of the Nation) within the ANC. Interestingly, women have also actively advocated for peace. A conference hosted by ZANU-PF Women's League, in Harare, Zimbabwe, in 1989, whose theme was "Women in the Struggle for Peace," drew women from all spheres of life and with a range of affiliations. These included women from the then-banned ANC, white South African women affiliated with the Black Sash, women engaged in community work, university lecturers, churchwomen, and many others interested in promoting peace in South Africa.

It needs to be noted that by and large, women's involvement in resistance movements initially derived from issues that directly impacted their lives as women and the lives of their families. Such issues were later perceived as "soft issues." Women's participation in broader national issues, those involving the well-being of everyone, began on a smaller scale, partly because the dominant ideology defined national political issues, "hard issues," as a male arena.[13] To illustrate, the *Who's Who in South African Politics*, presents biographies of only 7 women among its 122 entries.[14] In point of fact, white women, who have participated in the electoral process since the 1930s, in 1993 still had insignificant representation in government; for instance, they constituted only 3.5 percent of the Lower House, and 2.8 percent of the Upper House.[15] Overall, women's presence in most public institutions has been much smaller then men's, and increasingly smaller at higher levels of the hierarchies within the institutions.

In the rebuilding of South Africa, the gap between male and female representation in society's institutions needs to be addressed and redressed for several reasons. First, women have been negatively impacted by the apartheid order, like everyone else, and their situations and status in society need to be improved. Second, in various ways women have played a role in challenging apartheid laws, and have earned the right of full participation in a democratic society. Third, to build a democratic society, everyone's energy, effort, and input is critical, including women's. Said differently, involvement in the nation-building process should be open to everyone who is able and willing to be part of that process and not be subject to race or sex qualifications.

South African Political Parties on Gender

Eleven political parties campaigned for representation in the current government of national unity. Four have been identified as major parties in that they drew more support than the others from the electorate: the reformed Nationalist Party (NP), the Inkatha Freedom Party (IFP), the Pan Africanist Congress (PAC), and the African Nationalist Congress (ANC). In their history and evolution, each has dealt with the issue of gender in its own way. One can reasonably expect that their positions on gender will emerge during the process of nation-building and work to women's advantage or disadvantage.

The Nationalist Party, which historically represented white interests, in particular Afrikaner interests, has taken a structural-functionalist perspective on gender. This perspective has had much to do with shaping the nature of gender relations in the society. According to the perspective, men and women are biologically different: men have superior physical strength; women bear and rear children. These differences suit men and women "naturally" to different roles. Within the Afrikaner community, men are the family heads and, by extension, heads in the public sphere; women focus on the private and domestic sphere.

The pervasive gender arrangement supported by the Nationalist Party was neatly summed up in the now defunct males–only Broederbond. It worked for and symbolized Afrikaner male interests, aspirations, and politics. Participation in the national political scene by Afrikaner women was confined to voting and giving support to the political men in their lives. The women members of the Nationalist Party were part of what is known as the Women's Action group. At regional and national levels, they met as a constituency to discuss issues of importance to male political leaders or candidates and to raise funds. In short, their agenda was set by men. The meeting "chairlady" was usually the wife of a prominent politician.[16] In the forty years that the Nationalist party was in power, leadership in public institutions has been overwhelmingly male; in a Parliament with 103 National Party members, not one is female. Only one woman has been a member of Parliament: Helen Suzman, of British–Jewish heritage, representing the opposition Progressive Party. In sum, the Nationalist Party has supported a patriarchal society where ultimate control rests primarily with males.

The Inkatha Freedom Party has dealt with the gender issue in a manner that gives the appearance of being contradictory. Recognizing that African women in particular have suffered alongside men under apartheid and contributed toward challenging it, the party has publicly applauded women yet remains patriarchal and hierarchical in its treatment of gender. Chief Mangosuthu Buthelezi, its leader, in various speeches around Natal has clearly stated his view on the position of women in the party and society:

137

> My sisters, you are mothers in suffering inhumanity. Some of you are wives
> in an oppressed society and some of you are daughters in our oppressed so-
> ciety, and the full brunt of apartheid is borne by you more than by any
> other Blacks. . . . [W]hen others were quaking with fear, when others
> were intimidated . . . it was you who stood up to be counted.[17]

At the same time, Chief Buthelezi emphasizes that all party members
should be under the direct authority of his leadership, just as a woman
should be under a husband's authority at home. In one of the documents
publicizing the party's position on gender, a high Inkatha official wrote:

> In the family the man is the head. The woman knows that she is not equal to
> her husband. She addresses the husband as "father", and by so doing the chil-
> dren get a good example of how to behave. Women refrain from exchanging
> words with men and if they do, this reflects bad upbringing on their part.[18]

Of course, Chief Buthelezi sees himself as the ultimate authority of the
party, and on occasion he has chastised recalcitrant party members, male
and female, in these terms: "I want to make it clear that once I have defined policy as your leader, I expect the leadership to identify ways and
means of implementing it."[19]

Women in the party by and large accept their secondary position and
perceive their role as mother and defender of the home while men engage in public issues. They see their contribution in society to be for-
titude, forbearance, and unfailing support to loved ones. In a sense,
through the party, they have been trained to look upon themselves as the
power behind the male throne.[20]

In the literature of the Pan Africanist Congress, the party appears silent
on the question of women. Patricia De Lille, PAC secretary of foreign affairs, argues that historically the PAC has been anxious not to marginalize women by focusing on them separately from the overall population.
The PAC premise is that national issues invariably incorporate both sexes
and hence there is no need to address male and female equality. Curiously, after the lifting of the ban on all political movements in 1990, the
PAC set up a women's wing that would have representation in its National Executive.[21] In other words, the PAC recognized the need to assist
women's full participation in the public arena.

There is indication that within the ANC while it was a resistance
movement, the issue of male and female equality was one of lively debate.

As mentioned earlier, although racial equality was seen as primary, the gender issue lagged behind until it was brought to the front by the Federation of South African Women. Through women's insistence and persistence, the Women's Charter was written, highlighting the importance of gender equality. The Women's Charter begins by affirming the overriding commonality of interests women share with men:

> We women do not form a society separate from men. There is one society and it is made of both women and men. As women we share the problems and anxieties of our men and join hands with them to remove social evils and obstacles to progress.[22]

At the same time, the charter recognizes that women are discriminated against in society on the basis of sex, and commits women to working for the removal of discriminatory laws and practices. Throughout the charter, the dual nature of the women's struggle for equality is stressed:

> As members of the national liberation movements . . . we march forward with our men in the struggle for liberation. . . . As women there rests upon us also the burden of removing from our society all the social differences developed from past times between men and women which have the effect of keeping our sex in a position of inferiority and subordination.[23]

Needless to say, of the four major parties the ANC is the most progressive in regard to gender and could benefit all South African women regardless of racial background. The ANC policy guidelines unequivocally advocate women's equality in the public and private spheres, and encourage women's broad participation in postapartheid socioeconomic national development strategies.

> The emancipation of women must be an integral part of their lives, not just in legal statements, but in the reality of their lives . . . if women do not achieve equality with men, society will have failed. They have struggled within their homes, they have given their time, energy, and lives to the struggle for national liberation.[24]

The next, and most crucial, step for the ANC government is to move forward, to make certain that women are indeed part of the nation-building process.

139

Zengie A. Mangaliso

Toward Achieving Gender Equality in South Africa

A step already taken by the ANC government toward eliminating gender inequality was the introduction of affirmative action programs in all public institutions, ostensibly intended to encourage equal access to opportunities for all South Africans regardless of race and sex. Such programs elsewhere in the world, including the United States, do not translate into instant opportunities for the historically disadvantaged, and are also accompanied by a host of controversies.

Although the programs are welcome in that they indicate the willingness of the state to intervene to ensure equality, they are not by themselves sufficient. Women's representation in public institutions, particularly black women's, will not occur overnight. Some concrete steps are being taken to remove barriers created by apartheid, but cultural barriers remain largely untouched, and thus create circumstances unique to women.

Again, the South African culture clearly defines the positions of men and women in society: the public sphere is primarily the male sphere, and the private sphere is primarily the female sphere, and from birth everyone is socialized thereto. This pattern will not change soon because over time it has come to be perceived as "natural," the most convenient, and thus the most acceptable. Females may have access to quality public education, and, it is hoped, may have access to gainful work, but will run the risk of still having to fulfill customary domestic responsibilities. We are well aware of progressive family policies, such as those introduced in Nicaragua and Cuba, in which men are legally required to do their share of housework, but such measures have failed to alter gender socialization and gender relations within the household.

The home, where gender inequality begins and is reinforced, can remain mostly untouched by outside institutional forces, including government policy. Also, the economies of rural communities function effectively on the basis of a distinct division of labor that is based on sex. Rural economies for the most part still rely on traditional farming arrangements, whereby it is the males who supervise animal-drawn ploughs or drive tractors, and it is the females who do the planting and harvesting, as well as the managing of household. Gender equality is easier to advocate and implement in urban areas, where farming is not the means of subsistence and resources are in relative abundance. Further, historically in societies where liberation has been achieved, national leaders, who predominantly were male, spoke unequivocally on race equality, ostensibly because it benefited more members of the societies, but were largely silent on gender issues. Thus far in South Africa, one has not heard any statement of serious concern about gender inequality from any leader. The prevailing sentiment is that issues of race still dominate and deserve top priority. The problem too may be that the government itself, despite its progressive language on gender as reflected in the constitution, is still overwhelmingly a male province.

The pattern described above—government involving far more men than women—needs further discussion because it is universal. As indicated earlier, it is axiomatic that women in various ways had participated in resistance against unpopular governments, at independence found themselves relegated to the margins, if not pushed back into the private, domestic sphere. Why is this so? A possible answer:

> The mobilization of women during the struggle that is necessary to gain national liberation is usually annulled after this has been achieved, and the number of women who continue to participate in political power, in theorization and decision-making is very small. One reason for this is the fact that although women participated in struggles in large numbers, they left the development of theory and of strategy to the male experts.[25]

In other words, during the struggle women provide strength through numbers. In certain instances they tirelessly carry out the various day-to-day tasks such as walking from door to door recruiting and campaigning. In the press of daily activities, they overlook or neglect the need to prepare themselves, to be decision makers—or are not given opportunities to do so. Accordingly, they are not equipped for advancement in the public sphere.

It is imperative that more women acquire the skills required in the public sphere. Formal education provides women with specific skills and expertise; informal education can instill the motivation to move beyond the private sphere. Historically, women have played an important role in local community work, church work, and school committees. These are some of the areas that are deserving of acknowledgment and encouragement because they are "natural" sites where women can learn and improve leadership skills. Also, in most of Africa women have been disproportionately active in the informal sector largely because participation in the formal sector was unavailable to them because of lack of education. South Africa is the exception; its informal sector is dominated by women, in particular black women. Government policies that promote the informal sector would benefit women by increasing their earning capacity. Women's improved incomes would in turn increase their bargaining power within the home. In other words, could be used to persuade men to share household duties, which would enable women's greater participation in public life.

Conclusion

In sum, the inclusion of women in the democratic process in South Africa is still a challenge. Black women, in particular, who suffered the effects of apartheid and still face the daily pressures of a traditional culture, are doubly handicapped. Some expressed their condition pointedly on election day: they voted, and now have a government of their choice. The ritual of voting symbolized their political maturity and fulfillment. However, some still have to serve their white masters for a living, as well as manage their own homes.

Although the current ANC-led government speaks progressively on gender issues and has taken some steps toward gender equality in society, there is a long road ahead. Admittedly, the ravages of apartheid make racial equality more pressing than any other aspects of equality. Still, it cannot be assumed that women's meaningful participation in society will be a by-product of democracy for all. This has not happened even in socialist countries with clearly articulated principles of equality. Women's meaningful involvement in society has to be addressed within government, women's organizations, and the society at large.

Notes

1. The Constitutional Assembly charged with writing the permanent South African Constitution (completion deadline: May 1996), released a first draft and solicited comments and input from the general citizenry.

2. The use of the terms *sex* and *gender* highlights the prohibition of discrimination based on biological and cultural factors that prescribe men and women's positions in society.

3. The Anglo-Boer War arose out of the conflict between the British and the Afrikaners, the latter group then referred to as Boers, over the discovery of and access to diamond mines. The war also turned out to be a conflict between the two white groups for control over African land and labor. See Anne McClintock, "Family Feuds: Gender, Nationalism, and the Family," *Feminist Review*, no. 44 (Summer 1993): 62–80.

4. Ibid.

5. James Leatt, Theo Kneifel, and Klaus Nurnburger, eds., *Contending Ideologies in South Africa* (Cape Town, 1986.)

6. McClintock, "Family Feuds."

7. The benefits enjoyed by Afrikaner women were extended to white women in general. To the writer's mind, this condition makes a coalition between white and black women in South Africa an uneasy one, if not problematic. Despite this problem, however, it needs to be acknowledged that there are white women who have used their privileged position and mobilized to challenge the oppressive laws of South Africa, including labor and pass laws that perpetuated the oppression of maids. One organization of such white women is the Black Sash.

8. McClintock, "Family Feuds."

9. PAC Manifesto, 1962 (abridged).

10. Frene Ginwala. "ANC Women: Their Strength in the Struggle," *Work in Progress*, no. 45 (1986): 10–11.

11. Cherryl Walker, *Women and Gender in Southern Africa to 1945* (Cape Town: David Phillip, 1990), Ivy Matsepe Casaburri, "On the Question of Women in South Africa," in *Whither South Africa*, ed. Bernard Magubane and Ibbo Mandaza (Trenton, NJ: Africa World Press, 1988); Julia Wells, *We Now Demand! The History of Women's Resistance to Pass Laws in South Africa* (Johannesburg: Witwatersrand University Press, 1993).

12. M. Sutcliffe, "The Crisis in South Africa. Material Conditions and Reformist Response" (paper presented to the workshop Macroeconomic Policy and Poverty in South Africa, Cape Town, August 29–30, 1986; Jo Beall, Shireen Hassim, and Alison Todes, "A Bit on the Side? Gender Struggles in the Politics of Transformation in South Africa," *Feminist Review*, no. 33 (Autumn 1989). 32–56.

13. Casaburri. "On the Question of Women in South Africa."

14. Sheila Gastrow, ed. *Who's Who in South African Politics* (New York: Hans Zell, 1990).

15. Barbara Klugman, "Women in Politics Under Apartheid: A Challenge to the New South Africa," in *Women and Politics Worldwide*, ed., Barbara Nelson and Najma Chowhury (New Haven: Yale University Press, 1994).

16. Ibid.

17. Mangosuthu Buthelezi's speeches, various dates, quoted in Shireen Hassim, "Family, Motherhood, and Zulu Nationalism: The Politics of the Inkatha Movement's Brigade," *Feminist Review*, no. 43 (Spring 1993): 1–77.

18. Praisley Mdluli, "uBuntu-botho: Inkatha People's Education Transformation," Public Address No. 5, 1987.

19. See note 17, above.

20. Hassim, "Family, Motherhood, and Zulu Nationalism."

21. Klugman, "Women in Politics Under Apartheid."

143

22. Women's Charter; see Appendix, Cherryl Walker, *Women and Resistance in South Africa* (London: Onyx Press, 1982).

23. Ibid.

24. Zola S. T. Skweyiya, "Constitutional Guidelines of the ANC: A Vital Contribution to the Struggle Against Apartheid," *Sechaba* 23, no. 6 (1989): 5–10.

25. M. Mies, *Fighting on Two Fronts: Women's Struggles and Research* (The Hague: Institute of Social Studies, 1982).

Asia and the Pacific Islands

Feminist Struggles for Feminist Nationalism in the Philippines

Lynn M. Kwiatkowski and Lois A. West

The cultural production of a feminist nationalist ideology among "progressive" women's organizations in the Philippines has been an uneven process, contingent on historical and social conditions and prevailing cultural gender ideologies and structures. This chapter explores the historical and cultural production of feminist nationalist ideologies in the Philippines. It focuses on two sectors of the women's movement that are a part of the larger processes of the creation of feminist nationalist ideologies: the Women Workers' Movement (Kilusan ng Manggagawang Kababaihan—KMK), and women's organizations in the health sector.

Philippine feminism differ from feminisms in other nations through their emphasis on the development of a national identity common to both men and women; the collective or common good rather than individualism; the greater involvement of progressive religious movements in feminist theory-building and practice; and the centrality of family and kinship relations and roles. Some women's groups attempt to meld reformist strategies and goals with revolutionary ones. Feminists argue that nationalist, class, indigenous, and gender issues must be simultaneously addressed to challenge social inequality and Western capitalist values and systems. The progressive women's movement tends to be well organized and long-term in scope, with goals tied to an alternative and comprehensive social vision.[1]

Feminism has been generally understood in the Philippines as fundamentally entailing the ideas and organizational expressions or movements that seek in various ways to improve the status of women.[2] However, the feminists have not been homogeneously conceived because feminist ideologies, theories, and practices have been altered historically, contingent on political and material conditions. There is a plurality of women's organizations and beliefs that range from conservative to reformist to revolutionary. The contemporary women's movement has been influenced most greatly by ideological debates within the leftist national democratic movement, local political conditions, the uneven development of political consciousness among feminists, unpoliticized women,[3] religious fervor, and Western feminist movements and theory.

Nationalism in the Philippines has basically been understood in recent years as a collective response to problems created by modernization and intervention by foreign powers. Philippine nationalism aims toward freedom from national oppression, which involves liberation from foreign domination and intervention in the economy, politics, and culture.[4] Yet, again, the goals, theories, and practices of nationalism have varied historically, and among ideologically differing organizations.

A feminist nationalist ideology is a contested ideology within the Philippine women's movement, for conceptions of feminist nationalism vary among the wide array of women's groups and are always being refashioned as political and material conditions change. For example, a distinct form of feminist nationalism can be found among feminists in the Cordillera region on Northern Luzon island. Many feminist groups there construct a feminist ethnonationalist ideology that advocates gender equality as well as the cultural integrity and political and economic sovereignty of the region.[5]

Historically, although women appear to have been active participants in nationalist movements since the Spanish colonial period, women's issues were not really focused on until the current period. Since the 1960s, feminists have appropriated nationalist themes to argue that true liberation includes gender, race, and class, as well as nation to create a truly democratic national culture.[6]

Historical Background

The current women's movement has developed from a rich history of Philippine women's movements and experiences with foreign intrusion. Philippine mythology promotes a consciousness among women that men's and women's relations were leaning toward egalitarian during the pre-Hispanic period. A few women are believed to have held positions of power in certain communities.[7] Perceptions may not always be accurate, but it is significant that in the imaginations of Filipino women, reconstructions of their female ancestors represent women as strong, powerful, and equal to men.

The women's consciousness of their female ancestors' first involvement in activities approximating nationalist ideologies is a mythology surrounding female priestesses (*babaylanes*—Bisayans; *catalonan*—Tagalogs). These women are viewed as having occupied a position of power among precolonial ethnic groups. Jocano posited that they were the holders of wisdom, being the spiritual leaders, counsels, healers, and storytellers of a community.[8] They are reported to have been among the first to suffer oppression at the hands of the Spanish colonizers, beginning in 1521, as women of knowledge and proponents of local religions. They are also reported to have been among the first to lead the colonized peoples in uprisings occasioned by their opposition to imposed Catholicism or to avoid persecution. Although they had not developed a feminist or nationalistic ideological framework from which to operate, these women, in practice, resisted the incursion of foreign male domination of their ethnic cultural communities in an attempt to maintain their sovereignty and leadership roles.[9]

The main impetus for the formation of women's groups by the end of the nineteenth century was nationalist and anticolonial. The Spanish ideologies of machismo and the subordination of women to men diminished women's status, making women's participation in the nationalist revolution against Spain a significant beginning for women's involvement in nationalist movements and the political arena. Filipina Gabriela Silang, who is hailed as one of the first great female nationalist leaders, led Philippine soldiers in revolts against the Spanish.

Women were mobilized on a large scale in support of the secret Katipunan organization, the independence movement against Spain. Women also fought in the war of resistance against American colonizers, beginning in 1899. Women leaders in these wars were often the wives of revolutionary leaders, guiding women in humanitarian as well as military operations in their nationalist struggles. During each of these periods, the oppression of colonization was so severe and compelling that women were not yet able to focus on issues pertaining specifically to women.

149

During the American colonial period, women were allowed greater opportunities for educational advancement and employment. This mainly had an impact on upper- and middle-class women, leading to their greater participation in the political arena. Women of this period were also influenced by international women's movements, aided by the spread of literacy.[10] Many middle- and upper-class women's groups began organizing around women's suffrage. The first association to raise this issue was the, Asociacion Feminist Ilonga in 1906. Women's arguments to support their right to vote stressed that women have particular qualities and strengths different from men's that could enhance the political realm. Women's organizations, with the promotion of the movement by male political leaders,[11] gained women's suffrage rights in a national plebiscite in 1937. This was the first gender issue around which Filipino women's group had organized on a national scale.

Women's suffrage organizations fought to rectify the numerous laws held over from the Spanish period that diminished women's rights. It was only with the newly formulated Philippine Republic Constitution of 1947, following independence from the United States that the Spanish Civil Code was revised. Women's involvement in the suffrage movement urged women's participation in public life and advocated gender equality. Yet, in line with more recent arguments from members of the national democratic movement regarding the divisive character of the women's movement within the nationalist movement, some criticized the suffrage movement as having deflected attention from the independence campaign against the American colonizers. Thus, from the start of the women's movement, tensions existed between feminist and nationalist ideologies. The broader nationalist movement, led by men, contested the validity of women's claims to equality as being equally imperative and integral to the goals of the nationalist movement. Women involved in the suffrage movement had not yet formulated a class analysis of women's oppression and had not assessed the specific concerns of working-class or peasant women.

Anti-imperialist and nationalist groups formed during the U.S. occupation of the Philippines, including the Socialist Party and the Partido Komunista ng Pilipinas (PKP). Women's participation in these organizations was limited to intelligence work, cultural activities, and domestic labor. Even so, women's involvement in socialist-inspired trade unions in the early part of the twentieth century, marked the beginning of women's involvement in class issues.

Women fought alongside men in the Hukbo ng Bayan Laban sa Hapon (or Huk) guerilla resistance movement against the Japanese during World War II.[12] Again, some women were involved in military operations, but most served as couriers, intelligence agents, and as cooks and nurses for the soldiers. This was Filipino women's third substantial participation in a nationalist resistance movement, although, again, women's particular concerns were not raised at the time.

Women's involvement in the PKP in the 1950s marked the beginning of the influence of the Left on the women's liberation movement, and the prioritizing of class issues and nationalism over gender. Other women were actively organizing around mainstream party politics, but remaining as only adjuncts to male-dominated political parties.[13] Numerous women's organizations sprouted in the postwar period, including sociocivic, religious, trade union, and professional, predominantly among upper- and middle-class women. Women of the 1950s and early 1960s experienced a trend toward traditional gender ideologies, and reforms were generally made within the prevailing legal framework.[14]

Neocolonial structures imposed by the United States prior to its withdrawal as a colonial government in 1946 included the retention of military bases, the institution of economic provisions advantageous to U.S. business, and the promotion of International Monetary Fund and World Bank intervention in the Philippines. These impositions led to critiques of "imperialism" by Philippine nationalists. Increasing poverty, extreme social inequality, and lack of genuine land reform led to growing dissent in the nationalist movement in the late 1960s. Splits from the older PKP led to the formation of a new Communist Party of the Philippines (CPP), the New People's Army (NPA, the armed wing of the CPP), and the National Democratic Front (NDF, the broader political movement included the NPA and CPP). These organizations were strongly influenced by Marxist-Leninist and Maoist ideologies, which ultimately informed the incipient feminist movement.

With the declaration of martial law by President Ferdinand Marcos in 1972, a mass movement that became known as the national democratic movement, surfaced against the Marcos dictatorship. Women participated actively in the movement, particularly in urban areas and on college campuses. During the 1960s and 1970s, women began formulating an analysis of women's oppression in relation to capitalist class structures and imperialist, racist intervention, alongside a general resurgence of political activism. The nationalist and Communist movements during this period provided the basis for contemporary feminist nationalism. MAKIBAKA (Malayang Kilusan ng Bagong Kababaihan), the Free Movement of New Women, was formed in 1969 as a student women's organization; it was the first to articulate the ideology that women's liberation could be achieved only in the context of greater social liberation. For women in MAKIBAKA, total national liberation could be achieved only with the elimination of the "feudal," or patriarchal, treatment of women, commercialization of women's bodies, and other discriminatory practices and structures that inhibit women's full development. MAKIBAKA initiated reforms in this direction, beginning with a protest against a Miss Philippines beauty contest. Although MAKIBAKA articulated a relationship between women's oppression and class and national oppression, it was unique in viewing women's issues as related but distinct from these other oppressions.[16]

With the human rights' abuses of the Marcos dictatorship and the repression of progressive organizations following martial law, MAKIBAKA, as a part of the NDF, was forced to go underground. Pressures from the male leadership of the NDF urging the women of MAKIBAKA to concentrate on eliminating the dictatorship, U.S. imperialism, and class oppression caused MAKIBAKA to allow its focus on women's concerns to be subordinated to class and nationalist issues. Feminist scholar Salome Ronquillo argues that relegating women's issues to second place under national issues "eventually killed the growing women's movement in the Philippines" because men saw "no need for a separate women's organization, much more, movement."[17] Men argued that the promotion of feminism within the national democratic movement would prove to be divisive because it was perceived to be antimale and not culturally sensitive. These fears remain today among many Filipinos.[18]

The ideological debates among women involved in the nationalist movement during this period centered on the relationship between nationalism and feminism. Nationalist women

> accuse[d] the feminists of a tendency to isolate women problems from what they consider[ed] to be more urgent issues affecting the majority composed of the workers, peasants and urban poor. . . . The feminists run the risk of reducing the national movement to one of self-indulgence capable of dividing and bourgeoisifying the overall militant mass movement.

Feminists argued that this focus could "derail the present fight for women's issues."[19] The tension between the varying feminist and nationalist ideologies caused feminists working within the nationalist movement to attempt to meld feminism and nationalism.

Although male leaders of the CPP/NPA and NDF gave credence to the promotion of equality between men and women, in practice women's concerns were still considered to be secondary to the primary issues of class and nationalism. Women's equality was to be a concern following a successful socialist revolution. Women's organizing in the national democratic movement was viewed by male leaders mainly in instrumental terms, as a means of involving more women in the national democratic struggle, not as a means through which to address concerns particular to women. This inhibited some female nationalists from voicing concerns specific to women. For MAKIBAKA, the success of the national democratic struggle was necessary and sufficient for the liberation of women. It did not view women's liberation as having a central role in the national liberation struggle, which had seemed alien to their local experience during a period of great national repression.[20] Gender-specific forms of oppression were viewed as by-products of class and national oppression, and as problems that could be overcome primarily through education and cultural revival.

Nevertheless, other women's groups' continued to bring forth women's issues during the martial law period. Protests launched against organized sex tours, the mail-order bride trade; the export of women as overseas domestic workers whose wages would help repay the state's accumulating external debt; the exploitation of women workers in export-processing zones and in subcontracting arrangements; and reports of rape perpetrated by state soldiers in the rural areas.[21] Each of these issues was analyzed within the context of the political and economic structures of that period, including gender, class, racial, and national structures. Still, women's groups experienced tension between proponents of nationalist and feminist ideologies, and many were against the promotion of separate women's organizations.

By 1981, with the lifting of martial law, the mass women's movement expanded, particularly following the assassination of Marcos's opponent Benigno Aquino, Jr. This is considered by some to be the rebirth of the Philippine women's movement. Progressive women's organizations organized against the Marcos dictatorship and supported Cory Aquino as president of the Philippines.[22] Numerous women's organizations with a renewed vision of the liberation of women blossomed, such as KALAYAAN, PILIPINA,

NOW, KABAPA, SAMAKANA, AWARE, and WOMB.[23] The progressive groups among them (such as KALAYAAN and PILIPINA) were concerned primarily with the liberation of women in the context of nationalism and progressive social change. In this period to the present, women's liberation was no longer viewed as secondary to class and national liberation. The necessity of addressing women's subordination before national liberation was now stressed by many groups. Still, among the wide range of organizations, differing perspectives on how women's liberation could be accomplished generated a variety of feminist ideologies and some amount of tension and conflict among women's organizations.

KALAYAAN (Katipunan ng Kababaihan para sa Kalayaan) is a women's organization engaged mainly in research, writing, and education about women's subordination. It is noted for having been the first women's organization publicly to raise women's issues that cut across sectors and classes (such as rape, sexual harassment, domestic violence against women) during the period of the dictatorship. Prior to that time, women's personal issues had not been publicly addressed or viewed as political, nor was men's domination raised as an issue that was equally significant and related to, but distinct from, class and national domination. For the first time women openly expressed their view of the compatibility of feminist goals with the goals of national liberation and democracy. Some women's organizations followed a similar ideology; others remained more centrist, working within the established political framework.

The contemporary Philippine women's movement is characterized by being organized by sectors, including peasants, workers, urban poor, students, religious, health workers, and others. The intention behind this structure is to demonstrate how women are affected differentially by class position; and it enables women to organize around particular sectorial issues.[24] Social class divisions mark Philippine women's organizations, although some have attempted to address cross-class issues. Religious influence in women's organizations remains strong, although feminists are contesting churches' (especially the Catholic Church's) stance on reproductive rights, sexual orientation, and the role and status of women. Religious women have played a significant role in the Philippine women's movement. Utilizing a feminist theology of struggle, Filipino religious women tie women's liberation to total national liberation, with a focus on women's struggle through theology.[25]

By 1984, in realization of the need to organize women on a larger scale in the effort to oust the Marcos dictatorship, a national umbrella women's coalition was formed involving more than one hundred women's organizations. Named GABRIELA (General Assembly Binding Women for Reform, Integrity, Equality, Leadership and Action) after Gabriela Silang, the coalition initially concentrated on bringing women into the mass movement to oust Marcos, ending the worsening economic crisis, and obtaining justice for the victims of political repression. Thus, nationalist goals aided in developing a large national movement of women.

Although working for common goals, the women's organizations constituting GABRIELA had varying ideological and political perspectives. Tensions came to a head over whether to participate in or boycott the "snap" 1986 presidential election of Marcos, who was running against Aquino's widow, Corazon Aquino. Because of an inability to come to a consensus, the GABRIELA National Council ruled that member organizations could decide individually whether to participate.

Some grassroots women's organizations later counted the organizations that had decided to boycott the election and found them to be a majority, whereupon a resolution in favor of a GABRIELA boycott stand was passed. With this, a number of GABRIELA organizations, leaders, and members left GABRIELA, resulting in a fragmentation of the nationalist-oriented progressive women's movement.

Continued differences focused on approaches to the new government of President Aquino, who had been elected only after a historic People Power demonstration. Some advocated active engagement; others advocated a largely critical stance, given the continuation of human rights abuses, failed negotiations with the NDF/CPP, and ongoing International Monetary Fund & World Bank intervention in Philippine national affairs. Many women's organizations opted to participate actively in the formulation of the 1987 Constitution, lobbying congresspersons to promote women's equality within the document. Women's organizations came together with a huge "tapestry" of banners, a giant quilt, that expressed women's concerns for the constitutional commissioners.

Filipino women organizing around sectorial concerns continues today with local groups coming together to form networks. Women remain committed to furthering the goals of women's liberation but are divided in the realm of ideological perspectives and strategic means to carry this out.

Progressive women's organizations range from those that align themselves with the national democratic movement, the social democratic movement, and the old Communist Party (PKP). Other women's groups—comprising principally upper-and middle-class women—maintain a centrist ideology. Other grassroots women's organizations with a reformist orientation focus on sectoral issues or development work with women.

The rapid increase in nongovernmental organizations in the past decade has entailed growth for the women's movement. The Women's Network in Politics and Public Policy (Ugnayan ng Kababaihan sa Pulitika) got President Fidel Ramos to sign its ten-point political agenda. This included a pledge by the Ramos government to convert the National Commission on the Role of Women into the Philippine Development Institute for Women; to support increased participation of women leaders in the national and local governments; and to support legislation promoting women's rights. The organization was committed to "People's Power Politics," which would work to elect women at the local levels.[26] The National Network of Homeworkers, PATAMBA (Pambansang Tagapag-ugnay ng mga Manggagawa sa Bahay), represented "homeworkers" such as embroiders, weavers, and food producers in a national network. SARILAYA (kasarian-kalayaan, or gender liberation) began in 1994 as an activist vehicle for promoting a new socialist feminist nationalist vision of Philippine society.[27]

GABRIELA continues as a feminist nationalist organization, as "a movement integral to the national liberation struggle for sovereignty, a democratic and representative government and equality between women and men in all aspects of life." Women of GABRIELA "work for genuine national sovereignty in Philippine socio-cultural, economic and political life and freedom from all foreign intervention especially that of the United States."[28] In its analysis there are several systems of oppression: class, ethnicity, race, gender, and national. Women's leadership in the struggle for women's emancipation and equality is an integral part of the struggle for national liberation.[29] GABRIELA continues to align itself with the larger national democratic movement, which is not uniform on its women's positions: the National Democratic Front has taken the position that patriarchy is a problem for all classes, sectors, and genders, and upholds the right to sexual orientation; the Communist Party, on the other hand has tended to marginalize these issues.[30] GABRIELA's largest current membership base comes from the Women Workers' Movement.

The Women Workers Movement

From the beginning of the formation of the militant labor movement, the Kilusang Mayo Uno (KMU, May First Movement), in 1980, women workers struggled over whether they should remain in women's committees in KMU's "genuine" trade unions,[31] or form a separate women workers' movement. Women industrial workers decided to form the KMK in 1985 because, as one KMK leader put it, "the issues which are women-related are not given enough attention in the presence of other general problems of labor."[32]

KMK initially focused on organizing women factory and service workers but had expanded to peasant women, sugar workers, and miners' wives by 1988. An organizer said, "It's not easy to convince the women especially on equal rights. Because our society still remains a traditional society. . . . They say women are not tough so we must stay weak and obey rules and laws because we are women and not guys."[33]

KMK focused on grassroots organizing and gearing educational materials and training to the real-life, everyday struggles of working women in what they call their "women's orientations." These are educational modules focusing on the historical roots of women's oppression in the Philippines; how women workers are oppressed; the objectives of KMK; advice on how to form KMK chapters; and principles of national democracy and genuine trade unionism. Each module gets slanted to the specific production processes or places where women are employed; for example, department store workers' education and organizing differs from that of factory workers.

During the 1980s there was a continuing dialogue over the nature of women's role in labor movements. As a KMK president said, "Up to now, male trade unionists are still not convinced about KMK." In West's 1989 study of the KMU and KMK,[34] members were asked whether they thought men and women had different issues in the labor movement. All of the women sampled said yes; only 57 percent of the men said yes. As one male leader put it, "Women's lib has no way of organizing the union here, because the majority of our officers even from the very beginning are women and they hold key positions. Sometimes they are even more assertive than men. They hold tremendous power and sometimes they scold us men." However, when asked how many women officers there were in his union, he said two, but "they resigned because they want to take care of their families."[35] A KMK president said a series of "consulta-

tions" were necessary to convince most men of the importance of organizing around women's issues.

> The problem is not that KMU doesn't want women leaders, but it is more
> of developing and training women to be leaders. It really takes time on our
> part to develop women to become national leaders because of the "dou-
> ble burden" [housework and wage work] of women.[36]

Attitudes about gender relations go much deeper. Filipino professor
Belinda Aquino argued that for Southeast Asian women,

> the tendency is not as strong as in the West to confront the traditional so-
> cial structure and fault the family or male authority for injustice to women.
> The female self-concept is less individualistic and is defined by a more
> complex set of institutions that do not necessarily emphasize abstract no-
> tions of self-help, equality, independence, justice and control over one's
> life. Instead, such values as solidarity, reciprocity, cooperation, harmony
> and unity are stressed. One's family or kin group is paramount . . . family
> solidarity is still very much the norm. . . . Class, rather than sex, is the
> more significant variable in analyzing the role and status of women.[37]

This belief that women are part of a unit working for the common
good and the collective needs and class interests of the militant trade
union movement and the family rather than for individualistic interest
even gets reflected in how work is structured. The vice president of a garment company said of his attempt to start an incentive plan for women
workers to increase their productivity:

> We are going to have a contest on which is the best line for the day, or the
> best line for the month. And whoever is the best line gets something.
> There was a place wherein we were saying we have to work a second shift.
> Those people who are going to go on second shift will receive five pesos
> or ten pesos extra per day. The union rejected it, they said no. They said it
> is *not for the common good*. This undercuts productivity because when that is
> the thinking then individual effort is hindered.[38]

Philippine feminist nationalists see their interests as both women and
nationalists inherently linked to communities and to broader interests beyond individualism.[39] Additionally, Philippine feminists have historically

believed in gender difference rather than similarity.[40] A separate-spheres ideology remains important to cultural definitions.

KMK is interested in conserving the welfare of women as women maintain the cohesion of the family unit in traditional institutions. Its feminist agenda is reformist in that it promotes a social policy program demanding changes in state policy toward women. These include ensuring full employment, equal pay for equal work, abolishing the piece-rate system, extending maternity benefits, ensuring social services for working mothers, abolishing forced overtime, and punishing sexual harassment. Feminists attack what they call "sexual opportunism" among men, encouraging criticism when men sexually or emotionally abuse power and take advantage of women, especially in the "double standard" and in the prostitution associated with tourism. Women activists were able to pressure the Ramos government to act against child prostitution and sex tours in the mid-1990s.

As a nationalist organization that is part of the larger national democratic movement seeking to construct cultural identity and political and economic autonomy, KMK seeks fundamental structural change in the state and economy. It participated with the KMU in the 1980s rallies against U.S. bases and in human rights campaigns and campaigns for economic changes such as blocking oil price hikes and peso devaluations. The 1987 KMK president said,

> The women's movement will not win if the workers' struggle as a whole will not succeed. The women's movement is only an integral part of the bigger struggle which is why we should work hand in hand with other cause-oriented groups. The problem of women is not based in the factories only. So the participation of women should not be limited to workers' issues but to political and social issues.[41]

The charge that the militant workers' movement is not autonomous from the Communist Party and its political agenda has plagued KMU, KMK, and GABRIELA since their beginnings. In the early 1990s the Communist Party split into factions, which led to movement fragmentation, which was reflected in the labor movement and KMU.[42] However, GABRIELA's strong organization at the 1995 Beijing UN women's conference belied charges that it was simply a left-wing or nationalist "front," for it demonstrated there that its goals remain focused on women.

Although it represents a major block of GABRIELA members, KMK in the 1990s was a small women worker's movement with little political clout to influence state and management relations. Workers and feminists alike commented that it was easier to organize against Marcos in his waning years than it was against Aquino, and against Ramos today.

What does the future hold for the KMK? Socialist movements in other countries retrenched on the women's agenda once their leaders came to power. The KMK is progressive in representing and empowering working-class women, and is developing as a feminist organization during a time of an international feminist women workers' movement. The extent to which the KMK can retain its feminist goals without losing its nationalist agenda and can continue as a feminist nationalist organization during the wave of current labor repression and human rights abuses will be a sign of its survival as a social movement organization.

Progressive Women's Health Organizations

Just as women have been active in trade union work since the early nationalist revolutions, Filipino women have been active in providing health care services for members of national resistance movements. In the Philippine culture, women historically were associated with healing among ethnic groups during the precolonial and colonial periods, even when men were considered to be the ritual specialists. Indigenous women healers include the aforementioned *babaylanes* of the Bisayas, *catalonans* among the Tagalog, and the *mamao* among the Ifugao.

Although there are currently many male doctors and fewer male nurses in the Philippines, the majority of health care providers in the government NGO, private, and volunteer sectors are women. Culturally, basic biomedical and primary health care are generally gendered activities because Filipino women are considered to be responsible for the cultural role of health provider for their communities and families. In addition to professional female doctors, nurses, and midwives, poor women and fewer poor men are recruited by the government health department and NGOs to volunteer their time as community health workers.

Feminist and feminist-nationalist health organizations have broadened the biomedical conception of health care to one that views the linkages among health, illness, political economy, culture, gender discrimination, class oppression, foreign interventionism, and racism as integral. The mainstream national democratic movement has attempted to integrate

many of these factors in a number of NGO health programs implemented by a variety of organizations on national and local levels. Feminist health organizations such as WomanHealth have prioritized health
issues specific to women. Feminist-nationalist organizations, such as the
national health desk of GABRIELA and local women's organizations that
have health as a component of their programs, have also prioritized health
issues specific to women. Their activities include research, writing, education, legislative lobbying, and/or the provision of health services in local communities. There are also grassroots health organizations that do
not identify themselves as feminist but nevertheless are staffed predominantly by women who work through a feminist framework and engage in
feminist consciousness-raising among the local female volunteers with
whom they area associated. As in the feminist movement generally, there
are varying orientations to women's health among the women's organizations that either focus exclusively on health or have health as one component of a broader program.

GABRIELA created the Women's Commission on Health in 1987 to
provide a national democratic vision and program specific to women's
health. This was the first time women's health was conceived of as an important issue for GABRIELA. Some of the women working in the
GABRIELA health sector at the national level had been involved in the
NDF's health work during the Marcos and early Aquino periods. Their
work then sometimes involved the clandestine provision of health services
to members of the movement or to victims of political violence and human rights abuses in both urban hospitals and rural community settings.
Health work within the national democratic movement prior to
GABRIELA's formation had not focused on women's health issues:

> Today GABRIELA's Health and Reproductive Rights Commission in-
> volves itself in advocacy of issues affecting women's health such as a low
> government budget for health services; government population control
> program; consciousness-raising regarding women's right to decide on mat-
> ters affecting reproductive health; [and] assists in community based
> women's health committees.[43]

The work of GABRIELA that can also be considered as health-re-
lated, though not specifically defined as such, includes the work of the
Commission on Violence Against Women, which "addresses the issues of
prostitution, trafficking of women, domestic violence and coordinates a

network of centers for prostituted women in Olongapo and Manila."[44] All of these activities are conducted within GABRIELA's larger ideological framework of the resolution of women's problems in conjunction with class and national liberation. A GABRIELA member argued,

> Health work must be done in the context of the general [nationalist] movement. There should not be just a woman's health movement, but a health component in the general movement; like how poverty affects women. There is a women's health movement [within the Philippines], but a health movement should not be separate.[45]

GABRIELA confronts gendered problems that cut across class lines, such as violence against women, sexism in the media, rape, and others. Yet according to a GABRIELA member, "Some things GABRIELA does will be against the [economic] interests of upper class women. [So we] had to institute representation by sectors. . . . [Although GABRIELA] offices are mainly run by middle-class women . . . [in the] highest decision-making ranks, GABRIELA has tried to be representative sectorally."[46] The class-based nature and sectoral orientation of women's organizations is characteristic of the Philippine women's movement.

GABRIELA's orientation toward men stresses equality and cooperation, and religion and family are accorded importance and considered in the construction and implementation of programs. Politically, because of its alleged ties to the CPP, GABRIELA has faced harassment and surveillance by the male-dominated state military or police. Sectoral member groups of GABRIELA have experienced military harassment, and some women have been killed.[47] At the grassroots level, women engaged in volunteer health work sometimes encounter opposition from their husbands for spending too much of their energy and time away from home responsibilities and work.

GABRIELA emphasizes international linkages with other women's organizations. Yet feminism as constructed by members of GABRIELA must be viewed as having been forged within Philippine society and culture. As does KMK, GABRIELA interprets women's health in cooperative rather than individualistic terms. Women are educated and made conscious of women's and general health issues through GABRIELA organizations not only for their own sakes but also for the sakes of others in their families and communities. Women health workers are encouraged to share their familial responsibilities equally with their husbands.

With GABRIELA's perspective of health as being integrally linked to economic, political, and social factors, it advocates a nationalist orientation to the resolution of women's health problems. This is effected through the mass mobilization of women and men on issues such as International Monetary Fund and World Bank intervention, U.S. military and economic intervention, government land reform policies, government budget allocations, establishment of a nonalignment policy and a nuclear-free-zone provision for the Philippines, and other issues all of which are seen to impact directly on women's health, often to a greater degree than men's. For example, International Monetary Fund and World Bank loan programs, as well as others, have resulted in the enormous indebtedness of the Philippine government: U.S. $43 billion in 1994.[48] To reduce the external debt, 37 percent of the 1992 national budget was allocated for debt repayment; only 3.6 percent for health.[49] Women's health needs are not being met by government health programs, necessitating the work of NGOs. A feminist nationalist framework such as GABRIELA's, deriving from the social conditions particular to the Philippines, asserts that women's health problems cannot be resolved without simultaneously resolving larger political and economic issues such as class, state, and neocolonial oppression.

Numerous other women's health organizations and women's organizations emphasize a feminist orientation to women's health but place less emphasis on social class and maintain autonomy from the national democratic movement. One of these organizations, WomanHealth, has roots in organizations such as KALAYAAN, whose members had been active in promoting women's rights as human rights. These women had raised reproductive rights as human rights during the Human Rights Conference on International Human Rights Day, December 10, 1985. After the People's Power Revolution which deposed President Marcos in 1986, these feminists and other members of GABRIELA fought for prowomen provisions during the drafting of the Philippine Constitution. WomanHealth emerged from this loose network of women. WomanHealth is a national network of individual women, NGOs, and organizations committed to promoting the right to health and reproductive freedom. It is reformist in orientation, focusing on women's and men's equality, promoting legislative changes within the existing legal framework, and promoting education, consciousness-raising, and support and referrals for women around women's health needs and care.[50]

These different ideological approaches to women's health exemplify the diversity of feminisms in the Philippines. GABRIELA represents the largest feminist organization to advocate a nationalist perspective on understanding and resolving women's health problems in conjunction with the larger national democratic movement. Although GABRIELA seems to have made some headway in the NDF's orientation to gender problems, in practice women's concerns are largely marginalized to the women's organizations.

Pursuing Gender Equality Within a National Culture

Within the Philippine feminist nationalist movement, the debate continues in the larger arena as it did in the early 1970s over the primacy of gender versus nationalist issues and the reconciliation of both. Feminist nationalists say that

> all three dimensions of the women's struggle [national, class, and gender] must be simultaneously pursued. A women's movement which ignores national and class questions will remain limited, ineffectual, and isolated from the mainstream, from the motive forces which are the sources of structural change. On the other hand, a women's movement which permits the relegation of women's issues to the background is in fact delaying or negating the full liberation and empowerment of women as women—an end which can only be attained with the final uprooting of ideas and institutions which perpetuate inequality between the sexes even in independent and socialist societies.[51]

The alliance of progressive feminists with members of the mainstream national democratic movement has not always served to further feminist ideological goals, and at times has inhibited a gendered analysis of oppression in the Philippines. Due to resistance and pressures from both male leaders and female members of the movements to subsume issues of gender oppression under class and national oppression, women in progressive feminist organizations of the 1960s and 1970s tended to self-censor their activities as well as their aspirations for gender equality. By the 1980s, however, within a political climate of greater democratization, and with the recent upheaval in the national democratic movement, feminist organizations had begun to give increased attention to issues of gender oppression, some still focusing on the triad of gender, class, and national oppression. Yet the divisions created by strains in the broader Left may be creating stricter divisions among feminist organizations with some more feminist than nationalist.

A feminist nationalist image of Philippine nationhood envisions gender relations as well as class, national, racial, and ethnic relations as beginning to be equalized even prior to the total social and national liberation. In this feminist nationhood, women have self-determining power in all aspects of their lives and provide a contribution equal to men's in the processes of creating nationhood. The imagined nationhood is self-determined, no longer neocolonial, and class oppression is eliminated. Filipino women are actively changing structures of domination that affect them specifically as women, as well as those that affect men and women, prior to as well as following social revolution. Women's issues centrally permeate all components of social change and are not relegated to a marginal position in society.

While a feminist image of nationhood contests the mainstream nationalist ideology, feminist organizations have attempted to relate gender, class, and neocolonial oppression. One GABRIELA leader argued,

> Thus there can be no single women's movement in the Philippines solely on the basis of gender, to the negation of class . . . Thus the struggle for the freedom of all women is inseparable from the struggle of the working classes and from the global struggles of people the world over fighting racism and imperialism.[57]

The Philippine feminist nationalist movement provides us with an example of the sometimes slippery nature of the alliance between feminism and nationalism. Feminism in the Philippines, as held by progressive women's organizations, had historical roots in movements since the Spanish colonial period, when women organized in resistance against colonization. The most recent feminist organizations have been strongly influenced by the Left nationalist movement struggling against gender, class, and neocolonial exploitation. Some feminist organizations have additionally been influenced by local ethnonationalist movements for cultural integrity and regional autonomy while they simultaneously align with a broader Philippine feminist nationalist movement. Nationalism and feminism have been viewed by many women's groups as inseparable, but feminist groups' alliances with broader nationalist and ethnonationalist movements have not always advanced feminists' goals, nor has their integration as one movement been an easy process. This process continues, nonetheless, with feminists pursuing their ideal of a national culture that asserts gender equality.

Notes

1. Leonora C. Angeles, "Feminism and Nationalism: The Discourse on the Woman Question and Politics of the Women's Movement in the Philippines" (Master's thesis, University of the Philippines, 1989).

2. Ibid., p. 17.

3. Ibid., p. 63

4. Ibid. p. 242.

5. Lynn M. Kwiatkowski, "Feminism and Ethnonationalism Among Cordillera Women in the Philippines." Paper presented at the U.N. NGO Forum on Women, Beijing, China, 1995.

6. Ibid, p. 244.

7, Rosalinda Pineda-Ofreneo, "Tracing A Hidden Tapestry: Women and Literature in the Philippines," in *Women Reading: Feminist Perspectives on Philippine Literary Texts*, ed. Thelma B. Kintanar (Diliman, Quezon City: University of the Philippines Press and University Center For Women's Studies, 1992), p. 31.

8. F. Landa Jocano, ed., *The Philippines at the Spanish Contact* (Quezon City: R. P. Garcia, 1975), p. 41, cited in Kintanar, *Women Reading*, p. 10.

9. Marjorie Evasco, "The Writer and Her Roots," in Kintanar, *Women Reading*, p. 10.

10. Kumari Jayawardena, *Feminism and Nationalism in the Third World* (London: Zed Books, 1986) p. 7.

11. The first male political leader to propose women's suffrage publicly was Apolinario Mabini, one of the leaders of the Philippine revolution, in a draft of the 1889 Malolos Constitution that he prepared. Angeles, "Feminism and the Nationalism," p. 111.

12. Ibid., p. 248.

13. Ibid., p. 121.

14. Virginia A. Miralao, "Contemporary Women's Groups and Organizations: A Note on the Directions of the Philippines Women's Movement," *Social Science Information* 14 (October–December 1986): 5.

15. Angeles, pp. 147, 149.

16. Ibid.

17. Salome Ronquillo, "MAKIBAKA Remembered," *Diliman Review*, (May–August, 1984), pp. 52–53.

18. Maureen Pagaduan, "The Feminist Movement in the Philippines: A History of Searching," in *Reexamining and Renewing the Philippine Progressive Vision:*

Papers and Proceedings of the 1993 Conference of the Forum for Philippine Alternatives (FOPA), San Francisco Bay Area, California, April 2–4, 1993, p. 110. Unpublished manuscript. (San Francisco: FOPA, 1993)

19. Fe. B. Mangahas, "An Overview of the Militant Filipino Women's Movement During the Decade for Women" (unpublished paper, n. d.).

20. Angeles, "Feminism and Nationalism," p. 150.

21. Miralao, "Contemporary Women's Groups and Organizations," p. 6.

22. Angeles, "Feminism and Nationalism."

23. Ibid, p. 253.

24. Ibid., p. 219.

25. Mary John Mananzan, cited in Katahryn Poethig, "Sisters in the Struggle: Philippine Prostitution and Two Feminist Theologies in the 1980s," in *Papers and Proceedings of the 1993 Conference of the Forum for Philippine Alternatives,* p. 128.

26. Women's Network in Politics and Public Policy, "Women and the Ballot," flyer, United Nations NGO Forum, September 1995.

27. Joel Rocamora, *Breaking Through: The Struggle within the Communist Party of the Philippines* (Manila: Anvil, 1994), p. 208.

28. "GABRIELA, Women as a Political Force, Vital, Distinct, Integral," pamphlet (Manila, 1993).

29. Angeles, p. 217.

30. L. Kwiatkowski's interview with GABRIELA member, July 29, 1993.

31. KMU defines itself as "genuine" and "militant because it fights for the economic and political interests of the working class in conjunction with other oppressed sectors of society and relies on the collective strength and actions of workers and other sectors in pursuance of their interests." Lois A. West, "Political Unionism, Development and Democratization in the Philippines" (Ph.D. diss., University of California, Berkeley, 1989), p. 1. See West's discussion of the KMU and KMK in *Militant Labor in the Philippines* (Philadelphia: Temple University Press, 1996).

32. West, "Political Unionism, Development and Democratization," p. 243.

33. Ibid.

34. Ibid., p. 252.

35. Ibid., p. 253.

36. Ibid.

37. Belinda Aquino, "Feminism Across Cultures," in *Women in Asia and the Pacific: Towards an East-West Dialogue.* ed. Madeleine J. Goodman. (Honolulu: University of Hawaii Press, 1985), p. 342.

38. My emphasis. West's interview with a garment factory vice president in Taguig, May 15, 1987; West, "Political Unionism, Development and Democratization," p. 264.

39. See Virgilio G. Enriquez, *From Colonial to Liberation Psychology: The Philippine Experience* (Quezon City: University of the Philippines Press, 1992), for a

discussion of Western misinterpretations of Philippine culture. Aquino argued: "Filipino women . . . act more as partners or supporters rather than equals to men. They value complementary or compensatory roles rather than separate ones." Aquino, "Feminism Across Cultures," p. 342. Anna Fresnido disagreed: "A woman must learn to stand alone like an island. Only then will she be truly free. . . . A woman must then break away from the pervasive culture of dependence on the male. Separate but equal." Anna Marie Alvarez Fresnido, "Sugarland Hotel Tidbits: Women's Issues," (National Federation of Sugarworkers, Bacolod City, Negros) 1 (July 15, 1988): 4.

40. Uy, University of California, Berkeley, colloqium, December 1, 1988. This is GABRIELA's and KMK's position as well.

41. West, "Political Unionism, Development and Democratization," 244.

42. For a discussion of this fragmentation, see Rocamora, *Breaking Through*.

43. See note 22, above.

44. Ibid.

45. See note 23, above.

46. Ibid.

47. Ibid.

48. Women's Committee of the Freedom from Debt Coalition of the Philippines, "Focusing on Women, Debt and Structural Adjustment" (September 1995).

49. IBON, "Slice and Dice the 1992 Budget. IBON Facts and Figures." (February 15, 1992) 15, 3: 1–8. Manila: IBON Philippines Databank and Research Center.

50. "WomanHealth Philippines," pamphlet (1993).

51. The Philippine Women's Research Collective, "Alternative Philippine Report on the Impact of the Decade for Women (1976–1985)" (Quezon City, July 1985), reprinted in Amaryllis T. Torres, Ma. Luisa T. Camagay, et al., *An Anthology of Studies on the Filipino Woman* (Manila: UNESCO Regional Unit for Social and Human Sciences in Asia and the Pacific, January 1986), p. 227.

52. Fe Arriola (GABRIELA officer), "A Woman's Place," in *GABRIELA Convention Proceedings, 2–3 March 1985*, p. 18.

Integrative Feminist Politics in the Republic of Korea

Alice Yun Chai

Third World women and First World women of color have been developing diversified feminist perspectives through opening up the specificity of their realities. They argue that a concept such as race should not be considered as an added aspect of their experience but that we need to change our perception of the reality with a different consciousness.[1] Their insistence on defining feminism in its historical, social, and cultural contexts and interrelating various forms of oppression—discriminations based on race, class, gender, sexuality, nationality, religion, and ethnicity—contribute to comprehensive perspectives on women and multi-front strategies for social change.

Leaders of Third World women's movements insist that the theoretical framework of Third World women's liberation should be based on a feminism broad enough to deal with all inequalities of their respective societies. The movements, they assert, should direct their struggle not only to obtain sexual equality but to transform the aspects of their reality that are responsible for the oppression of women and people in other disadvantaged groups. This means that in the Third World context national liberation and human rights struggles are seen as interconnected with women's liberation movements.[2]

The form women's movements take at a particular time and place is generally related to the multiplicity of women's experiences: (1) the historical development of gender and production relations; (2) the transformational political consciousness of these relations; and (3) the autonomy, legitimacy, and strength that women's movements have created in their relations with other concurrent social movements.[3] Therefore, there is a need for feminism to recognize both the separateness of women's movements and their linkages to the larger struggles to eliminate the total structure of inequality.

A number of Third World countries experienced increasingly repressive militarized governments in the 1970s and 1980s. Hence, there was a critical need for Third World women to make connections with larger social movements for national and social liberation from dictatorial militarism and the new international division of labor created by the global political economy. [4] Similarly, the current women's movement in Korea has been characterized by the necessity to make connections with larger movements for national and social liberation from foreign domination and from the military regimes.[5] Because of this interrelatedness and simultaneity of many aspects of women's oppression and the existence of inequalities and conflicts among different groups of women, feminism for Korean women can be best defined as a theory and politics that seek to remove all forms of inequalities, domination, and oppression interconnected on a global level.[6]

Since the latter half of the 1980s, the women's movement in the Republic of Korea has been developing out of the realization that the vulnerable conditions of working-class Korean women were tied to the entire social structure of oppression and the global political economy. This led many Korean feminists to engage in multifront struggles and seek total societal transformation.[7]

This newly emerging women's movement blossomed into creative and strategic coalition politics in the form of the Korea Women's Associations United (KWAU) during the spring of 1987. This coincided with the beginning of the democratization movement, where feminist issues were dealt with in the context of the national political transition from authoritarianism to democracy.

KWAU was based on the belief that women's problems cannot be separated from social movements that seek to change the contradictions of the political, economic, and social structures. Changes were to be carried out as a part of the democratization movement. To illustrate how this belief was approached in practice, the following are the priority issues of

KWAU in 1993: (1) the introduction of special legislation on sexual violence; (2) demands for reductions in the military budget; (3) employment issues of women workers; (4) organizational expansion of regional, grassroots, women-based movements; (5) coalition advocacy and research work on military sexual slavery "comfort women"—women who were used as sex slaves drafted by Japan during World War II; and (6) national unification and world peace through democratization.[8]

Several factors influenced the development of the current Korean women's movement: (1) the political instability resulting from the division of Korea into North Korea and South Korea in 1945; (2) post-Korean War industrial development; (3) authoritarian militarism; (4) the globalization of feminist agendas since the United Nations Decade for Women (1975–1985); and (5) the emergence and the globalization of the Asian Women in Solidarity for "Comfort Women" movement, which originated in South Korea and Japan and has spread to the rest of the Asia and Pacific region since 1990.

National Division and the Political Economy

On August 15, 1945, Korea was liberated from Japan with Japan's surrender to the United States and its allies. On September 2, 1945, the peninsula was divided at the 38th parallel: the southern half was occupied by the United States; the northern half by the USSR. South Korea became politically independent with the establishment of the First Republic of Korea on August 15, 1948, and the inauguration of President Rhee Syngman (1948–1960).[9]

The new president adopted a strong anticommunist national security policy toward the North, which resulted in the tragic Korean War of the 1950s. His government received extensive military aid from the United States, in both weaponry and personnel. Although North Korea declared its political independence from the Soviet Union (and China) in 1966, the United States maintains a military force of 37,000 in South Korea against what the government sees as a continuing communist threat from the North.

Political instability marked several decades following the war, including a series of coups d'etat. The student movement forced the resignation of Rhee Syngman, and the Second Republic was established in 1960, with a new president, Yun Bo Sun (1960–1963). A coup d'etat in 1961 orchestrated by a new military leader, General Park Chung Hee, resulted in the Third Republic in 1963. Rising protests against his authoritarianism led him to impose military rule in 1972 and to ban all political opposition in 1975. Park, actually a dictator, introduced the Yushin system, which literally means "restoration" or "making anew," and broke his promise to resign at the end of his second term in 1971.[10] In 1979, after sixteen years in office, Park was assassinated by the head of the Korean intelligence forces. The chief commander of national security, General Chun Doo Hwan, formed a group that succeeded in taking over the interim civilian government after a six-month democratization period, commonly called the "Spring of Seoul."

Another military government was formed, under Chun Doo Hwan, with the declaration of martial law on May 18, 1980. A day later students in the city of Kwangju, Cholla Namdo Province, began demonstrations against the coup, demanding an end to martial law and the resignationof Chun. They were later joined by citizens shocked at the brutality that left 500 people dead and 960 reported missing, in contrast to the official figure of 170 casualties. [11]

Chun was "formally" elected president in 1981 for the full seven-year term, which brought into being the Fifth Republic. Political dissidents staged what came to be known as the June 1987 Revolt, an antigovernment mass protest that led to the election of a new president, General Roh Tae Woo, who negotiated a truce with the political opposition. For the first time in South Korea's twenty-year history, its people had a direct presidential election (December 16, 1987). In 1992 the first civilian president in thirty-two years, former dissident Kim Yong Sam, was elected. Many felt that the event marked the beginning of true democratization.

Because of the Kwangju massacre, many people continued to seek justice and this partly led to the 1995 indictment of the two former presidents Roh Tae Woo and Chun on charges of extreme bribe taking from big business executives, *chaebol* (rich capitalists/owners/board members of large business conglomerates as well as conglomerates themselves and the equivalent to *zaibatsu* of Japan), involvements in the Kwangju massacre; and against Chun for the mutiny stemming from the December 12, 1979 coup.

Between the beginning of the Yushin period (1972–1979) and the spring of 1987, political instability and the hostility of the military governments toward unification made open debate on national unification impossible. However, in 1992 South Korea established diplomatic relations with China, North Korea's only major ally.

During the rapid industrialization of the 1970s and 1980s, South Korea became one of the "Little Four Dragons" in Asia, along with Taiwan, Hong Kong, and Singapore. In these Newly Industrializing Countries (NICs), women workers, who toiled long hours for low wages, were the backbone of the export-oriented textile, garment, chemical and electronics industries. South Korea's rapid economic growth could not be divorced from the linkages between militarism, political repression, and the global economy. Its militant women's union organizers disproved the stereotype of docile Asian women workers. While the military regimes (1961–1986) kept labor costs low and repressed organized labor to spur economic development, the Korean women workers were spearheading the 1970s labor movement.[12]

Social movement grassroots organizing led to the severe repression of South Korean human rights activists, who argued that the unification of Korea was a fundamental requirement for justice and peace, both of which are possible only through self-determination and changes in the priorities of the South Korean state.[13]

While the middle and upper classes prospered under the government's economic development policies, the poor and the working class believed the policies to be harmful and disruptive, for example, in the conversion of farm lands to industrial sites. This, coupled with the lowering of prices for rice and other farm products by the government in order to meet the foreign competition for exports, impoverished rural people who were forced to migrate to urban slum areas to find unskilled, low-paying jobs in the informal sector of the labor market. Such dislocation in the name of "development" is no better exemplified than in the government's actions prior to the 1988 Olympics in Seoul; for "the beautification of Seoul," wholesale government evictions were carried out.

President Roh was faced with many politically sensitive and important demands of the people, such as prosecution of the former president Chun, exposing truths about the Kwangju massacre, release of political prisoners, elimination of prison torture, ending the power of the military government in the name of the national security policy, and initiation of a North-South dialogue for a peaceful unification. Under the current president Kim Yong Sam, social movement activists continue to demand justice against the abuses of the military regimes and an initiation of a North-South dialogue for a peaceful unification under the current president.

Alice Yun Chai

The South Korean State and Women

All things considered, one would not expect the South Korean government to take on the issue of sexual equality in the politically turbulent
1960s, 1970s, and 1980s. A series of five-year Economic Development
Plans during 1960s and 1970s have been concerned with women mostly
in relation to national family planning policies and the integration of
women into overall economic development.[14] In 1984, however, the
National Assembly ratified the UN Charter on the Elimination of All
Forms of Discrimination Against Women, a charter the United States has
yet to ratify. Also in the 1980s the government established the National
Committee on Women's Policies and the Korean Women's Development
Institute (KWDI). The former is in charge of planning and coordinating
national policies for the enhancement of women's status among various
administrative agencies related to women's issues. The latter was originally under the Ministry of Health and Social Affairs but was transferred
to the Ministry of Political Affairs in 1991. KWDI was created to prepare
for the 1985 Nairobi UN International Women's Decade conference,
but now conducts comprehensive research projects and educational and
training programs, and also initiates various action-oriented programs.[15]

In 1988 the Second Ministry of Political Affairs (originally called the
Ministry of Political Affairs Without Portfolio) was established, headed by
a woman cabinet-level minister. She is responsible for formulating and
implementing policies related to sexual equality by promoting women's
active participation in social, economic, and political reforms and in democratization and globalization processes. In 1991, pressured by the
women's movement activists, the government organized an all-women
police squad to deal with crimes of violence against women. The next
year, the ministry announced a plan to eradicate violence against women.

According to a recent report by the UN, Korean women's overall status
ranked 90th among 116 nations surveyed. The low representation of
women in the administrative, legislative, and judiciary branches of government has been of great concern to the women's movement activists
since the democratic transition period (1987–1992). In 1995, there was
only one woman minister and one woman vice minister in the cabinet. In
1996, nine of the 299 members of the National Assembly are women.
Seven were elected in a proportional representation system of the political
parties rather than being elected from electoral districts by direct popular
vote. Although sexual discrimination was prohibited in the employment of

civil servants by the 1989 Equal Employment Opportunity Act, in 1993 only 1.9 percent of the civil service positions above grade five were women. Only 5.6 percent are women in local councils, 9 percent are women on various government committees.[16]

Through the concerted efforts of women's organizations and women legislators, the Special Committee on Women in the National Assembly was created in June 1994 to be the liaison between the National Assembly, the government, and women's organizations. The committee's main and immediate tasks are revision of the law on the prohibition of marriage between persons of the same surname with the same ancestral origin, and laws on child care and domestic violence.[17]

During the democratic transition period in the 1980s, there was a keen awareness of the importance of women's political participation in the democratization process. Some of the results of a research project on female voting behavior in local elections held June 27, 1995 were: (1) the women voted according to their independent and individual opinions; (2) the women did not necessarily vote for candidates from the conservative ruling party; (3) the women voted for more women candidates than did the men; and (4) women's interests and participation in politics showed no difference from men's.[18] In the light of these findings and because women voters are 50.7 percent of the total voting population, each party platform incorporated women's issues, such as child care at the workplace, to attract the female vote in the next election.

After thirty-seven years of persistent struggle, the National Assembly in 1989 amended the Family Law. The United Coalition of Women for the Revision of the Family Law had been organized in 1984, and the Special Committee on Family Law Reform had been appointed by the KWAU. The amendments, which became effective in January 1991, made it possible for (1) a divorcing woman to seek a share of the couple's property in proportion to her contribution; (2) child-custody arrangements in divorce settlements not to favor the father automatically; and (3) all surviving children to inherit equally regardless of gender. The law's controversial provisions on succession to house head as male still stand, but in the case of a male house head, some of the duties and responsibilities of the head can be shared with other family members.[19] Further, the prohibition of marriage between persons of the same surname and same ancestral origins was left untouched.

The Equal Employment Opportunity Act (EEOA) was passed abruptly by the Assembly in 1987 by a majority of the ruling party in order to win the women's votes in the upcoming presidential election.[20] The act was not effective for women, however, because it has had no teeth; employers who contravened its provisions were subject to only a small fee. Revisions made in 1989 defined discrimination and added provisions concerning equal pay for comparable work. Amendments in 1995 helped to ensure more stringent enforcement. For example, the penalty for noncompliance was raised from 3,000,000 to 5,000,000 won (800 won is approximately U.S. $1). The amendments also include mandatory paid maternity leave provisions for child-care leave for both parents during the child's first year. More important, the 1995 amendments prohibit employer application of sexual double standards; specifically, using the criteria of physical appearance and marital status in reference only to women applicants. Amendments in 1995 to the 1991 Child Care Act require companies with three hundred (reduced from five hundred) or more female employees to provide child-care facilities.

Because only 1.9 percent of civil service workers above the grade five were women in 1995, women's organizations have begun to press for a ratio (quota) system in hiring for grades five to seven. They want to increase the proportion of females to 15 percent by 1998, and 20 percent by the year 2000 to correct for past discrimination.[21]

The Korean Women's Hot Line began an active campaign in 1991 to eradicate sexual violence. Working with KWAU's Special Committee for Legislation on Sexual Violence, the group was able to see the Act Relating to Punishment of Crimes of Sexual Violence and Protection of Victims (commonly known as the Special Law Against Sexual Violence) enacted in December 1993. The act covered forms of sexual violence other than rape, such as sexual advances in public places and pornographic computer messages. The period for reporting to the authorities has been extended from six months to one year.[22] There are now some provisions that enable third-party reporting of instances of rape by a relative and of sexual assaults against the physically challenged.[23]

There is an urgent need for a new coalition movement for legislation concerning violence against women in the household, such as wife battering, incest and marital rape. KWAU member organizations are working on having legislation introduced that would cover such issues. Because the 1994 Prostitution Prevention Act was not effective in criminalizing customers of prostitution, its revision in 1995 gave prostitutes more legal rights and human dignity. The 1994 Social Security Act for Korean military sexual slaves/"Comfort Women" provides those who survived a monthly allowance of 200,000 won, free medical care and the right to apply for public rental housing.

The South Korean Women's Movement

The early Korean women's movement emerged from the establishment in 1886 of the first school for women, the Ewha Hakdang founded by American missionary women. Young Korean women not only learned to read and write there but also were introduced to the concepts of political, religious, and personal freedom. On March 1, 1919, a large number of female students and women all over the country participated in the nationwide uprising against Japanese colonial domination. Thereafter, Korean Christian women educated in mission and church schools acted as the main force in a series of anti-Japanese political activities. Christianity, by raising consciousness through education, empowered Korean women to become leaders in the national liberation movement during the Japanese colonization period, 1910 to 1945.[24]

Since the 1970s a new wave of the women's movement has come along, concurrent with political and economic developments, democratization, and the national unification movements.[25] The grassroots women's movement not only challenged political repression but also took on other structural restrains, such as environmental pollution and sexual exploitation in the labor market.

In the 1980s the Korean women's movement entered another stage, during which new organizations emerged to empower the *Minjung* women, that is, the alienated women in poverty, and rural and industrial working-class women who were struggling for economic survival and for labor organization. *Minjung* consists of such grassroots people as the workers in the agricultural and industrial sectors who resisted military authoritarianism, foreign cultural imperialism, and economic exploitation.[26] It can also include intellectuals, writers, politicians, professionals, and student protesters and their mothers of the 1970s and 1980s who participated in collective actions for democratization and national unification. Likewise, the Korean women's movement of the 1980s and later can be called "*Minjung* feminism" because it has been carried out by persons whose political consciousnesses have been raised: women student and intellectuals working for the social and economic liberation of the poor, urban working-class and rural women who are at the bottom of the social hierarchy.[27]

The Korean upper- and middle-class older women, highly educated women intellectuals, and young women, who had participated in direct collective actions against the military government in the 1970s and in the 1980s, founded autonomous women's groups, such as the Korean Women for Equality and Peace (1983), the Korean Women's Hot Line (1983), Another Culture (1984), the Korean Women's Association for Democracy and Sisterhood (1987), and other grassroots women's organizations. In the midst of such organizational energy the Korea Women's Associations United (KWAU), composed of more than twenty member organizations, was founded in February 1987, a few months prior to the 1987 June Revolt. The spur was the belief that the women's movement should not be separate from the social movements attempting to bring about changes in the political, economic, and social structures.

The member organizations of the KWAU were determined to effect changes in the social structures characterized by institutional sexism. They challenged sexual discrimination in the workplace, such as the prohibition or hindrance of women workers' union organization; public policies discriminating against working women in employment opportunities, advancement, and retirement; and violence against women in the household, in the workplace and in the larger society.

Defining the women's movement as a part of the larger nationwide mass-oriented human rights and democratization movement, the KWAU strove to achieve women's liberation, national unification, and democratization simultaneously through coalition strategies in the midst of the democratic transition period in the late 1980s. This integrative strategy gave women great political momentum and a unique opportunity to link their movement to the labor, democratization, and national unification movements. Coalition work has made women's agendas visible in the broader political arena by mobilizing a substantial number of women including middle-class housewives and mothers of student activists for direct action, such as staging the first protest against the police use of tear gas during the 1980s student protests.

To promote consciousness-raising and solidarity among women of various backgrounds, the KWAU inaugurated the annual Korean Women's Conference (KWC) on International Women's Day, March 8, 1985.[28] In 1987 it initiated the Woman of the Year Award to a woman or a group in recognition of contributions to women's liberation. The first award was given to a former student activist and union organizer, Kwon In Sook, who had filed suit charging rape against a police officer in the

Inchon local court. Her decision to reveal the incident was one of a series of events that triggered the June 1987 Revolt, which in turn brought about the change in the constitution that made possible a general presidential election. In 1995 the KWAU celebrated World Women's Day with the forum Women and Men as Equal Voters for Peace and Unification.

The post-1980s women's movement has another component: an alternative/feminist cultural movement, represented by such groups as Another Culture. Feminist arts and criticism which emerged in the 1980s such as fine arts, indigenous folk and shaman rituals, literature, drama, music, dance, and audio-visual materials, all helped to create an alternative women's culture. In 1989 the KWAU proclaimed the last week of September to be National Women's Week; many women's cultural events were held nationwide. Women artists organized the Society for Feminist Culture and Art in 1992.

Ever since a course in women's studies was inaugurated in 1977, and an M.A. program in 1982, and Ph.D. women's studies program in 1990 were established at Ewha Women's University, Korea is one of the leaders in Asia in feminist teaching and research. In 1984, the Korean Association of Women's Studies was established to provide a basis for the nationwide development of feminist research and education. Currently, approximately 70 universities in Korea are offering Women's Studies courses. Marking the establishment of the Asian Center for Women's Studies at Ewha Women's University, the center published the first annual issue of *Asian Journal of Women's Studies* in 1995.

There are also educational organizations for women in the community such as the Women's Center for Social Education and specialized feminist professional organizations such as the Korean Association of Women Theologians which publishes a quarterly journal, *Hankuk Yosong Shinhak* (Korean Feminist Theology).

Women's movement organizations have worked together since the 1980s on a series of sex discrimination cases by forming *ad hoc* committees composed of women's and other social movement groups. The first case that prompted cooperation concerned the police rape of a female student-prisoner arrested on a charge of demonstrating against the government in 1984. A committee composed of eleven women's organizations brought a charge against the minister of internal affairs, and the chiefs of the Chongyangree and Sodaemun police stations, who were accused of the crime. The group held large meetings to discuss rally strategies and published newsletters critical of the government.

Other such committees put together the Special Committee for the Legislation of Special Laws Against Sexual Violence (1992) and the Joint

Committee on the Sexual Harassment Case of a Seoul National University (SNU) Research Assistant (1993). The latter was formed by university students and twenty-seven women's organizations and brought the first workplace sexual harassment case in Korea.[29] In 1995 the committee Women in Solidarity for the 20 percent Ratio System to Increase Women in the National Assembly was founded by fifty-six women's organizations to prepare for the June local elections.[30]

In the 1990s women's movement workers have been actively involved with violence against women as one of its top-priority issues. Violence against women generally includes date rape and marital rape; battering; incest; sexual harassment; trafficking in women, including prostitution and sexual slavery; and pornography. Several women's organizations were founded in relation to sexual violence, such as the Korean Council for the Women Drafted for Sexual Slavery by Japan (1990), the Korean Sexual Violence Relief Center (1991), the Crisis Center Against Sexual Violence (1993), and the Counseling Center for Family and Sex opened by the Women's Association for Democracy and Sisterhood. Summarizing the work of these organizations, the Korea Women's NGO Committee issued the booklet, "Violence Against Women and Women's Human Rights in Korea," for distribution at the 1995 Beijing NGO Forum.

In legislative coalition work, beginning with the 1990 Public Forum for Legislation on Gender Violence, the Committee for Legislation on Gender Violence was formed at the initiative of the Korean Women's Hot Line. Later, the national campaign for legislation on sexual violence was launched by forming the Special Committee for Legislation on Sexual Violence by KWAU member organizations.[31]

The "economic miracle" of export-oriented development under the authoritarian regimes in the 1960s and 1970s resulted in the continued expansion of the sex industry in Korea. Moreover, because of the media exposure of the purportedly high numbers of HIV-positive prostitutes in the Asian sex tourist industry, there has been an increased demand for young "virgin" girls. The shortage in the supply of such girls is one of the reasons for the greater use of violence during recruitment, such as luring and kidnapping. It was estimated in 1995 that approximately six thousand women and young girls were in virtual imprisonment, locked into "involuntary" prostitution.[32]

Movement women have also been involved in the resistance against the presence of the U.S. military and the foreign interference that hinders unification. Unification is based on principles of one nation, self-determination, and democracy. There is cooperation as well with foreign feminist activists and researchers who are concerned with military prostitution.[33] Korean Church Women United, a member organization of the KWAU, has been working on the issue of sex tourism and prostitution since 1970, and in 1988 organized the International Conference on Women and Tourism on Cheju Island, Korea. There, Professor Yun Chung-Ok, the pioneer researcher on military sexual slavery, presented a report on the issue, the first since the end of World War II. Some of the most important reasons behind the Asian Women in Solidarity for Military Sexual Slavery/"Comfort Women" movement were: the first public testimony made by a Korean military sex slave/"comfort woman" survivor, Kim Hak Soon in 1991; and consciousness-raising brought about by making the historical connection between the military sexual slavery/"comfort women" system and sex tourism.[34]

The 1992 sexual assault and murder of Yu Keum Hee and a series of other violent attacks perpetrated by U.S. military personnel against Koreans ignited the anti-American movement of recent years. Protesters demanded revision of the Status of Forces Agreement (SOFA) and the withdrawal of the U.S. forces.[35]

The 1995 rape of an elementary school girl by three U.S. marines on Okinawa caused an uproar in Korea over the U.S./Japanese fifty-year-long militarization of the island. Such incidents raised the consciousness of women in Korea, Okinawa, and Japan, and made them see the interconnection between militarism, commodification of female sexuality, racism, and class oppression. In consequence, violence against women in war and peace has become the focal point of the Korean women's movement in recent years. Movement workers believe that peace in Asia depends on Korean unification. They have been active in the group Peace and Unification for Human Rights of Korean Women in coalition with women in other Asian countries.

KWAU member organizations have been in the forefront of planning and participating in the annual meetings of Women and Peace in Asia held in Tokyo, Seoul, and Pyongyang, which opened a dialogue on women's responsibilities in achieving Korean unification and peace in Asia. The initial meeting , the first such to be authorized by the two Korean governments since division, was held in Pyongyang in 1992. Four South Korean and four North Korean military sexual slaves/"comfort women" survivors burst into tears there, embracing after sharing their stories.[36] In 1993, 1995, and 1996 the group's meetings were held in Seoul, Tokyo and Manila. Korean activists believed that unless Japan resolved the issue there would be no peace in Asia.[37]

In 1993 at the UN World Human Rights Conference in Vienna, and in 1995 at the UN NGO Forum on Women in Beijing, KWAU member organizations worked with the Korean Council for the Women Drafted for Sexual Slavery by Japan to present international symposia on the military sexual slave/"comfort women" issue with supporters and survivors from North Korea, the Philippines, and Japan. In Beijing they demanded that the Japanese government give up on the idea of privately funded reparation and make survivor compensation a state responsibility. They also appealed to the women in all of the victimized countries to join the Asian Women in Solidarity for military sexual slavery/"comfort women" movement. The four-year international campaign and intensive lobbying at the UN Commission on Human Rights resulted in the adoption of the Special Rapporteur on violence against women, its causes and consequences by the 52nd session of the UN Commission on Human Rights on April 19, 1996 in Geneva, Switzerland. It was the first major UN condemnation of sexual slavery since the end of World War II which called for a public apology and payment of redress by Japan to the individual survivors.[38]

The military sexual slavery/"comfort women" issue enables us to confront women's sexual oppression in its totality, that is, in all its historical, political, economic, and social contexts, by relating it to the structures of colonial, military state, race, and class oppression.[39] Indeed, in the 1990s, the Asian Women in Solidarity for Military Sexual Slavery/"Comfort Women" movement is the cutting edge of the emerging global feminist movement against violence toward women.

Conclusion

The modern Korean women's movement has been successful in raising the issue of women's rights in the context of the struggle for democracy and national unification and in bringing about changes in women's condition and position in the family workplace and in the larger society. It has changed the definitions and agendas of human rights and "politics" in the context of women's everyday lives by making connections between the repressive state and women's economic and sexual inequalities. Direct political actions against the state, capitalist interests, and male-dominant union management gradually resulted in the emergence of a broad-based grassroots women's movement.

The KWAU developed female solidarity among different groups of women, both nationally and internationally, such as between Christian and non-Christian women, between the poor working-class women, rural women and middle-class women. This was possible because college-educated, middle-class women organizers who worked as clandestine union factory workers in an earlier period were able to see the connections between their own lives and those of factory women.

By developing assertive strategies and carrying out direct feminist actions as integral parts of the larger democratization movement, the KWAU has made linkages with members of other social movement groups. The realization that dictatorial military governments were mainly responsible for the social, economic, and sexual oppression of the masses, including women, gave all social movements a strong impetus to engage in a common struggle for justice and peace. Therefore, the efforts of the KWAU to liberate working-class women and to bring about larger societal change set in motion a new era for the women's movement by making women visible in the process of the national democratization movement, and the struggle against the economic and sexual exploitation of women.

Because feminism is a transformational politics and worldview, and women's economic and sexual freedom cannot be achieved in a society such as Korea without simultaneously achieving political democracy and national unification, Korean feminists have been concerned with the removal of all forms of inequalities and oppressions in the society that they believe to be interrelated and globally linked. From the outset, globally conscious feminists in Korea analyzed their political actions in a worldwide context to bring about more profound change. They adopted multiple goals and integrative strategies by building coalitions among women's groups. The women's labor movement and the political democratization and national unification movement groups have worked to eliminate militarism, economic exploitation, and sexual oppression. Thus, Korean feminists have developed a global feminism while engaged in their political struggles. They make connections between the macro- and microlevel political, economic, and sexual inequalities in their society and in the world.

Notes

This chapter is a revised and updated version of a paper coauthored with Sung Sook Cho and Sook Ja Kang of Seoul, Korea, that was presented at the National Women's Studies Association annual conference, June 1987.

Korean personal names appear unpunctuated in order of one word last name followed by given names, generally two words with or without hyphenation, as customary among Koreans. Or a name may appear in the order chosen by the person.

Since it is more accurate to use the term "slavery," the combined term "military sexual slavery/'comfort women' " will be used instead of the single term "comfort women," a euphemism used by Japan during World War II.

1. Joanna K. Gajardo, *Has the UN Decade for Women Done Anything for Latin American Women* (New York: Women's International Resource Exchange, 1986).

2. Charlotte Bunch, *Passionate Politics: Feminist Theory in Action* (New York: St. Martin's Press, 1987), p. 302; Sun Ai Park, "Behold I Make All Things New," *Asian Women Doing Theology, A Report from Singapore Conference, November 20–27, 1987* (Kowloon, Hong Kong: Asian Women's Resource Centre for Culture and Theology, 1989), pp. 11–14; bell hooks, *Talking Back: Thinking Feminist, Thinking Black* (Boston: South End Press, 1989), pp. 19, 25.

3. Saskia Wierinega, ed., *Women's Struggles and Strategies* (Brookfield, VT: Gower, 1988), p. 1.

4. Jane S. Jaquette, ed., *The Women's Movement in Latin America: Feminism and the Transition to Democracy* (Boston: Unwin Hyman, 1989), pp. 1–15.

5. "A Glimpse at Asian Women's Movements from the Group of Desary Meeting," *In God's Image*, (September 1987), pp. 39–44; Yayori Matsui, *Women's Asia* (London: Zed Book, 1989), p. 143.

6. Kamla Bhasi and Mighat Said Khan, *Some Questions on Feminism and Its Relevance in South Asia* (New Delhi: Kali for Women, 1986), pp. 2–6, 19–21.

7. John C. B. Webster and Ellen Low Webster, eds., *The Church and Women in the Third World* (Philadelphia: Westminster Press, 1985), pp. 11–12.

8. Myeong Sook Han, "Himchan chunjin-uiro yosong undong-ui saejipyong yolja" (Let's powerfully march on to open a new horizon for women's movement), *Minju Yosong* (Democratic Women; newsletter, Korea Women's Associations United) 14 (March 29, 1993): 2–3; Na Young Hee, "1993 nyondo saop banghyang-kwa kwaje" (The direction and task of 1993 activities), *Minju Yosong* (Democratic Women; newsletter, Korea Women's Association United) 14 (March 29, 1993): 4–9.

9. *Yonhap Yongap* (Yonhap annals) (Seoul: Yonhap Tongshin, 1995).

10. George E. Ogle, *South Korea: Dissent Within the Economic Miracle* (London: Zed Books Ltd., 1990), p. 32.

11. North American Coalition for Human Rights in Korea (Washington, D.C.), "Reports from Kwangju," September 1980, p. 21.

12. Jeong-Lim Nam, "Women's Role in Export Dependence and State Control of Labor Unions in South Korea," *Women's Studies International Forum* 17, no. 1 (1994): 57–67.

13. "Declaration of Korean Women Theologians on the Peace and Reunification of the Korean People," *Women's Forum Report* (International Christian

Consultation on Justice and Peace Conference, sponsored by Korean National Council of Churches, Inchon, April 24–25, 1988), p. 160.

14. Hye Kyung Lee, "Gender Division of Labor and the Authoritarian Developmental State: Korean Experience," in *Gender Division of Labor (In) Korea*, ed. Cho Hyoung andChang Pil-wha (Seoul: Korean Women's Institute Series, Ewha Women's University Press, 1994), pp. 292–323.

15. Korean Women's Development Institute, brochure (1995).

16. Mikyung Lee, "Korean Women's Movement and Its Tasks in the 1990s," *Proceedings of the International Workshop on Evaluation and Future Direction of Korea Women's Association United, November 9–11, 1995, Seoul, Korea*, pp. 3–15, at p. 11.

17. Republic of Korea, *Korean Women Now* (Seoul: KWDI, 1994), p. 41.

18. *Center for Korean Women and Politics Newsletter*, summer 1995, pp. 12–13.

19. Republic of Korea, *Korean Women Now*, pp. 32–33; Sei-wha Chung, "Women's Movement and Girl Scouts: Yesterday, Present, and Tomorrow," *Women's Studies Review* (Korean Women's Research Institute, Ewha Woman's University) 5 (December 1988): 281–331; Lee, "Gender Division of Labor and the Authoritarian Developmental State," pp. 292–323.

20. *Far Eastern Economic Review*, September 1988, pp. 97–98; Pong-yul Kim, "Hankuk nodongyosong-ui shinsang bunsok," (Analysis of actual condition of Korean working women), in *Ilto-ui moksori* (Voice of Workplace) (Seoul: Chiyang-sa, 1984), pp. 268–323.

21. *Yosong Kaebal Soshik* (KWDI newsletter), November 1995, pp. 2, 12.

22. Hei-soo Shin, "Highlights from the Women's Movement: Overview of 1993 and Prospects for 1994," *Korean Women's Hot Line Newsletter* 3 (June 1994): 2–4.

23. Republic of Korea, *Korean Women Now* (Seoul: KWDI, 1994), pp. 37–38.

24. Committee for the Compilation of the History of Korean Women, *Women of Korea: A History from Ancient Times to 1945*, ed. and trans. Yung-Chung Kim (Seoul: Ewha Women's University Press, 1976), pp. 210–212, 217–266.

25. Hyo-Jae Lee, *Hankuk-ui Yosong Undong* (Women's movement in Korea) (Seoul: Chongusa, 1975); "A Glimpse of Asian Women's Movements from the Group of Desaru Meeting," *In God's Image*, (September 1987), pp. 39–40.

26. Kenneth M. Wells, ed., *South Korea's Minjung Movement: The Culture and Politics of Dissidence* (Honolulu: University of Hawaii Press, 1995), p. 2; Byung Moo Ahn, *Minjung Shinhak Iyaki* (A story of Minjung theology) (Seoul: Research Center for Korean Theology, 1987), pp. 27, 33.

27. Hae-joang, Cho, "The 'Woman Question' in the *Minjok-Minju* Movement: A Discourse Analysis of a New Women's Movement in 1980's Korea," in *Gender Division of Labor (In) Korea*, ed., Cho Hy-oung and Chang Pil-wha, pp. 324–358; Miriam Ching Yoon Louie, "*Minjung* Feminism: Korean Women's Movement for Gender and Class Liberation," *Women's Studies International Forum* 18, no. 4 (1995): 417–430.

28. Hyo-Jae Lee, "Yosong undong-ui seroun jipyong eul yolja!" (Let's open

the new horizon of the women's movement!), *Minju Yosong* (Democratic women; newsletter, Korea Women's Associations United) 1 (July 10, 1987), p. 3.

29. *Yosong-ui nuneuro* (Through women's eyes; newsletter, Korea Women's Hot Line), nos. 10–11, 1995, p. 54.

30. *Minju Yosong* (Democratic women; newsletter, Korea Women's Associations United) 18 (April 1995): 124.

31. Hei-soo Shin, "Legislation on Sexual Violence," in *Proceedings of the International Workshop on Evaluation and Future Direction of Korea Women's Association United, November 9–11, 1995 in Seoul, Korea*, pp. 41–45.

32. Hei-soo Shin, "South Korea" (paper presented at the International Movement Against All Forms of Discrimination and Racism (IMADR) workshop Against Trafficking in Women in Asia, UN NGO Forum, Beijing, August 31, 1995.

33. Saundra Pollock Sturdevant and Brenda Stoltzfus, "Tong Du Chun: The Bar System," in *Let the Good Times Roll*, ed., Sturdevant and Stoltzfus (New York: New Press, 1992), pp. 176–179.

34. Alice Yun Chai "Asian-Pacific Feminist Coalition Politics: The *Chongshindae/Jugunianfu* ("Comfort Women") Movement," *Korean Studies* (annual publication, Center for Korean Studies, University of Hawaii) 17 (1993): 67–91, at p. 79.

35. Woo Sop Chun, "Doisang uri-reul seulpuge haji-malra! (Do not let us be sorrowful again!), *Betheul* (newsletter, *Korea Women's Hot Line*), 68 (January 10, 1993): 6–7.

36. Mikyung Lee, "Asea-ui pyonghwa-wa yosong-ui yokhwal: Pyongyang toronhwe-ui songka-wa jonmang" (The achievement and future direction of the Pyongyang forum Women and Peace in Asia, September 1–6, 1992), *Minju Yosong* (Democratic women; newsletter, Korea Women's Associations United) 13 (October 1992): 32–37; Yun Chai, "Asian-Pacific Feminist Coalition Politics," pp. 67–91, at p. 83.

37. Hee-Soon Kwon, "International Solidarity Activities of KWAU," in *Proceedings of the International Workshop on Evaluation and Future Direction of Korea Women's Associations United, November 9–11, 1995 Seoul, Korea,* pp. 67–74, at pp. 69–70.

38. UN Economic and Social Council Commission on Human Rights Fifty-second session, Item 9 (a) of the provisional agenda, *Report of the Special Rapporteur on Violence Against Women, Its Causes and Consequences*, Ms. Radhika Coomaraswany in accordance with Commission on Human Rights resolution 1994/45: Report on the Mission to the Democratic People's Republic of Korea, the Republic of Korea and Japan on the issue of military sexual slavery in wartime, (E/CN. 4/1996/53/Addol, January 4, 1996, 37 pp; Associated Press, Geneva, "U.N.: Japan Must Pay, Apologize to Sex Slaves," *Honolulu Star Bulletin*, February 6, 1996, p. A-6.

39. Alice Yun Chai, "The Struggle of Asian and Asian American Women Toward a Total Liberation," in *Spirituality and Social Responsibility*, ed., Rosemary Skinner Keller (Nashville: Abingdon Press, 1993), pp. 249–263, p. 255.

Feminism and Indigenous Hawaiian Nationalism

Haunani-Kay Trask

Ahoa Mai, Aloha kakou.

In Pacific Island cultures, genealogy is paramount. Therefore, I greet you with my family origins. I am descended of the Pi'ilani line of Maui and the Kahakumakaliua line of Kaua'i. I am Native Hawaiian, indigenous to Hawai'i.[1]

My people were born of Papahanaumoku—Earth Mother—and Wakea—Sky Father—who created our bountiful Hawaiian islands. From these islands came the taro, and from the taro, our chiefs and common people.

The lesson of our origins is simple. The land is our mother, and we are her children. If we care for our mother, she will care for us in return. The relationships is more than reciprocal; it is familial.

Like most Native peoples, Hawaiians lived in our mother's keeping for millennia until the fateful coming of the haole—Western foreigners—in 1778. Then our world collapsed from the violence of contact: disease, mass death, and land dispossession; evangelical Christianity; plantation capitalism; cultural destruction including language banning; and, finally, American military invasion in 1893 and forced annexation in 1898. During the course of little more than a century, the haole onslaught had taken from us 95 percent of our Hawaiian people, 99 percent of our lands and waters, and the entirety of our political sovereignty. As the twentieth century dawned, we were but a remnant of the great and ancient people we had once been.[2]

During the long suppression of the territorial period (1900–1959), Hawaiians lived under martial law for seven years during the Second World War, suffered increased land confiscations for military bases, and fearfully watched as the vicious process of Americanization created racist political, educational, and economic institutions. By the time of my birth in 1949, being Hawaiian was a racial and cultural disadvantage rather than a national definition. The U.S. federal government had officially classified our people by blood quantum in 1921: those of us with 50 percent Hawaiian blood quantum were Native, and those of us with less than 50 percent were not Native. "Fifty-percenters," as they are known today, have claims to land; "less-than-fifties" do not have such rights. In this way, our nation was divided by race, a concept and reality foreign to our way of thinking. Thus was I born into captivity, a Native child in a racist, non-Native world.

Under the power of colonialism, I was sent to missionary schools, both Catholic and Protestant, when I was young. Then I went on to "higher education" on the North American continent in 1967. As I journeyed across the huge land masses of the western states to take up residence in the frigid Midwest, my little island home in the Pacific seemed small indeed. The size of the United States was reflected in its dominance in world affairs; our fragile archipelago was matched by our own powerless conditions. Everywhere, I saw and felt inequality. People of different colors and economic status were partitioned off from one another into better or worse urban areas. African Americans, in particular, were treated with a nonchalant violence that personally frightened me. For a while, I attended the University of Chicago and witnessed the rioting and shooting and casual cruelty that has since become a hallmark of American culture. I learned about and supported the Black Panthers because they seemed so rational in a time of purposeful, institutional cruelty against their people.

But Chicago was too harsh for me. Exhausted by the fear and violence there, I transferred to the University of Wisconsin. As my years in Madison lengthened into graduate education through the mid-1970s, I began to understand how capitalism and racism sustained each other, how the world of hatred the haole had made in the United States originated in the colonial period when the Native American tribes suffered an onslaught of genocide under the "freedom-loving" presidents Washington, Jefferson, and the rest. An adoration of violence had driven the United States into war after war. After the Native Americans were exterminated or confined, then island nations in both the Atlantic and the Pacific were occupied and annexed. By the time of my sojourn on the continent, Americans were engaged in another war, this time in the Far East. Because the University of Wisconsin was a bellwether campus for the antiwar front, I was able to participate in huge student protests against what the "greatest democracy" was doing to the Vietnamese people.

In class, I added to my formal studies of Third World politics the new field of feminist theory. While the antiwar and African-American resistance efforts were enlarging the arena of contested issues, women were loudly asserting an alternative vision of life through the power of creative imagination. Inspired by this ferment, I identified myself with the rising tide of feminism. My intellectual interest expanded outward from Third World, anticolonial politics to encompass feminist theory. I saw then, as I do now, that the oppression of women is connected to larger cultural postures regarding the value of life, of the living earth, and her bounty. Determined to link this life force, this Eros, to the power of political liberation, I focused on the growing field of feminist women's poetry—from writers like Adrienne Rich, Robin Morgan, and others—as the best expression of an alternative vision of society. In the feminist imagination, life was honored and power reshaped into an enabling force for the protection of both the human and the natural world. I named this creativity the "feminist Eros."

Enlivened by revolutionary ideas, and chafing under the long apprenticeship of graduate school, I decided to return home to Hawai'i in 1977. I had been gone from my family, my people, and my islands for a decade. My reentry was long overdue.

The great ferment on the continent had barely touched my homeland, but another resistance front was brewing in our islands, one that would take center stage all over the world in the last quarter of the twentieth century: indigenous sovereignty.

Without a moment's hesitation, I committed myself to a Hawaiian movement focused on land rights, language assertions, and finally, self-determination in the form of Native sovereignty. Two of my sisters, also educated on the continent, had preceded me in their return home. They were both active, both nationalist, and both feminist.

My vision of political power imbued with a feminism Eros was seemingly fulfilled by the struggle for my people's sovereignty. Out of the university, in opposition to the dominant world of Americanism I imagined a linking of feminism with indigenous nationalism.

But as I decolonized my mind and my commitments, the political and cultural environment at home splintered my acquired feminism from my Hawaiian existence. I recognized that a practicing feminism hampered organizing among my people in rural communities. Given our national-ist context, feminism appeared as just another haole intrusion into a be-sieged Hawaiian world. Any exclusive focus on women neglected the historical oppression of all Hawaiians and the large force field of imperi-alism. Now that I was working among my people, I saw there were sim-ply too many limitations in the scope of feminist theory and praxis. The feminism I had studied was just too white, too American. Only issues de-fined by white women as "feminist" had structured discussions. Their lan-guage revolved around First World "rights" talk, that Enlightenment individualism that takes for granted individual primacy. Last, but in many ways most troubling, feminist style was aggressively American.

But I was no longer in America; I was in my Native country. And there, in Hawai'i, we were asserting our cultural posture, including our own style and language of argument, as defining of the political arena.

American feminism, in contrast, had evolved in the First World and was informed by the long genocidal heritage that created the United States and made it the preeminent cultural and military force around the globe. Worse, American feminist ideology assumed the essential value of individual accomplishment and ambition. It viewed the liberal state as the proper arbiter of rights and privileges. It accepted capitalism as the de-spised but inevitable economic force. And finally, it insisted on the pre-dictable racist assertion that all peoples are alike in their common "humanity"—a humanity imbued with Enlightenment values and best found in Euro-American states. Indeed, even socialist feminism was of Western origin, with white women as the agents of action.

As our Native movement gained ground, and as I took my stand alongside other Hawaiian leaders, I realized that all American ideolo-gies—feminist or otherwise—are foreign to us. Feminism and white fem-inists are out of place here, that is, out of geographic and cultural and historical place. Clinging to their accustomed cultural ways, white femi-nists in Hawai'i have retreated to the defensive position that Hawaiian sovereignty is anti-haole, meaning racist, not merely anti-American. Worse, they often contend, we Hawaiians are actually oppressing feminist haole by asserting our claim to indigenous political and economic power.

Thus, justice for our Native people in the form of our own land base, cultural integrity, and government is generally perceived as an injustice to non-Natives, particularly white people who keep publicly asserting, in their own words, that "Hawai'i is, after all, part of the United States."

Of course, who better knows this than my own people! Our entire movement is based on ameliorating our historical subjugation. But here is precisely the deep-rooted problem. White American women are *American*, not Hawaiian. White American feminist women are still *American*. Their loyalties are to the *United States of America*.

In the First World view of such women, we Hawaiians seem particularly ungrateful for the gifts of Americanism. That the United States invaded our country, overthrew our government, occupied our lands, and remains here to this day is, to these women, a wholly peripheral issue. What frightens these affronted Americans is our assertion of Hawaiian cultural primacy through the process of peeling off the mask of American colonialism. Put bluntly, we are rejecting the United States and its dominance. For most Americans, especially white folks, an attack on the United States is a personal attack.

Now, while I am, as always, an advocate of women's power and claims, my context is Hawaiian and not American culture, and my political work is based on Hawaiian self-determination. This focus includes all our people, not only our women. Traditional women's issues—reproductive rights, equal employment, domestic violence—are obviously part of the struggle for our homeland and our integrity as an indigenous nation. Nothing has escaped the ravages of colonization, including the lives of our women. But the answers to the specifics of our women's oppression reside in our people's collective achievement of the larger goal of Hawaiian self-government, not in an exclusive feminist agenda.

As my scope has enlarged over the years to encompass international linkages with indigenous women in the Americas, in the Pacific Basin, in the Arctic, and elsewhere, feminism seems more and more removed from the all-consuming struggle against our physical and cultural extinction as indigenous peoples. Issues specific to women still inform our identity as Native women leaders, but our language and our organizing are framed within our own cultural terms, not within feminist American terms.

The problem of culture, of course, is where the greatest disjunction occurs. First World feminist theory is incapable of addressing indigenous women's cultural worlds. How could it be otherwise? This is just another way of arguing that theories hatched in universities two thousand or more miles away on the continent have only theory-making as their praxis. First World universities give rise to First World theories. First World feminists create First World feminism.

But our indigenous women struggle to create our own history in our own country. Our collective lives lead to a different order of understanding than the praxis of First World individual feminists in the university and elsewhere. For us, it is not theory that gives rise to praxis but the reverse. Indigenous women in struggle fashion indigenous-based views of what constitutes women's issues, about how women should lead our indigenous nations, and about the role, if any, of feminism.

An example, Hawaiian women suffer one of the highest breast cancer rates in the United States. Like our Maori sisters to the south of us, we have been forced into a system of food distribution that is supermarket-oriented. Our land has been taken from us, our people proletarianized, our fertile valleys and bays polluted by development. Because our disastrous health profile resulted from colonialism, our condition is not simply a "women's issue." Poor Hawaiian health for both our men and women is directly traceable to Americanization of our country, including theft of lands where we once grew healthful Native foods. Like our other health problems—for example, high infant mortality, low life expectancy, high adolescent suicide rates—Hawaiian women's health profile is a result of colonialism and the subsequent loss of control over our islands and our lives. Thus does a "women's issue" become a sovereignty, not a feminist, problem for us. Our experience as indigenous people determines the way we view our lives. This is also true for the way we view feminism.[3]

The conflict between haole and Hawaiian is illustrated in the conflict between haole feminists and Hawaiian women. Generally, haole feminists in Hawai'i are ignorant of, or indifferent to, the causal connection between our oppressed life conditions—poverty, poor housing, high levels of imprisonment, low educational attainment, an enlarging diaspora— and our status as colonized people. The feminist failure of vision here is a result of privilege—an outright insensibility to the vastness of the human world—because they are white Americans. White people's survival does not depend on knowing daily life with a decolonizing mind or sensing reality as a menacing place that must be negotiated with great skill and a discriminating step. We indigenous people occupy two cultural worlds; white people occupy only one. We are the colonized; they are the beneficiaries of colonialism. That some feminists are oblivious to this historical reality does not lessen their power in the colonial equation.

While few haole, male or female, comprehend their ruling-class status in Hawai'i, we subjugated Hawaiians have a very clear understanding of white people's dominant cultural and physical place in our country. Our survival depends on a kind of second-nature knowledge of everything haole.

Unlike most Americans, we know the only reason haole are physically present here is because Hawai'i was missionized, colonized, and eventually annexed by the United States in 1898. In other words, imperialist privilege has allowed haole to take up residence anywhere in Hawai'i without one moment's consideration about how the United States came to rule our exquisite islands. Moreover, this characteristic American ignorance does not vary by class. Even poor haole take for granted their freedom of travel, power of purchase, and the familiar intercourse of their own language and institutions and customs in my homeland. American citizenship is the passport of our country; the American dollar is the economic and political currency; English is the official as well as everyday language. Indeed, Hawai'i is the fiftieth state of the United States of America. What better indication of American superiority!

Thus does imperialism benefit the people of imperialism, including haole women. That most haole fail to comprehend (or refuse to address) this large imperialist reality is irrelevant to the continued dominance of their culture and the exploitative effects of their freely exercised power over our people, our lands, and our place in our own country. All haole in Hawai'i benefit from American control of our islands. Period.

If the very presence of colonials in the colonies indicates their status, then their relationships with the colonized are reiterations of that status. An obvious illustration is the insistence by haole feminists about what constitutes the feminist agenda: so-called women's issues. In this view, our own indigenous concerns—for example, land and sovereignty—are clearly secondary.

But why is land, our mother, not a women's issue? The answer, almost too obviously, is that Hawaiian land—this land that all of us in Hawai'i enjoy—is not the mother of haole feminists because haole are not born of this land. Culturally, Papahanaumoku is not the mother of Americans. So, haole may see Hawai'i as beautiful, or exploited, or crowded, or expensive, or hostile, or even a haven for racism, but they cannot ever see our land as familial. This is to say, haole can never know what we know, or feel what we feel, about our mother, the land. Thus does history—and genealogy—separate our politics, and our analysis.

Predictably, then, what concerns white women of the ruling culture is rarely what concerns Native women in colonized cultures. When Hawaiian land is destroyed by development, by resort complexes, by military installations, it is our family, our history, our past, and our future that are destroyed. No non-Hawaiian can understand this. Nor do most non-Hawaiians acknowledge that we suffer a horrific grief and anger, because they do not feel these emotions themselves. To our colonizers, this familial sense is nothing but mixed-up romanticism, a yearning for the past that is a kind of convoluted nostalgia. Even to sympathetic haole, our people seem strangely focused on that which is lost.

But in our language, the past is our future. We face our past: *ka wa mamua* —the time before. The past holds our wisdom and our *kupuna* (elders') knowledge. As our culture tells us, we are guided in the present on the path so well followed by our ancestors in the past.

Here, the cultural perspective on the "past" is stunningly different for Hawaiians and for haole. Because haole misunderstand this, they believe we are strangely inferior, in the sense of "undeveloped."

It is a short step from being viewed as inferior to being treated as inferior. Haole in Hawai'i—whether feminist or not—display an appalling, aggressive disregard grounded in a fundamental racism that views Native history, culture, and ways of life as simpleminded and, in the case of the Hawaiian people, particularly infantile and ornamental. As I say, everything Western is hegemonic in Hawai'i: styles of speech, television, radio and film, clothing, dance, food, habits of daily life, and more. So, too, the monsters of concrete, high-rise urbanization, land development, mass-based tourism, naval and air force bases, and so on. Such is the Gargantua of capitalism and its safeguard, militarism.

Given tremendous Americanization, why should non-Natives try to understand our culture when theirs has been so superbly "successful" in Hawai'i? To meet us as fully endowed peoples with histories, and genealogies, and cultures presumes some form of equality as human beings. It also requires acknowledging the oppression of our world because of the dominance of the American world. But how does the ruling class actually see beyond its luxury? What ruling class ever has?

No, the posture of most Americans in Hawai'i, in the Pacific, and in the world, is one of assumed superiority, an envelope of security and distance that is crucial to daily power. Racism is just one aspect of this; cultural hierarchy is another. White feminism has escaped neither.

Donna Awatere, Maori nationalist and author of the pathbreaking work *Maori Sovereignty*, has written of Maori women's experience with white feminists in much the same way I have here. She argues:

> The first loyalty of white women is to the White Culture and the White Way. This is true as much for those who define themselves as feminists as for any other white woman. This loyalty is seen in their rejection of the sovereignty of Maori people and in their acceptance of the imposition of the British culture on the Maori. This is to be expected as the oppressor avoids confronting the role they play in oppressing others. . . . White feminists do this by defining their "feminism" for this country [New Zealand] and by using their white power, status and privilege to ensure that their definition of "feminism" supersedes that of Maori women.[4]

What is true in New Zealand is true in Hawai'i. The divergent path of Native movements in the Pacific Basin from haole-defined issues and movements (for example, feminism, environmentalism, socialism) confirms Awatere's analysis. In our political experience, self-determination for Hawaiians, or other indigenous people, has never been a goal for haole, whether they identify with feminism or Marxism, or some other First World ideology.

This does not mean haole, including feminists, have no role to play in our movement. They have the role we assign to them, and no more: to support our efforts publicly, to form antiracist groups that address our people's oppression through institutional channels, and to speak out in our defense when we are attacked by white people. These are the roles white people can and should play. And they should do so under our direction.

In Hawai'i, there are haole women and men who have supported our struggles in just this capacity. They do not harbor the kinds of individualistic and racial resentments that so plague Americans in general. And they willingly follow our lead because they live as uninvited guests in our country. To put it simply, they have learned their place.

At this stage in our collective lives, Hawaiians are determined to make our own history, with or without white feminist support. We will do so as Hawaiian people, not only as Hawaiian women. Feminists, as other white people, must understand that our sovereignty struggle requires working with our own people, including our own men. This is preferable to working with white people, including feminists. Struggle with our men occurs laterally, across and within our movement. It does not occur vertically between white women and indigenous women on one side and white men and Hawaiian men on the opposing side.

The reasons for this are many. Sovereignty for our people is a larger goal than legal or educational or political equality with our men. As we struggle for sovereignty, our women come to the fore anyway. We Hawaiian women are made of strong stock; our presence on the front line of resistance proves this. But we also share many more similarities, both in struggle and in controversy, with our men and with one another as indigenous women than we do with white people. The familiar point, here, is that culture is a larger reality than women's "rights."

Beyond strategic questions are the familiar feelings and realities of struggle. Vast differences in heritage, in genealogies, and in collective and familial suffering exist between haole and Hawaiian. The cultural lines are drawn deep and fast across two hundred years of history. Therefore, we make common cause with our own people and other Native peoples before we join with non-Natives, especially those living in and profiting from our country.

For most haole, feminist or otherwise, my stance appears to end any potential coalition work or even a meager understanding across our barriers of culture and history. In reality, however, the opposite is true. We confront each other, warily, carefully, every day. Occasionally, we work together. But struggle is what we do, not what we meditate on in some quiet remove from the heat of political and cultural battle. In a life of indigenous struggle, questions regarding relationships between theory and praxis recede into the clouds. I work with haole, and fight with them, all the time. How can I not since haole *and* haole institutions determine so much of Hawaiian life?

But I do not engage feminist theory every day, or even once a month. Nor do I want to. Like most peoples in struggle, I take my support where I find it. I know full well, as do my compatriots, that struggle creates strange bedfellows. When disagreements arise, we try to work through them. Or, we part company and change strategies. But I do not doubt my leadership, nor that of our other women.

As for feminist theory, I rarely think about it. I have lost the patience, and the time, to do so. But I am also not particularly interested in the subject. The request for this article occasioned the first moment in many years that I have seriously considered the relationship between feminist theory and feminist praxis. More than a feminist, I am a nationalist, trained by my family and destined by my genealogy to speak and work on my people's behalf, including our women. I am a leader, and my obligation is to lead, both our women and our men. This is my duty to our people—all of them: the ancestors, the living, the yet to be born. I am comfortable with that.

Notes

1. I capitalize the word *Native* for complex reasons. The word is colonial in origin, like *Black* as a description of Africans transplanted to the United States. But just as *Black* was politicized, used for self-identification, and capitalized, so *Native* has undergone similar transformations. Therefore, I capitalize the word to emphasize the political distance between that which is Western and that which is Native. I also capitalize *Native* to highlight the word and therefore its referent. In Hawai'i, we generally call ourselves Hawaiians. But since the sovereignty movement, the consciousness that we are Natives and not immigrants to Hawai'i has meant a greater identification than the term *Native*, especially because immigrant history here has been glorified and falsified at the expense of Natives. It is characteristic of American ideology to reiterate that "we are all immigrants. "Capitalizing the word *Native* reminds the reader that some of us are not immigrants. Thus, my usage is political on a geographic level: we are Native to Hawai'i and not the United States. It is political on an ideological level: we are neither Western nor Eastern but Native to the Pacific Islands. And it is political on a cultural level: we are not transplants from somewhere else but indigenous to our archipelago, Hawai'i.

2. For a discussion of the large Hawaiian population's contact with the West, and the subsequent catastrophic decline due to introduced diseases, see David Stannard, *Before the Horror: The Population of Hawai'i on the Eve of Western Contact.* (Honolulu: Social Science Research Institute, 1989.) For an account of the land dispossession suffered by Hawaiians in the nineteenth century, and the resulting taking of lands by American Calvinist missionaries, see Lilikala Kame'eleihiwa, *Native Land and Foreign Desires* (Honolulu: Bishop Museum Press, 1992). Regarding the conditions of reservation lands in the twentieth century, see U.S. Department of the Interior, 1983, *Federal State Task Force on the Hawaiian Homes Commission Act* (Washington, DC: Department of the Interior, 1983). Also see U.S. Civil Rights Commission, *A Broken Trust: The Hawaiian Homelands Program, Seventy Years of Failure of the State and Federal Governments to Protect the Civil Rights of Native Hawaiians* (Washington, DC: U.S. Civil Rights Commission, 1991). For a lengthy analysis of the overthrow of the Hawaiian government by U.S. marines and missionary-descended sugar barons, see *Report of the Commissioner to the Hawaiian Islands* 53d Cong., 2d sess. (Washington, DC: Government Printing Office, 1893). Called the Blount Report, after the commissioner sent by Presi-

dent Grover Cleveland to investigate the overthrow, the report runs to 1,400 pages in two volumes. In its conclusion, the report indicts the United States for the invasion of Hawai'i, for the support given the all-white group of businessmen who took the throne, and for the undisguised effort to annex Hawai'i against the overwhelming opposition of the Native people. For a discussion of the banning of the Hawaiian language, see Larry Kimura, "Native Hawaiian Culture," in *Native Hawaiians Studies Commission Report*.(Washington, DC: U.S. Department of the Interior, 1983), 1:173–97.

3. For statistics on Hawaiian health, see *Native Hawaiian Health Data Book* (Honolulu: Papa Ola Lokahi, 1991).

4. Donna Awatere, *Maori Sovereignty* (Auckland: Broadsheet, 1984).

The Americas

Nationalism, Feminism, and Revolution in Central America

Norma Stoltz Chinchilla

During the 1960s the first wave of armed guerilla movements based on the "foco" theory, popularized by Regis Debray's account of the Cuban Revolution, emerged in Latin America. Small bands of full-time "professional" guerilla fighters ("focos" or "ignitors") attempted to overthrow what were assumed to be relatively weak, externally dependent dictatorships or oligarchic governments, relegating presumably sympathetic beneficiaries of the revolution—workers and peasants—to a relatively passive role of support.

The number of women who participated in the armed revolutionary movements of the 1960s in countries like Nicaragua and Guatemala was relatively small. Among these, few, if any, transcended the gender division of labor reproduced within the movement (that is, men as combatants; women as couriers, spies, or consorts). And rarely were the women viewed as independent members of the guerilla forces (rather than as the "partner of" or "sister of" a male member). To the extent that the participation of women in revolutionary groups was known outside their organizations, they were viewed as "highly unusual" or "exceptional" women, at best, or as women of questionable judgment (that is, communists and prostitutes), at worst.[1]

Few accounts of women's participation in these early movements exist. Those available are heroic and highly idealized, even when based on interviews or letters left by the women themselves. The emphasis on the exceptionalism of women revolutionaries in firsthand accounts yields little insight into how daily life in the movement differed for men and women or the reasons that so few women were involved compared to subsequent movements.

Ernesto "Che" Guevara, the Argentinean who died fighting in Bolivia after participating with Fidel Castro in the Cuban Revolution, is one of the few who discuss the role of women in these early guerilla movements, based on his experience in the Cuban Revolution which came to power in 1969. Che supported women's involvement but justified it with the relatively traditional, uncritical, and ultimately essentialist arguments common among male leftists at the time. This master theorist and practitioner, revered by subsequent revolutionary movements for his ideas about the non-materialistically motivated "New Man" as the ultimate goal of the revolution and his personal example of hemispheric solidarity, wrote in *Guerilla Warfare*, his classic treatise, that

> the part that the woman can play in the development of a revolutionary process is of extraordinary importance. It is well to emphasize this, since in all our countries, with their colonial mentality, there is a certain underestimation of women which becomes real discrimination against them . . . Women are capable of performing the most difficult tasks, of fighting beside the men.[2]

"Tania," the German-origin woman who joined Che in his ill-fated attempt to liberate Bolivian peasants in the late 1960s, was one of those women "capable of performing the most difficult tasks." Tania had to march in men's oversized military boots, and sources close to Che said he believed that her "presence in the group served to show that a woman could endure what those miserable guys who had given up couldn't. She never lost her spirit."[3] The Bolivian government, responsible for annihilating her guerilla column, insisted on giving her (and only her) a Christian burial after her death on August 31, 1967. Castro enshrined her memory with the nickname "*la Guerilla Inolvidable*" (the unforgettable guerilla).

Despite the potential of Tania and others for transgressing traditional gender roles, Che believed that women's "indispensable characteristics" meant that women combatants would "naturally" be a minority. A woman in the guerilla forces might occasionally "perform a relief role" for the male fighter but her principal tasks ordinarily would be in communications (because women inspire less fear of danger in the enemy), transportation of arms, and teaching literacy and revolutionary theory, and as nurses or doctors (because women have "a gentleness infinitely superior to that of her rude companion in arms").[4] Woman revolutionaries could also

> perform [their] habitual tasks of peacetime; it is very pleasing to a soldier subjected to the extremely hard conditions of this life to be able to look forward to a seasoned meal which tastes like something. One of the great tortures of the [Cuban] war was eating a cold, sticky, tasteless mess. Furthermore, it is easier to keep her in these domestic tasks; one of the problems in guerilla bands is that the men are constantly trying to get out of these tasks.[5]

Thus, in the powerful legacy left by Che Guevara, the ultimate Latin American revolutionary hero, armed struggle became the highest form of political struggle and the military activities that were at the core of armed struggle were "naturally" masculine activities. Women could complement or even share in guerilla warfare but not lose their "inherently feminine" qualities. The prototypical guerilla soldier remained a courageous, daring, virile, self-sacrificing man, unconcerned with the details of daily life.

The only modification of this image, prior to the revolutionary movements of the 1970s, occurred within late-1960s urban guerilla movements in Brazil, Uruguay, and Argentina. There, mostly young women students of middle-class origin functioned as "soldiers" in the execution of bank robberies and kidnappings with their equally young and mostly middle-class-origin male comrades. Unlike the rural guerilla movements, however, the urban fighters were not full-time revolutionaries. Rather, they used the urban setting, social networks, and daily routines to blend into the population and thus escape detection by the police, at least in the early stages of their movement. Miller observes that

> although the urban guerilla movement employed military languages ("soldiers," "operations," etc.) it did not involve uniforms or barracks-style living or other military activities so strongly identified with masculinity; women could belong as women, not as women who were like men.[6]

Despite their direct participation in military activities and seemingly more egalitarian relationships with male comrades, women in the urban guerilla movements of the late 1960s, like women in left political parties, did not achieve positions of leadership and were excluded, by and large, from policy and decision making.

The reluctance of revolutionary organizations and political parties of the Left to investigate critically the reasons for unintentional reproduction of gender ideologies and hierarchies, especially in the access to power and decision making, was an important concern of the generation of relatively well educated women activists who split off from Left parties and movements in the late 1970s to create the second wave of feminism in a number of Latin American countries (particularly Mexico, Peru, Colombia, Brazil, Argentina, Uruguay, and Chile).[7] But leftist movements in those countries at the time, like most of their predecessors since the Stalinist period of the Russian Revolution, saw feminism as a "bourgeois" or "middle-class" preoccupation that would, if advocated, break the unity of the working class and peasantry in their pursuit of national sovereignty and social revolution. Accentuating this tension was the fact that the revolutionary movements that emerged in the 1970s in countries such as Nicaragua, El Salvador, and Guatemala came of age in a virtual vacuum of feminist theory or practice in the region, even of the upper- or middle-class variant.[8]

Thus, the new strategies and underlying theories guiding Central American revolutionary movements of the 1970s were new, coming out of a critique of strategic and tactical failures of the past; their view of the class struggle as the fundamental contradiction in society to which gender and race/ethnicity is inevitably subordinated remained relatively intact. There was little awareness of a need to examine critically gender ideology, culture, and symbols inherited from the past. The only models for incorporating women into the revolution came from the Soviet experience in the early part of this century; the Cuban Revolution, which took place in the midst of the 1950s social conservatism and the Cold War prior to the emergence of second wave feminism in the developed countries; and the Communist Parties of China and Vietnam, whose historical origins and cultural contexts were quite distinct from those of Central America. The precise implications of these deficiencies, from the point of view of some of the women participants themselves, will be explored below.

Nationalism and the Ideologies of the Central American Revolutions

Before analyzing the nature of women's involvement in Central American revolutionary movements, and some concepts and practices that stood in the way of greater gender equality, it is important to attempt to understand the relationship of these movements to nationalism, so as to connect feminism back to nationalism later in the discussion.

It might appear, at first glance, that class-based and internationalist ideologies derived from the Marxist tradition have been more important than nationalist ones in Latin American revolutionary movements since the 1960s.[9] But nationalism, in one form or another, as Mexican political scientist and journalist Jorge Castenada has argued, has remained a consistent underpinning of Latin American revolutionary thought for more than a century, including recent decades.[10] Dependency theory, on which the Cuban-influence revolutionary models of the 1960s and 1970s were based, embodied a particular form of nationalism that posited the "virtual neo-colonial status of the hemisphere" and the "consequent historical impotence of the local business classes." The latter were seen just as irrevocably tied to that which was foreign and external as their nineteenth-century and colonial period counterparts had been. Elite ties to that which was external to the country were seen as the main obstacle to development and greater social justice.

In this thesis of total continuity between colonialism and neocolonialism in Latin American history—which Castenada views as "contain[ing] its grain of truth though . . . factually false"[11]—"elites are seen not only as incapable of completing the unfinished task of nation building but as not really even part of the nation. It is "the people," that is, the destitute and excluded from society, "the misbegotten and banned, dark-skinned and ethnic," who constitute "the real nation" or "its soul." The educated, lighter-skinned elites, then, are the true "other."[12]

The task of leading the recovery of the nation "for the people," of nation building and national consciousness-raising, has traditionally been assumed to fall primarily (though not exclusively) on the shoulders of radicalized intellectuals. Nationalism has been traditionally weak or nonexistent among the broad masses with their "religious myth, syncretism, and tribal or regional loyalties," and church and business elites have been seen as "unsuited for the chore."[13] For radical intellectuals to carry out the task, however, a popular constituency is needed, implying that any nationalist campaign must take up the social demands of that constituency.

The interpenetration of arguments for social revolution and nationalism in post–World War II Latin American revolutionary movements brings with it an inevitable confrontation with internal defenders of the status quo. And discussions of national identity and citizenship become part of the larger question of dignity for the poor and marginalized as revolutionary movements in the 1970s and 1980s attempted to win the support of Indians in Guatemala or peasants in Nicaragua by putting forth social and economic demands that spoke to their conditions. The strongest constituency for nationalist appeals in Latin America, especially the single-minded anti-Yankee version of which Castenada is critical, probably continues to be the educated middle classes. The inseparability of arguments for social transformation and national dignity (equated with dignity of the "other") has meant that in contrast to the United States and much of western Europe, "there [are] no social leftists who are not convinced radical nationalists."[14]

Women and the Revolutionary Movements of the 1970s

The revolutionary movements of the 1970s in Nicaragua, El Salvador, and Guatemala emerged out of an analysis of the failures of the Cuban-inspired revolutionary movements of the 1960s. They represented a new type of revolutionary movement, much larger and more mass-based, and with significant participation of "new" social sectors, such as Catholics influenced by liberation theology and Indians in the case of Guatemala. In each case, unarmed civilian (that is, mass or "popular") organizations were linked, to differing degrees, with political-military (that is, guerilla) organizations that drew on diverse sectors of the population for active participation and support (urban, rural, peasants, workers, students, Christians, professionals, and others).

The conditions under which the movements developed and the stages of evolution they went through differed by country because of variations in national history, the relationship with the United States, and the social and cultural composition of the population.[15] In spite of these differences, there were important similarities. In each movement, the degree and type of participation by women were without historical precedent in Latin America. Unlike the Cuban Revolution, women, particularly young women, joined the FSLN, what came to be the FMLN (the Farabundo Marti Liberation Front of El Salvador) and what came to be the URNG (National Revolutionary Unity of Guatemala) as militarily trained combatants, urban commandos, radio operators, intelligence gatherers, purveyors of supplies and infrastructure, propagandists, and medical teams. Other women actively contributed to the revolutionary movement as noncombatant grassroots activists, organizing their neighborhoods, unions, student groups, peasant organizations, or Christian base communities, and providing food, medical care, refuge, intelligence, and homemade weapons for the combatants, many of whom were friends and relatives.[16]

The transformations in women's political involvement occurred rapidly and, by and large, pragmatically, with few previous political models to emulate. There was little scholarly or theoretical understanding of the multiple determinants of women's subordination in dependent capitalist societies or the concrete reality of women's lives—in all their diversity—in the country. There was little awareness of the ease with which gender inequalities can be reproduced in revolutionary organizations and the potential between participation and full citizenship in the revolution.

In all three countries, there was virtually no previous feminist movement tradition to build on—not even the early-twentieth century upper- or middle-class feminist movements that had existed in other Latin American countries. The Cuban and Soviet bloc's rejection of what was viewed as "First World or bourgeois" feminism made the tiny handful of women who could be said to be conscious feminists prior to joining the revolution leery of pursuing the topic theoretically or politically.[17] In addition, the majority of women revolutionaries were relatively young adolescents at the beginning of their involvement, having been socialized into relatively traditional Catholic-influenced cultural definitions of masculinity and femininity.

In all three movements, women generally did not reach the top levels of organizational leadership (despite a few well-known exceptions in the Salvadoran case). And the proportion of women in middle-level leadership levels did not match their relatively high levels of participation. But in all three countries, this historic shift in women's political involvement has left an indelible mark on the consciousness of the women themselves, their families and close friends, and, undoubtedly, on the course of any future movements for social change.

Based on some sixty interviews with Salvadoran women who were active participants in all levels of revolutionary activity, Murguialday and Vasquez draw conclusions that could apply to any one of the three revolutionary movements:

> The most favorable consequence of these women's participation in the war appears to be the symbolic and practical questioning of conservative frame-

works regarding what women are and are not permitted to do. The war showed them and the rest of society that women could fight and conspire [to overthrow the established order], that they are capable of participating in the most unexpected fronts, and of efficiently carrying out tasks thought to belong to men. It also appears to have left them with the view that if women did reach the highest levels of decision-making in the military and party structures, it was not because they were not qualified but because sexist prejudices still predominated in the FMLN.[18]

Obstacles in the Path of Women's Search for Equality and Power Through Revolutionary Change

By the middle of the 1990s the period of strength of the armed revolutionary movements in Central America was at its end. Only one of the three movements, the Sandinistas in Nicaragua, achieved its goal of capturing state power (by overthrowing the Somoza dictatorship on July 19, 1979) and remained in power until its electoral defeat by a coalition of opposition parties on February 25, 1990. Although the Sandinistas carried out some important reforms, including land reform, during the decade they were in power, many of their initial gains were eroded and others never realized because they were forced to defend the revolution against a U.S.-financed counterrevolutionary force ("The Contras") for seven of their ten years in power. Even more disappointing to many women activists was the failure after the electoral defeat to modify the all-male Sandinista top-level leadership, which dated back to the overthrow, and undertake internal democratic reforms.

What most recruits to the revolutionary movement in El Salvador thought would be a short and decisive battle to overthrow the old regime (akin to that of the Sandinistas against Somoza in Nicaragua) turned into a costly decade-long war (with some seventy thousand or more lives lost), ending in a military stalemate and a negotiated a settlement under which future competition for power would take place through the electoral process.

After three decades of armed struggle and the loss of more than one hundred thousand lives, many of them Indian, the Guatemalan revolutionary leadership is in the final stages of negotiation with representatives from the strongest counterinsurgency army in the hemisphere and relatively intransigent business and political elites. Although peace cannot be

achieved without the Guatemalan revolutionary movement's cooperation, the position its leadership brings to the bargaining table is much
weaker than that of its Salvadoran counterparts because of the relatively
greater stake many sectors of the elite seem to have in preserving the status quo. Many Salvadoran women activists have been disappointed by the
exclusion of the rural women who served as cover and infrastructure for
young revolutionary activists from the benefits afforded other partisans in
the peace agreements, and the lack of gender-specific demands in the accords and validation of women's efforts in revolutionary party discourse.[19]

At this crossroads in the history of movements for social justice and
political power for the masses in Nicaragua, El Salvador, and Guatemala,
a number of women participants are examining critically, for the first
time, the conditions that favored or inhibited their access to lasting improvements in more equal gender relations and access to power and decision making. All agree that it is their experience that has made possible
their critical evaluation of movement shortcomings now. Without the
revolutionary movement, feminism would undoubtedly still be the
province of a privileged few. At the same time, however, the emergence
of feminism as a priority political identity—sometimes prefaced with the
descriptors "popular," "revolutionary," or "socialist"—and the insistence
that consciousness of and mobilization around gender issues are essential
for and do not distract from any project of social transformation have put
many women at odds with the revolutionary organizations—that is, the
substitute families in which they "came of age." Despite the resistance
of the leftist tradition to what was once viewed as a "bourgeois" or "middle-class" political identification, women's participation in the revolution
has unintentionally created the conditions for women's and explicitly
feminist movements that are probably the most vital of any currently existing in Central America.

Because the evolution of women's gender and feminist consciousness
during different stages of Central American revolutionary movements,
particularly in Nicaragua, has been amply explored elsewhere,[20] the discussion that follows will focus on identifying some key ideological and
cultural barriers that kept women from achieving greater lasting equality
and access to power—which may be instructive for similar movements in
the future. The analysis is grouped around several themes: (1) the lack of
a gendered analysis of the revolutionary movement and the society it
wanted to change; (2) the role of masculinist culture in the "genderless"
vanguard party; (3) the principle of absolute self-sacrifice and obedience

to authority; and (4) a weak understanding of the importance of democracy and the role of civil society in the creation of a new society. It is based on my discussions with Central American women activists over several decades, in person and at conferences, and my own observations and conclusions.[21]

The Lack of a Gendered Analysis of the Revolutionary Movement and of the Society to Be Transformed

Many observers, including this one, have argued previously that the pragmatism, flexibility, and, for lack of a better term, empiricism for which the Central American revolutionary movements of the 1970s were known should be seen as strengths, that is, as welcome antidotes to the rigid imported dogmas of the Soviet Stalinist era. This relative openness to analyzing the particularities of "the national reality," for example, made the Sandinista leadership relatively responsive to the popular will for much of the Sandinistas' time in power and made the Guerilla Army of the Poor patient and respectful of local indigenous cultural differences in the early days of its implantation in the Western highlands. And given that the new-type Central American revolutionary organizations arose before the emergence of a second wave of Latin American feminism, it was probably better to have little or no theory than an outdated one to be used as a straightjacket for interpreting new experiences.

The lack of theoretical and empirical attention paid to the ways in which men's and women's lives are materially and culturally structured by gender, however, had its cost, as several feminist, former revolutionary activists have pointed out. In the absence of new understandings of daily life, gender ideology as a societal framework, and the ways in which social, economic, and political contradictions (around class, race/ethnicity, and gender) interact in dependent capitalist societies, economistic and reductionist conceptions (of gender contradictions as inevitably subordinate to class contradictions, for example) and traditional religious views of sexual morality and motherhood held sway in the minds of important sectors of the leadership of the movement and among many women militants themselves. As a result, many women found themselves in sharp conflicts between old moralities or theories and new situations that they were often left to resolve on their own. And women activists who did push for open discussion and debate on controversial issues (such as women's right to control their reproduction, domestic violence in Nicaragua, or the relationship of Marxism to feminism, an issue of concern to Salvadoran and Guatemalan women militants in exile in the 1980s) were often silenced or marginalized, their revolutionary credentials in doubt.

To the extent that the lives of women in the society at large were analyzed, often in response to the need to speak at international conferences or on tour in search of solidarity, the emphasis was on public-sphere activities and on working-class, peasant, and poor women. Private or domestic life and the subjective dimension of the gendered experience remained an enigma.

Writing about the Salvadoran experience, Murguialday and Vasquez observe:

> Intolerance of different views occurred when there was an analysis of reality that did not place the class struggle and the urgency of the revolution at its center. Feminism, for example, as a theoretical explanation of unequal and hierarchical relations between the genders, was dismissed by the political-military organizations as an idea derived from imperialist countries, raised and debated in order to distract attention from the true interests of the people. Women were taken into account only in terms of their membership in the exploited classes which, in effect, does form part of the identity of a large number of Salvadoran women but does not define them in their totality.

The Role of Masculinist Culture in the "Genderless" Vanguard Party

Related to the weak theoretical understanding of the causes of gender differences and a lack of awareness of the concrete conditions of the lives of ordinary women in their multiple dimensions was a lack of understanding of how inequalities might be unintentionally reproduced within vanguard revolutionary organizations.[22] As a result, the goal of a gender-equal new society was confused with the reality of unintentional gender inequality among militants. Because equality was deemed to reign among comrades, especially among those with access to military training and the use of arms (supposedly erasing physical differences between men and women), women activists often did not raise concrete demands for greater equality

211

or modification of certain weaknesses in the culture or policies in vanguard organizations. Those who did were viewed as too radical and rebel-
lious. According to Murguialday and Vasquez,

> Women in high level leadership positions in party structures during the
> war did not raise demands related to the discrimination they suffered in
> such structures. Some limited their activities to orienting the work of dif-
> ferent women's organizations and attending to the demands of interna-
> tional aid agencies and international feminist solidarity groups, maintaining
> a considerable distance [from], if not explicitly [rejecting] feminism.[23]

This failure to discuss openly the implications of policies and practices
with implications for gender inequality was especially critical in the areas
of maternity and sexuality. Women were officially discouraged from becoming pregnant and urged to use contraceptives, which the organization
usually provided. In reality, however, women became pregnant frequently,
either because of unplanned sex or a desire to consummate a relationship
with a child when the survival of either partner was so uncertain.

During the long wars waged by Guatemalan and Salvadoran revolutionary organizations, pregnancy appears to have been the most important reason for women's "falling behind" in relation to their male
counterparts. Women were offered the "option" of not getting pregnant
(and thus to be "New Women"), but when they didn't "choose" this option (which was understandable because of their "nature"), it was basically their responsibility to deal with the consequences. Women militants
received contradictory messages about pregnancy: on the one hand, plans
were upset and training invested was seen as "lost," at least temporarily,
when pregnant militants had to be reassigned, but on the other hand,
women were celebrated in slogan and song for "bellies that give birth to
more revolutionaries."

There was little discussion in the revolutionary movements of alternative models of paternity and maternity or child rearing. Women who
chose to stay in the rearguard with an infant were often resentful at being
expected to take care as well of children of other members of the organization. Women who left their children to be cared for, often in precarious
or less than desirable circumstances, suffered pangs of guilt that they often
never overcame. Frequently, when they went to recover a child after the
war was over, the child resisted leaving those who had become his or her
de facto family. No public acknowledgment of the traumas connected

with wartime sexual or maternal experiences has been made by leaders of the movement.

Either way, it was usually women's responsibility to resolve the dilemma of maternity, even though men often pressured women to have sex or have a child with them. Nicaraguan women, although not faced with the dilemmas of a long guerilla war, suffered a high level of domestic violence, including at the hands of comrades in the struggle, and a historically high rate of paternal abandonment. These issues could be and were discussed openly in Nicaragua under Sandinista rule because of the pressure of Sandinista feminists, but the lack of official understanding of the link between gender ideology and revolutionary transformation meant that the issues were often relegated to the back burner rather than seen as part of the whole process of transformation, especially during the Contra War.

Likewise, the sexual double standard often came into play when women were being considered for leadership or tasks implying great responsibility. Men's sexual practices were rarely discussed (unless they involved rape, which was generally punished when brought to the attention of the leadership), but women were, on the one hand, in an environment with much sexual freedom and pressure by men to have sex, and judged, on the other hand, as somewhat unreliable if they were known to have had multiple partners.

The underestimation of the degree to which men's and women's experiences differed in relation to the revolution, even within the vanguard parties, led to the socialization of both men and women into an unconsciously masculine revolutionary culture. Women and men were urged to "be like Che," that is, to be daring, heroic, and self-sacrificing. Thus,

> women militants were socialized as a group under the concept of "revolutionary" ("*revolucionario*"—the masculine form of the word in Spanish) and "New Man"; the implications of these concepts expressed in the masculine form were not limited to linguistic convention; they were also observed in the political lines and practices created on the basis of the illusion that differences can be suppressed by not recognizing them.[24]

If the very concept of the vanguard was unconsciously gendered, so was the relationship of mass to vanguard: in mass organizations, women were assumed to be numerous and indispensable. The vanguard, however, to which the mass organizations were seen as subordinate, was assumed to be predominantly masculine because of the difficulty of women's full incorporation into its activities. In practice, the military predominated over the political (particularly, for example, in El Salvador in the period between the two offensives, 1981–1989, when the vanguard became highly militarized; in Nicaragua during the Contra War; and in Guatemala during the army's bloody post–1982 counteroffensive).

The pressures of war, compounded by the principles of compartmentalization, clandestinity, and the collective over the individual, discouraged women from sharing problems and experiences. Problems were seen as "personal" or were not shared for fear they would be considered signs of "deviation" or "ideological weakness." Although men suffered from these restrictions too, whole segments of women's lives and subjectivities were inadvertently defined as nonpolitical and nonpriority despite the fact that they constituted part of the core fabric of the society they aspired to transform. The result was reenforcement of masculine culture and discourse, which, consciously or unconsciously alienated women from the revolutionary project.

Absolute Obedience to Authority

Although a balance between democracy and centralism was the stated ideal, obedience to centralized authority regularly triumphed over internal democracy, especially in times of crisis and war. The two-way transmission belt for ideas and information frequently functioned in only one direction, discouraging open debate and criticism of leadership errors. The lack of a culture nourishing internal democracy only served to reinforce the hierarchy of traditional elite political and economic culture and the Catholic Church out of which many of the militants had come. Sofia Montenegro, an ex-Sandinista feminist, actually compares her former revolutionary organization, which was probably more internally democratic and pluralist than its Guatemalan and Salvadoran counterparts, to a religious order complete with a charismatic savior (Sandino), an apostle (Carlos Fonseca, the founder of the Sandinista Front in the 1950s), disciples, novitiates, vows of obedience, and a priestly class.[25] Her assessment is undoubtedly influenced by her reaction to the pressure to "close ranks" during the Contra War and the Sandinista leadership's resistance to internal reform since the election, but there is no question that adherence to "the revolutionary mystique" often substitutes for the development of cadre who can think independently even while acting as part of a collective. Montenegro concedes that this might have been justifiable during the period of clandestinity and armed struggle and even perhaps during the first few years after taking power. But, she argues,

> it is an anachronism and senseless that fifteen years after, when the organization is a civil organization, an institutionalized political party and a democratizing force, in spite of itself. The FSLN as a political group is not (nor has it been) a space of equals where all its members are viewed as subjects, that is to say people whose capacity to analyze, participate, and decide in conditions of equality is recognized.[26]

Montenegro concludes that, in official Sandinista discourse, women were granted the right to be "compañeras" alongside men in the struggle or reproducers of revolutionaries but not autonomous women, capable of their own self-determination.

Feminism, Nationalism, and Revolution

The experience of women in the revolutionary movements of Nicaragua, Guatemala, and El Salvador during the 1970s and 1980s yields important insights into the conditions under which women's involvement in revolutionary movements—whether nationalist or class-nationalist—leads to greater gender equality and a transformation in gender relations.

The first and most important point is that participation, in and of itself, even participation in nontraditional gender roles, does not result in the transformation of gender ideology and culture. It is a crucible for such transformation, creating the possibility of accelerating change dramatically, but without a direct attack on gender ideology, culture, and practice, based on a holistic and multidimensional understanding of the concrete conditions of women's lives, tolerance of women's transgression of gender roles can be temporary, despite the best intentions of leaders and the participants themselves. Wars may "bring women out of their kitchens," but the end of the war may just as easily pressure women to return to them if the process has not been accompanied by major transformations in men's and women's consciousness.

Second, the gender dimension of social classes, ethnic or racial groupings, and the nation itself must be explored and understood so that the vision of change for which the seeds are planted in the revolutionary movement can include women and the public as well as domestic lives of people. Gender and ethnicity cannot be reduced to social class or nation but must be understood to have some degree of autonomous effect on social structure and political struggles. Personal or sectoral expectations—that is, social and personal liberation—must be seen as the powerful motivators they are for individuals' willingness to sacrifice for social transformation rather than being dismissed as "deviations or "petty-bourgeois weaknesses." To the understanding of political economy and the power of social structure to shape behavior must be added the power of culture, subjectivity, and the unconscious, concepts traditionally missing from orthodox Marxist analyses.

Third, the struggle of women and other disenfranchised groups is very much tied up with respect for democracy, pluralism (including among vanguard or leadership organizations), and the potentially powerful social transformation role of civil society (that is, those nonstate, nonmilitary institutions and organizations). The movement must be a social laboratory for tolerance of differences and the widest possible access to avenues of decision making and power.

Finally, although women have demonstrated their capacity to sacrifice and succeed as direct participants in armed struggle, it must be clear that women's demands and access to power almost always suffer as the military aspect of struggles for fundamental social transformation take precedence over political struggle, negotiation, and dialogue. The glorification of that which is directly connected to armed struggle almost always brings with it a devaluing of the reproductive tasks traditionally assigned to women, with the exception of those carried out in direct support of the war. The identification of the hero as one associated with arms rather than with child rearing reinforces traditional gender divisions and the hierarchies that accompany them.

Feminism, therefore, is not an automatic consequence of women's involvement in political struggle or of men's experiences with women doing things they were not expected to be able to do. Feminism comes from direct challenges to gender ideologies and practices and giving women the autonomy, within mixed political organizations and outside them, to share experiences with other women and collectively decide on leadership and priorities for demands. Feminist nationalism and feminist class struggle imply a transformation of that struggle in the direction of greater democracy, tolerance, and respect for daily life than has traditionally been the case.

Notes

1. Linda Labao, "Women in Revolutionary Movements: Changing Patterns of Latin American Guerilla Struggle," in *Women and Social Protest*, ed. Guida West and Rhoda Lois Blumberg (Oxford: Oxford University Press, 1990); Jane Jaquette, "Women in Revolutionary Movements in Latin America," *Journal of Marriage and the Family* 35 (May 1964): 344–354.

2. Che Guevara, *Guerilla Warfare* (New York: Vintage Books, 1967), p. 86.

3. Antonio Arguedas, quoted in *Tania: The Unforgettable Guerrilla* eds. Marta Rojas and Mirta Rodriguez Calderon (New York: Random House, 1971), p. 918.

4. Ibid. p. 918.

5. Ibid., p. 87.

6. Francesca Miller, *Latin American Women and the Search for Social Justice*, (Hanover, NH: University Press of New England, 1991), p. 172.

7. Virginia Vargas, one of the most notable of these new feminist theorist/activists, discusses the feminist critique of Left parties in several of her publications: "The Feminist Movement in Peru: Inventory and Perspectives," in *Women's Struggles and Strategies*, ed. Saskia Wieringa (Brookfield, VT: Gower, 1988). For an overview of the development of thought among Left Women in the 1970s, see Cornelia Butler Flora, *Socialist Feminism in Latin America*, Working Paper No. 14 (East Lansing: Michigan State University, 1982).

8. *Feminist* here means something more than work with women or for women, it means an explicit critique of the gender hierarchy and a commitment to activities directed toward overcoming it.

9. The Cuban Revolution, for example, advocated the view that objective conditions in 1960s Latin America were ripe for revolutions if only the subjective conditions — the formation of the vanguard party—could be advanced. The revolutions they envisioned were characterized by the hegemony of the working class or a worker-peasant alliance with the inclusion of national capitalists or nationalist reformers only when the coalitions were under the hegemony of the revolutionary vanguard party. The goal of such revolutions was seen as the destruction of the administrative and military apparatuses of the bourgeois state and the redistribution of wealth, not simply the elimination of dictatorship or recovery of national sovereignty. Overcoming external dependency and extremes of wealth and poverty, in this view, required a socialist economy and state. The Soviet-aligned Communist Parties' history of cross-class alliances in pursuit of national capitalist development was dismissed with disdain. Formal independence from European colonialism had come to most Latin American countries more than a century ago (the majority in the 1820s, with notable exceptions, such as Cuba), and most nation-states had more or less existed since that time. From this point of view, nation-building or the establishment of a national identity would not seem to be a priority on the revolutionary agenda.

10. Jorge Castenada, *Utopia Unarmed: The Latin American Left after the Cold War* (New York: Knopf, 1993), pp. 70–71.

11. Ibid., p. 278.

12. Ibid. p. 273.

13. Ibid., p. 182.

14. Ibid., p. 277.

15. The National Sandinista Liberation Front (FSLN) in Nicaragua, for example, sought to put an end to the forty-year rule of the Somoza family dynasty directly supported by the United States. The Farabundo National Liberation Front (FMLN) in El Salvador struggled against direct and indirect dictatorial and pseudo-democratic oligarchic rule by a small number of coffee-growing families dependent on a military propped up by U.S. "advisers" and arms. The Guatemalan National Revolutionary Union (URNG) struggled against the de facto military dictatorships supported by the United States and its allies, such as Taiwan, Israel, and South Africa, which had placed actual military dictatorships in place since the CIA-sponsored overthrow of a democratically elected government in 1954. In Nicaragua, the revolutionary movement included mestizos and some Indians but very few Miskitos from the Atlantic Coast. In contrast to the relatively homogeneous mestizo population of El Salvador, a number of the twenty-two ethnic groups of Guatemala became part of a leftist revolutionary opposition movement for the first time in history. In Nicaragua, the recovery of a national hero, Agusto Cesar Sandino, who had resisted the intervention by the U.S. marines in the 1920s, gave the revolution a vaguely defined "populist" nationalist symbol. In El Salvador the elevation of communist Augusto Farabundo Marti, who died leading strikes and uprisings in the 1930s, emphasized the class aspect of the revolutionary philosophy. And in Guatemala, the revolutionary leadership attempted to remain nonindividualized and invisible in order to avoid repression, much like the Indian population itself.

16. See Margaret Randall, *Sandino's Daughters* (Vancouver: New Star Books, 1981); Clara Murguialday Martinez, *Nicaragua, revolucion y feminismo, 1977–89* (Madrid: Editorial Revolution, 1990); as well as my previous writings on the subject: "Revolutionary Popular Feminism in Transition in Nicaragua: 1979–1994," in *Women in the Latin American Development Process*, ed. Chris Bose and Edna Acosta Belen (Philadelphia: Temple University Press, 1995); "Feminism and Democratic Transitions in Nicaragua," in *Women's Movements and the Transition to Democracy in Latin America,* ed. Jane Jacquette (Boulder: Westview Press, 1994); "The Evolution of Revolutionary Popular Feminism in Nicaragua: Articulating Class, Gender and National Sovereignty," *Gender and Society* 4, no. 3 (September 1990): 370–397; "Marxism, Feminism, and the Struggle for Democracy in Latin America," *Gender and Society* 5, no. 3 (September 1991): 291–310.

17. The most bold in this respect were some of the women Sandinistas whose efforts to press feminist issues are described in the writings of Margaret Randall,

my own writings, and other sources. As the war against the Contras wore on, however, and military strategy was allowed to dominate over the political struggle and open debate that had made the Sandinista movement strong in popular support in its early stages, the women who consciously identified as feminist felt increasing intolerance of pluralism among the support base of the FSLN and diminishing tolerance of criticism of the leadership, which remained all-male. It is their belief that these were some of the same weaknesses, in addition to failure to retain strong support from women, that caused the Front to lose the 1990s elections unexpectedly. Many of these women are no longer members of the Sandinista Front, having left after their efforts (and those of others) to reform the Front internally and make it more democratic after the elections failed.

18. Clara Murguialday and Norma Vasquez, "El impacto de la guerra en las concepciones y practicas de la sexualidad y la maternidad de las mujeres Salvadorenas" (preliminary version presented to regional forum A Feminist Look at the Participation of Women in the Armed Conflicts in Central America and Chiapas, San Salvador, December 4–8, 1995).

19. Ibid.

20. See 16, above.

21. Of particular importance to the topic here was a forum sponsored by Las Mujeres por la Dignidad y la Vida (the first autonomous explicitly feminist group to come out of the Salvadoran Revolution) in December 1995: A First Feminist Look at the Participation of Women in the Armed Conflicts in Central America and Chiapas. The majority of the invited participants were activists with notable trajectories in the different revolutionary movements. Several publications are expected to come out of the discussions that took place at this conference.

22. I use the term *vanguard organizations* without questioning, in this essay, whether they fulfilled all the conditions of a vanguard in Marxist theory, whether the Marxist theory of the vanguard is a useful one, or whether the populations' view of the organizations and their own view of their role as in the vanguard of leadership was the same. In other words, I am using the term they use without subjecting the term to scrutiny.

23. Marguialday and Vasquez, "*El impacto*," p. 49.

24. Ibid., p. 30.

25. Sofia Montenegro, "Es revolucionario el FSLN" (paper presented at the regional forum A Feminist Look at the Participation of Women in the Armed Conflicts in Central America and Chiapas).

26. Ibid., p. 1.

Feminist Nationalist Movements in Québec:
Resolving Contradictions?

Patrice LeClerc and Lois A. West

Feminism and nationalism have thrived in Québec since the turn of the century, when their ideologies took form as social movements.[1] Their ideological roots were formed much earlier: for nationalism, when French Canadians lost their wars with the English over territorial control and then spent centuries exerting minority rights within a majoritarian society; for feminism, when the development of industrialization institutionalized a separate-spheres ideology at the same time that the English law superseded the previously more egalitarian French law.

This paper examines the themes and contradictions between feminism and nationalism within the formation of Québec as a territory until its struggle for sovereignty during the early 1990s. It examines the ways in which feminism and nationalism have coexisted as ideologies and social movements, sometimes quietly, other times with blaring contradictions, rarely as monoliths. Feminism links with conservatism; nationalism with liberal/conservative or federal/separatist ideologies. Feminism struggles with definitions of women's individual rights as citizens seeking autonomy and independence in liberal developed societies while seeking to maintain women's rights within the collectivity—be this the family or the state, where women have traditionally been defined as the mothers of the nation upholding and maintaining its language, tradition, and culture. Nationalism also must confront contradictions between individual rights, the rights of the nation-state, and the rights of minorities versus majorities.

This chapter is limited to the experience of the French within Québec; Aboriginal Canadian nationalism and feminism are beyond its scope, and a separate study awaits them. In Québec, Aboriginals are represented by fourteen nations (some 52,000 people) and a smaller Inuit population. Of French-speaking Canadians (francophones), nearly 90 percent live in Québec; only 4 percent of the population in the rest of Canada speak French as a first language, and 89 percent speak English.[2] By territory, history, and language, francophone nationalism has been aided by the relative smallness of the society and its close-knit character. But from its beginnings, Québec was involved in conflicts over resources and between competing groups.

The Foundation for Feminist Nationalism in Early Québec

The historical context of the settling of Québec set the stage for nationalism. During the seventeenth century, King Louis XIV wanted to exert direct French governmental control over New France and encouraged French immigration to the new colony. Although this French interest did not last, by the late seventeenth century New France had its distinctive French Canadian character, which became the basis for French Canadian nationalism.

Competition over fur resulted in wars with Aboriginal peoples, particularly the Iroquois, and with the British. By the late 1750s, these wars resulted in the defeat of the colony by the British. In 1760 Montréal surrendered and New France was renamed Québec under the Treaty of Paris of 1763, which put Québec under British control. However, early French nationalists forced the British Parliament to pass the Québec Act in 1774, which gave the Roman Catholic Church official recognition, and began the tradition of the myth of the *idéologie de la survivance*, the ideology of survival and perpetuation of French culture and tradition in North America against the British attempts to obliterate them. The French Canadians, unlike the British, had communities based on strong Roman Catholic support structures but had no representative political institutions. The Québec Act also endorsed the French language and restored French civil law in place of English common law. French law, known as the Coutume de Paris, made marriage an equal partnership (unlike English law) and gave the wife right to half of the husband's property, which guaranteed wives and children property rights after the husband's death.

Noel argued that women in New France held a privileged position compared to their counterparts elsewhere: ideas about women's roles were flexible. Women were not relegated to the domestic sphere because it did not exist, even though family was the basic economic and political unit. Female immigrants had advantages not available to their European counterparts. The French nuns established an educational tradition that was favorable to the education of girls. In 1663 Montréal had a school for girls but not for boys.[3] Marriageable females were in such short supply that they had a wider choice in marriage, and many who came from France were urbanites with greater cultural sophistication. The emphases on war and the fur trade gave women opportunities as they carried on business while their husbands were involved in or were killed in the wars.

In 1791 the Constitutional Act divided the territory into Upper and Lower Canada. French Canadians gained their first representative body and the assembly became the center of francophone political activity with a French political party, the Patriotes. Under the act, all property owners could vote and no distinction was made by sex. Some women property owners had the right to vote until 1849, when the right was withdrawn.[4] (The Patriotes were afraid that the women's vote would lose them seats in the opposition.)[5]

The Patriotes spurred an armed rebellion in 1837 in Lower Canada. In its aftermath, the Act of Union of 1840 joined Upper and Lower Canada and encouraged French Canadian assimilation by placing French Canadians in a minority position. In 1867 the Act of Confederation integrated what is now Québec, Ontario, Nova Scotia, and New Brunswick into Canada. Québec was guaranteed its local autonomy and made officially bilingual. However, the Québec Civil Code of 1866 eroded women's previous marital rights by giving women the same legal status as minors and persons with mental disabilities. A wife was no longer coequal but subject to her husband's authority.[6] Thus, while French Canadians were being forced to maintain a precarious balance between their nationalism and the various acts of confederation, Québec women saw their rights gradually eroded.

The first French Canadian prime minister of Canada, a Liberal, was elected in 1896, and the Liberals took over from the Catholic-supported Conservatives and governed Québec from 1897–1944.[7] Nationalists continued to be concerned with maintaining their provincial rights within the federalist system and as guardians of francophone interests outside Québec. For example, during the late nineteenth century and early twentieth, when Manitoba and Ontario attempted to limit Catholic schools, Québécois were concerned with the rights of Francophones outside Québec to be educated in their own language. French Canadians resisted attempts to conscript them during World War I, and this split the country along nationalist/federalist lines.

From Canada's earliest history, French Canadians struggled to maintain their autonomy and traditions and early forms of nationalism under English domination. Women who lived under French rule fared better until English law took away some of the rights they once enjoyed. Although there was no "feminist" movement until the late nineteenth century and early twentieth century, the lack of the relegation of women to a private sphere in preindustrial Québec ensured women's strong roles, which formed the basis for a later feminism. The struggle over both nationalism and feminism became institutionalized with the social changes facing the Québécois during the rise of industrialization.

Early French-Canadian Feminism

By the late nineteenth century, Québec was rapidly industrializing. By 1891, 20 percent of factory workers in Québec and 28 percent in Montréal were women.[8] These changes set up contradictions for women, who, at least from the mid-nineteenth century on, were viewed as the maintainers of the home, the *guardiennes de la race* (guardians of the race).[9] Their lives centered on pleasing a husband, in most cases working on a family farm, regular worship at the Catholic church, and the production of many children.

This view affected early Québec feminism, which began in the late nineteenth century with the "social feminism" of women involved in charity work. These feminists believed in the gender differences between men and women and the complementarity of roles.[10] Their early activism was motivated by their attempts to confront the social problems created by the rise of industrial capitalism. They struggled to confront the rise of the "separate-spheres" ideology by creating strong public roles.

In 1907 the Fédération Nationale Saint-Jean Baptiste, was founded as a Christian women's organization to focus on issues of charity, education, and working women, issues compatible with a "clerical-nationalist ideology."[11] The largest number of its affiliated women's organizations were those run by nuns.[12] The archbishop of Montréal defined Christian *féminisme* for this group as "the zealous pursuit of all the noble causes in the sphere that Providence has assigned to her. . . . There will be no talk in your meetings of the emancipation of woman, of the neglect of her rights, of her having been relegated to the shadows, of the responsibilities, public offices and professions to which she should be admitted on an equal basis with man."[13]

Lamoureaux argued that nationalism was founded on Roman Catholic interpretations of the New Testament that set up a distinction between the Kingdom of Caesar and the Kingdom of God. On the economic level, this meant reserving agriculture and the liberal professions for the francophones, industry and commerce for the anglophones. This also logically translated into the nineteenth-century ideology of separation of spheres: women in the private sphere, men in the public, by which, as the Kingdom of God dominates the Kingdom of Caesar, the men's sphere should dominate the women's.[14] Yet Trofimenkoff argued that during this period, Québec's clerics, nationalists, and feminists shared similar concerns: all were concerned with being guardians of the social order, with education, and with preserving the family as the foundation for religion and morality and the center of social organization. Each believed that the francophone family had a "peculiar essence" that distinguished it as superior to Anglo families.[15]

Because the feminist label implied that women would move outside their "proper sphere," early feminists sought to define their feminism within terms acceptable to the clerics and nationalists who were threatened by women's new public roles in the factories and more visible roles in educational institutions. The Fédération Nationale Saint-Jean Baptiste supported the rights of working women and had intellectual clerical and secular women as "strong women" role models which contradicted the images of women in limited mother and religious roles among the early nationalists.[16] An inherent contradiction existed between the ideology of traditional roles for women and the early feminist attempts to advocate political rights for women.

Feminist efforts to bridge feminism and nationalism did not always work. In 1913 a cleric invited to speak at the Fédération lambasted feminism as violent and brutal to men, leading to unnatural demands and the breakup of the home. In a separate attack in the nationalist Montréal daily, *Le Devoir*, the paper's editor criticized feminism as a foreign, Protestant import that would destroy French Canadian civilization because women were the keys to the survival of religion, morality, education, and the family.[17]

This conservative tone helped to delay suffrage for Québec women until 1940. However, feminists worked to regain the citizenship rights lost under the English domination of Québec; in 1912 the Montréal Suffrage Association was formed to seek the vote for women in federal elections except Aboriginal people living on reserves. By 1918 all Canadian women could vote in federal elections, although Québec women could still not vote in provincial elections. In 1922 feminists met with the premier of Québec, Louis-Alexandre Taschereau, to advocate voting rights for women, but their efforts were rebuked. Taschereau argued that women have a "ministry of love and charity" to fulfill, which makes politics more appropriate for men.[18]

In 1927 Idola Saint-Jean founded the Alliance Canadienne pour le vote des femmes du québec (the Canadian Alliance for the vote for Women of Québec). This organization and the Ligue des droits de la femme (League for Women's Rights) founded in 1929 by Thérèse Casgrain worked for women's right to a provincial vote until suffrage was finally gained in April, 1940. Up until this time the Catholic clergy opposed suffrage "because it goes against the unity and the hierarchy of the family."[19]

Although it can be argued that when the provincial vote finally came, it was the Québec government's effort to encourage women to move out of their traditional roles for the war effort, French Canadians were opposed to their own involvement in World War II. Despite this, by 1942 the government was training women to be mechanics, electricians, and welders in war factories,[20] as North American women were brought into the work force to support the war effort. The war demonstrated the continuing struggle over women's family and nationalist roles and the needs of the marketplace. The federal government established a government-sponsored day-care program to meet the needs of working mothers. Interestingly, while Ontario established twenty-eight day nurseries, Québec only established six, and of those six, French Canadians used only one. The clergy and nationalists emphasized that government day care was a communist plot. There was pressure for women to stay in the home, for they argued that women who worked outside the home were undermining the family. French Canadian Catholic women who did work, usually out of economic need, were more likely to put their children in family or private care.[21]

When the war ended, women who worked outside the home were

encouraged to return to their roles as *guardiennes de la race*. The premier, Maurice Duplessis,[22] set the stage for a modernization of the economy by encouraging further industrialization. He also encouraged the authority of the clergy in medicine and education, and increased the number of *instituts familiaux*—"domestic science" schools run by the clergy and designed to train girls for domestic life, femininity, and the family. During 1957, of four thousand hours of instruction in a four-year program, more than half were devoted to sewing, cooking, French, child psychology, and religious education.[23] The ruling ideology was on maintaining the province as a traditional society, with French survival depending on maintaining *la foi, la langue, la race* (the Catholic faith, the French language, French Canadian ancestry). Interestingly, although there was an immediate postwar "baby boom," family size had reduced from an average of six or more children during the nineteenth century to an average of from two to four during the twentieth. Instead of women having more children, the number of children per woman was reduced. More women had children which accounted for the postwar boom.[24]

Despite the conservative, probusiness nature of the Duplessis government, women who did work for wages organized some major, postwar strike campaigns. In 1946 several thousand workers (of whom at least a third were women) waged a long and bitter strike against Dominion Textile's Montréal mills, which inevitably resulted in a labor contract. In 1951 women workers of Imperial Tobacco went on strike and had their demands met. In 1952 women struck a Montréal department store, Dupuis Frères, and got a collective bargaining agreement. The increasing public roles for women, however subtle, and increasing prosperity helped set the stage for the Quiet Revolution.

The Quiet Revolution

After decades of elite and provincial leadership that inhibited modernization and encouraged Catholic Church domination over aspects of daily life, a new premier brought the province into the modern world. Upon Duplessis's death in 1959, the Liberal Party under Jean Lesage took over the country and escalated socioeconomic changes. The years 1960–1966 became known as the Quiet Revolution because of the number of "revolutionary" changes, including the resurgence of nationalism and feminism. While Lesage continued Duplessis's attempts to modernize the economy, he encouraged French Canadian control of industry through public ownership. He made some dramatic changes in education, civil service administration, and tax structure. In 1964 control of the educational system by the clergy ended and a ministry of education was created. Women who had once attended the family institutes were now attending the Colleges d'énseignment général et professionnel, which were provincially sponsored community colleges. After 1965 many women returned to school to get professional and academic training in continuing education programs for women.[25] The civil service expanded, creating positions for the newly educated and creating a substantial French-Canadian middle class.[26] Lesage redefined Québec's relationship to the federal tax system, asking for a bigger share of the total revenues, although he also raised taxes to pay for provincial changes. The Québec state had now taken over many aspects of daily life that had previously been controlled either by the Catholic Church or the family, such as health care, education, and pensions."There were sudden changes in all aspects of identity, culture, and politics.[28]

With the Liberal government, nationalism took on a socioeconomic face, focusing on economic and cultural matters.[29] Nationalists were concerned with the dominance of anglophones in the economy.[30] Separatist tendencies motivated the formation of a separatist political party in 1962, and led to the formation of the Front de Libération du Québec (FLQ) in 1963. Separatist nationalists of the FLQ were radicalized by anticolonial movements and theories from the Third World. The *Parti Pris*, a nationalist journal, argued that the history of colonialism in Québec made it akin to the colonization of Third World nations.[31] In what came to be known as "the October Crisis" of 1970, FLQ separatists kidnapped the British trade commissioner, followed by Québec's labor minister, whom they later assassinated. This provoked Pierre Trudeau, a Québec Liberal and Canada's prime minister, to invoke the War Measures Act during peacetime—emergency powers that included the suspension of some civil liberties and the arrest of four hundred people without warrant.

Not all separatists were as militant. Rene Lévesque began the nationalist Parti Québécois (PQ) in the late 1960s; it advocated Québec's political and cultural autonomy as an equal partner within a common market. As a more reformist, legalistic arm of the nationalist movement, the PQ organized at the grassroots level, using consciousness-raising techniques that focused on nationalist issues at the same time it condemned the violence of the FLQ. This strategy paid off, and in 1976 Lévesque became premier. The Québec government was moving from being a province to becoming a "national government."[32] As Denis Moniere put it, "*On ne parle plus de province mais de l'Etat de Québec*" (One no longer speaks of the province but of the state of Québec).[33]

As nationalism was becoming increasingly institutionalized, women's changing roles were stirring a new form of feminism. The Catholic Church was taken out of the realm of family with the inauguration of civil marriage in 1968 and divorce courts in 1969, which led to a rising divorce rate.[34] Between 1939 and 1969 the birth rate was cut in half. By 1970 Québec had the lowest birth rate of any of the provinces (15 per 1000).[35] With mechanization of agriculture, increasing urbanization, a change in women's education, the increasing availability of birth control and use as women rejected the church's birth control prohibitions, and a rising women's work force, large families were no longer needed.

Demographer Jacques Henripen created a stir among nationalists in the late 1960s when he suggested that this drastic decline in the birth rate would result in francophones becoming a minority in their own province. To the nationalists, the *revanche des berceaux* (revenge of the cradle),[36] a high fertility rate, was the only way to ensure cultural survival. These predictions led to a call for a sovereign state where francophones would control language policies and policies affecting their *survivance*. Another major point of contention was that of power over migration: Québec wanted control in order to encourage immigration of French-speaking persons from Vietnam, Haiti, and Lebanon to increase further the number French-speakers in the province.[37] French was made the official language of Québec in 1974, and the use of English was restricted in education, business, and government.

At the beginning of the sixties women's issues were not in the public eye, but there were some important changes that gave rise to the resurgence of the women's movement by mid-decade. Clare Kirkland-Casgrain was elected the first member of the National Assembly of Québec. In 1964 she sponsored a bill that ended the legal incapacity of married women, who could now launch lawsuits or act as executors on their own behalf. Women were becoming politicized. In 1966, to celebrate the twenty-fifth anniversary of suffrage, the Fédération des femmes du Québec (FFQ, the Women's Federation of Québec) was founded as an umbrella group of women's associations to promote women's rights. It identified itself as "feminist," was multiethnic, included anglophone groups as well as francophone, and was secular, unlike most earlier feminist groups.[38]

By the late sixties, Western radical feminism had affected the more radical women of Québec. Anglophones founded the first radical feminist group in 1969, the Montréal Women's Liberation Movement, and opened a center in Montréal with funding from Dr. Henry Morgentaler, a physician who was willing to perform abortions, although they were illegal. Francophone feminists were not affiliated with this movement,[39] although they, too, worked for liberalized birth control and the legalization of abortion. The Quiet Revolution laid the basis for the feminist nationalism of the 1970s.

Feminism and Nationalism in the 1970s

Nationalism provided francophone feminists with the political vocabulary to analyze their oppression, and many women came to feminism through their involvement with nationalism. Many felt women's liberation would come with national liberation.[40] The link was created between independence and autonomy—for the country and for women within the family.[41] By the late sixties, a common slogan was "*Pas de libération des femmes sans Québec libre, pas de Québec libre sans libération des femmes*" (No women's liberation without a free Québec, no free Québec without the liberation of women).[42] Both francophone and anglophone feminists founded the Front de libération des femmes (FLF) in 1970, but the francophones who were more concerned with the nexus between nationalism, feminism, and class politics, ousted the anglophones soon after. In response to an FLQ manifesto, two radical feminists published the *Manifeste des femmes Québécoises* in 1971, in which they denounced working with anglophone women "*parce qu'elles sont dans une position dominante par rapport à nous*" (because they are in a position of domination over us).[43] They criticized radical groups like FLQ for their treatment of women while asserting the need for independent women's organizations. Yet their reference to anticolonialism and the "struggle for women's national liberation" demonstrated the prioritizing at this time by many feminists of the nationalist struggle over the feminist.[44]

The FLF fell apart in 1971 and members began a new organization in 1972, the Centre des Femmes (Woman's Center), which lasted until 1975. Where the FLF had a particularly nationalist focus (refusing to work

229

with anglophone women's groups who organized an abortion rights march on Ottawa in May 1970 because they did not recognize the government of Ottawa and wanted a strictly Québécoises march),[45] the center identified itself as socialist feminist and prioritized the working-class, socialist struggle over the nationalist. The center published a journal, *Québécoises Deboutte!*, and was active in the Comité de lutte pour l'avortement et la contraception libres gratuits (Action Committee for Free Abortion and Contraception), including setting up abortion services.[46]

Trofimenkoff argued that second-wave feminists still shared many tenets with nationalists.[47] Many were the same persons, and others shared origins, social class and occupation. They both drew analogies with other movements and spoke for a broader clientele, and their demands were similar in that they both wanted the same problems solved: wage parity, access to professional training, a position in the economy, and political power. Both said they merited special consideration because of past inequities. They looked to the state as the instrument of liberation, and they welcomed the dissolution of the power of religion in civil society.

Despite these similarities, Couillard argued that Québécoises feminists defined themselves in relation to their historical context of time.[48] Although the militant nationalists, socialists, and feminists shared the concept of oppression and were movements of liberation, militant male nationalists and socialists refused to integrate the feminist struggle into their own, necessitating women's formation of autonomous groups.

Women's struggles were to be the center of independence politics, and women challenged Québec to be more responsive to women than the federal government had been.[49] On the Québec policy front, the Conseil du statut de la femme (CSF) was established in 1973 as an advisory board to the government on women's issues. Initially (until 1980), the leadership of the CSF used its resources to help women organize networks between women and to help with the development of services for women, such as rape crisis and battered women's shelters.[50] With the advent of Parti Québécois leadership in 1976, the budget of the CSF increased from several hundred thousand Canadian dollars to more than a million, and its 1978 report put forward a number of proposals for improving the status of women.[51] Between 1970 and 1979, the Parti Québécois platform had changed from peripheralizing women under "family and childhood" to attempting to accommodate women in their dual roles as worker and housewife-mother. But this created somewhat of an ideological tension in the nationalist and modernization theory, which valued motherhood at the same time as employment and abortion.

Lamoureaux criticized the CSF for focusing its women's-rights perspective on women's family and maternal roles. She argued that it existed to appease the modern factions of the PQ and co-opt women through policy making, creating something of a "state feminism."[52] However, Di Domenico pointed out that the services that the CSF provided constituted one part of the women's movement that took over services to women once provided by the women religious.[53] Other parts of the movement were pressure groups for women. None of which had much relationship to the nationalist movement. The majority of women identified with the women's movement's service tendency. Union leader Monique Simard also argued that the feminist movement, at least within her union the Confédération des Syndicats Nationaux (CSN), was always more practical than ideological—focusing not only on worker's rights issues such as equal pay or the right to work but also on feminist issues such as abortion rights for women. CSN women negotiated abortion leaves in unions as a form of education even before Québec legalized abortion. Simard believed CSN women unionists held "a more global vision of women in society" because they negotiated both as workers and as women.[54]

Feminists initially had held out great hopes for the Parti Québécois government when it came to power in 1976. There was more confidence and pride in the government as it took over many of the functions performed by the traditional instruments of nationalism—religion, language, and the family.[55] It appeared as if the question of the status of women was gaining increasing importance in the social, political and ideological life of Québec.[56] Feminists thought political parties, the government, the Catholic Church, unions, and business were beginning to take women into account. Women participated in government and business and were integrated into the policy process.[57] Women were involved in the new economy, entrepreneurship, access to professions, and increasing income.[58] Many Québécoises felt that with these changes they were ahead of the rest of Canada.[59]

For more radical feminists, however, the government and political parties were not doing enough and were continuing to peripheralize women's concerns. Yet the tension and contradictions between women's dual roles as mothers and workers, and the struggles between social movements with different priorities—be they nationalist or feminist—came to a head over the 1980 referendum on Québec autonomy.

Solidifying Contradictions: The 1980 Referendum

When the Parti Québécois came to power in 1976, it promised a referendum on independence in 1980. As the referendum on what was finally called "sovereignty-association" with Canada approached, women were torn in several directions. Although some felt the Parti Québécois government had done a great deal for women, there was fear of their nationalist, pronatalist policies coming into effect. Many feminists were socialists, and they supported the PQ for its socialist ideology but were dismayed at the slowing down of progress for women. Publicly, the PQ was committed to the liberation of women, but it was still traditionally nationalist in many ways, especially in viewing women as mothers of the nation.[60] The PQ assumed that all feminists supported their party, but many women, and many feminists were federalists, supported continuing federation with Canada. The contradictions and ambivalence between feminism and nationalism can be exhibited in two very different ideological social movements: one radical feminist, the other conservative.

In response to the demise of the FLF and Women's Center, the Regroupement des femmes Québécoises (RFQ) was organized in 1976 to bring together the ideological tendencies of both movements—feminist, and nationalist and socialist. Unlike the other two movements, the RFQ prioritized feminism over nationalism and socialism, and affirmed the organization to be radical, autonomous and, as a pressure group, independent from any political party. They felt the Parti Québécois did not go far enough on women's rights, and worked on issues of violence against women.[61] At its height in 1978, the RFQ had more than five hundred members. The RFQ's undoing came over the issue of the 1980 referendum on Québec's independence. The RFQ wanted to make the referendum one for women. Its referendum committee felt that the national liberation struggle had been made without the active participation of women and asked women to write in *FEMME* (WOMEN) on their referendum ballots rather than voting yes or no on independence.[62] The majority of the RFQ rejected this proposal as one of letting their votes be wasted and of giving force to the no voters. The committee resigned, which effectively helped to demobilize the movement, and membership dwindled considerably between 1980 and 1983.

Couillard argued that the RFQ failed because it never built a mass movement.[63] It could not resolve the tensions between being action-oriented and ideological, and could not resolve the contradictions between radical feminism, socialism, and nationalism. One problem was that in equating women's struggle with socialism, women became a social class analytically and class differences between women were ignored. The contradiction between feminism and nationalism came to a head in the referendum vote where there was a tension or lack of coherence between the actions of voting in the referendum and the feminist ideology. RFQ members did not want to prioritize being a feminist over being a nationalist.

A contrasting struggle over the referendum occurred with what has been called the "Yvette phenomenon," a collective behavior example of women's movements. During the campaign for the referendum the Minister Responsible for the Status of Women, Lise Payette, a member of the Parti Québécois, made an off-the-cuff remark that the leader of the Liberal Party (which supported federalism), Claude Ryan, had a wife who was an "Yvette." Payette said Ryan wanted all women to remain "Yvettes." Yvette was a little girl in primary school textbooks who helped her traditional mother in the household while her brother, Guy, had exciting adventures elsewhere. According to Payette, "Yvettes" were afraid to take Québec out of Canada.

Within a week, fourteen thousand women who identified themselves as "Yvettes" rallied at the Montréal Forum in support of federalism. They were addressed by prominent Québec women who appealed to women's traditional values of moral responsibility and family loyalty to support maintaining the confederation. Despite perceptions elsewhere, they never attacked feminism and at least one speaker said women wanted equal opportunities and respect for decisions to stay at home.[64] Unbeknownst to the group, the Liberal Party had orchestrated the rally, which left bad feelings among many feminists.[65]

The outward recognition that one could be a feminist and still support federalism created a new mood in the province. Until then, the polls had shown almost even distributions between those who would vote *Oui* (Yes) or *Non* (No). Many analysts believed that the Yvette issue swung the vote. The nationalist image of women as mothers upholding the nation took hold and ironically led to an antinationalist vote—60 percent against a change in status to 40 percent for separation. Women's political input was great in defeating autonomy.[66] The aftermath of the Yvette phenomenon reverberated throughout the political process. The PQ platform during the 1981 election supported a pronationalist position by offering financial rewards for having children instead of for more child care.[66] Some feminists viewed the Yvette phenomenon as part of the beginning of a backlash against feminism that has continued into the present.[68]

Both the feminist and conservative movements demonstrated the difficulties women had in linking feminism with nationalism. Radical feminists balked at being asked to prioritize nationalism over feminism. Traditional women resorted to traditional nationalist ideology on women to defend their position, while taking an antinationalist position on provincial autonomy. Both resorted to elements of nationalism but refused to give up those aspects of tradition that feminism challenged. In their analysis of the Yvette phenomenon, Jean and colleagues speculated that Québec "has had to cling to collective values in order to survive. It is quite possible that such a society would be less likely to espouse the new individualistic values, which often have antifeminist connotations."[69] Perhaps both movements represented an attempt to come to terms with the ambiguities between feminism and nationalism. It was left to the rest of the eighties to resolve these contradictions.

The Constitution—Women's Equality versus the Distinct Society?

Simard argues that the loss of the referendum created something of a "national nervous breakdown" in the province as people turned away from the national debate and forms of political activism until the late 1980s.[70] Trade unions were having to organize a new constituency, not the traditional Catholic francophone men but now women and the young within a time of economic crisis and change.

The feminist movement changed strategies as well. By the early 1980s, de Sève argues, there was an end to the *idéologisme* of feminists.[71] Where feminists were once dogmatic, they now began to form coalitions that were facilitated by the smallness and closeness of the francophone society.[72] The Conseil du statut de la femme withdrew from women's organizing and returned to its original mandate of research and legal analysis, working to facilitate coalition-building between existing women's groups.[73] The Confédération des Syndicats Nationaux worked in abortion and pay-equity coalitions with feminist groups seeking to change legislation.[74] Women worked on resolving issues of diversity within the movement through consensus. The coalition-building paid off when confronted with the debate over the Constitution.

The Parti Québécois was defeated in the 1985 elections even after taking a rightward turn during the campaign, and the Liberal Party under Robert Bourassa came to power. Although nationalism had appeared to peak over the issue of the referendum, it was the federal government's response that led to a new movement by the end of the 1980s. On the heels of Québec's referendum, the federal government passed the Constitution Act of 1982, which included new definitions of the division of power and a Charter of Rights and Freedoms. It also meant that any further changes to Canada's constitution took place in Canada and did not require approval by Great Britain (called "repatriation"). In 1981 Québec's National Assembly had voted almost unanimously to repudiate this repatriation, fearing French-language laws and other rights would not be respected. Nonetheless, the Ottawa government adopted the changes without Québec's participation.

One of the new Québec Liberal government's first tasks was dealing with the constitutional questions. It informed the federal government that in order for Québec to support the new act conditions must be met: there must be constitutional recognition of Québec as a "distinct society"; Québec must be allowed broader powers in the field of immigration and labor market training; programs falling under Québec's jurisdiction must get limited federal spending; and Québec must be allowed to participate in appointing judges from Québec who sit on Canada's Supreme Court.[75] Québec felt that the charter was based on a principle of multiculturalism, a "national Canadian identity" in which French culture would be one of many cultures represented. Québec's distinct status would not be recognized and the "levelling effect" would overlook the inequality created by linguistic majorities.[76]

The federal government's attempt to deal with these conditions came to be known as the Meech Lake Accord of 1987. It recognized Québec as a "distinct society," and agreed to some of the changes in the federal and provincial division of power. The accord had to be approved by the Canadian Parliament and all the provinces by 1990 in order for it to be ratified. Québec was the first province to approve it.

The entire debate presented a problem for Canadian feminists' relations to Québécoise feminists. Pan-Canadian Women's groups had lobbied to have Sections 15 and 28 of the Charter of Rights and Freedoms, which guarantee equal rights for women and men, written into the Constitution. Canadian feminists who had worked diligently for these sections feared that the Meech Lake Accord would override portions of the guarantees of equality rights, especially if the "distinct-society" clause came into conflict with the equality clauses. The threat was that there was no specific understanding of which, if either, would take precedence, and the belief was that gender equality rights might not be upheld.[77]

Québec feminists were less concerned. They trusted their provincial government to protect their rights more than the federal one.[78] There was an empirical basis for this belief: Québec had adopted the Charte Québécoise des droits et libertés (the Québécoise Charter of Rights and Liberties) in 1975 during the United Nations International Women's Year. For the first time, it officially prohibited discrimination based on sex. In 1988, despite the Church's position, abortion was legalized and it became easier to get an abortion in urban Québec than in other parts of Canada. The government-supported Conseil du statut de la femme had helped in the process of legalization by promoting abortion as a health issue, not as a conflictual issue over women's rights for autonomy.[79] Based on these perceptions of their rights, Québec feminists did not feel that the accord would threaten their cultural or equality rights,[80] and felt that women's equality rights were "an inherent part of the distinct society of Québec."[81]

Tension was focused in the two major women's groups, the National Action Committee on the Status of Women in Canada (representing 543 women's groups) and the Fédération des femmes du Québec (FFQ; representing 115 associations and 100,000 individuals). Québec feminists felt they were unfairly placed in a position of having to make a choice between Canadian feminism and Québec nationalism. Additional tensions resulted from the fact that the FFQ was unable to receive direct federal funding, as the committee does, because it was not considered a "national" group. Québec feminists felt that the FFQ was a national organization.

After much discussion the FFQ and the National Action Committee worked out a compromise on women's equality that would not affect the distinct-society clause of the Meech Lake Accord.[82] The compromise mainly consisted of the Québec women's groups saying that although they did not find it necessary, it would be acceptable to include a statement of guarantee of equality rights in the accord. Despite the compromise, there were still differences of opinion between Canadian women's groups over whether the distinct-society clause threatened Sections 15 and 28. There was concern that a "hierarchy of rights" would be established that would threaten women's equality.[83]

The federal government held public hearings on the Meech Lake Accord and listened to the presentations of various groups, including Québec's women's groups. The Committee on the Constitution's majority report concluded that it did not believe that either gender equality or distinct-society rights would supersede the other, and decided ultimately to leave the matter to the courts.[84] Canadian women who thought that women needed protection that the accord did not guarantee found the issue unresolved. Some Québécoise women felt the Anglo Canadians were inconsiderate and should have stayed out of the issue. They held some resentment at the Canadians' protectionist attitudes.[85]

In 1990, in spite of the support from some Canadian provinces, the Meech Lake Accord was not approved. Québec's immediate response was to form a commission and hold public hearings on the future of Québec. The Commission sur l'avenir politique et constitutionnel du Québec (Commission on the Political and Constitutional Future of Québec) included representatives from the business, trade union, cooperative, educational, and cultural sectors of the province. It received 607 briefs and heard 267 presentations, including many from women's groups.[86] Based on this information, the commission recommended a referendum to be held in 1992 on the question of whether Québec should stay in the federal union or secede. If passed, Québec would become a sovereign state.

Most feminist groups were supporting sovereignty after the failure of the Meech Lake Accord, although some groups did not want to take a stand on the issue.[87] The Fédération des femmes du Québec supported sovereignty. It planned regional meetings in 1992 to outline a coalition and consensus for what feminists were calling *un projet féministe de société* (a feminist project for a new society) that would delineate feminism and women's citizenship within the concept of "distinct society."[88] This project would be an attempt to link feminism, social questions, and independence.[89] FFQ argued that a sovereign Québec must conform to principles of equal rights between women and men, universal suffrage, a political plan that would include decentralizing regions to facilitate more political involvement and equal representation for women, a plan for the judiciary that would include legislation about maternity rights and pornography, and an economic plan that would ensure full employment, fiscal reform, and an attack on poverty and would deal with the international community from *"une perspective pacifiste."*[90]

The Confédération des Syndicats Nationaux (CSN) also favored sovereignty. It felt there were more possibilities of creating social changes through independence than through the centralized government.[91] Their *projet de societé* of its Comité de condition féminine called for equal rights for women, the rights to remunerated work which included equal pay, maternity rights, universal child care, and abortion rights.[92]

In the 1990s many feminist groups were coming together on the issue of sovereignty, but not all contemporary Québec feminists as individuals were in agreement about Québécoise feminist nationalism. Some feminists opted out of the debates and focused solely on feminist struggles because they no longer believed in collective, political action.[93] Some became disenchanted, fearing that the history of women and nationalism meant a return to women's traditional roles, such as the emphasis on natalism to curb the dwindling birth rate.[95] Others believed that the focus on nationalism relegated feminism to secondary status, "in the belief that 'when Québec separates,' women will have absolute equality." They saw the nation-state as patriarchal and pernicious and felt that feminism need not be carried out in relation to a state apparatus.[95]

Dumont argued that the questions facing the constitutional debate necessitated sorting out issues of women's personal and individual citizenship rights from the problems of women's being defined in relation to Québec culture. Nationalist myth views the Québec family as the transmitter of culture, but this confronts actual family realities of spousal and child violence and problems of family economic development.[96]

Some construct their own necessary conditions for a resolution of the issue: Augerot-Arend argued for an "ecofeminism," a concern not only with Québec as land but for an environmental love of land that would protect it from exploitation and domination.[97] Some feminists saw women's values as a form of political power that developed in the context of women's involvement in the private sphere as influential in the development of nationalism—not only through culture transmission, but through networks of solidarity developed to oppose such things as military conscription.[98] For these feminists, women's values (love, compassion, solidarity) must override patriarchal values in order for feminism to be reconciled with nationalism, with some preferring the term *independence* to *nationalism*.[99] Some thought feminism had made such an inroad into society that a backlash was resulting,[100] particularly where men felt changes in the laws regarding separation and child support. Interestingly, men now made their personal experiences with these laws into political issues.[101]

Although there may be some disagreement over analysis, ideologies, and praxis, over the issue of the Constitution and sovereignty there has been coalition-building and action among Québécoises feminists. Unlike early feminists, there is a deepening understanding of the contradictions between feminism and nationalism, although the mainstream Québec women's groups ignored the contradictions in their pragmatic approach to the Constitution.

The contradictions and themes outlined above came to the fore again in the 1995 referendum. Québecers voted in October on a question of whether to form a "new partnership" with Canada, a question that most saw as a *OUI* or *NON* about Québec's sovereign future. Many women's groups openly supported the *OUI* side, some did not take a position, but the referendum barely went down in defeat.

During the referendum debate there were several instances that particularly concerned women. Lucien Bouchard, leader of the *OUI*, stated that the birth rate in Québec was one of the lowest in the world, and that francophone women were not having enough babies (unspoken: to preserve the race). He later tried to explain his statement as a purely demographic observation, to the satisfaction of the president of the FFQ, who appeared with him two days later. However, after this statement, women's presence at the *NON* rallies increased. There were special efforts made on the part of both sides to attract the women's vote, including rallies specifically for women. The *OUI* side had four posters promoting its position, one of which had the "woman" symbol.

As of this writing, it is still unclear exactly how the gender gap played out in the referendum vote. Polls prior to the vote showed that more women intended to vote *NON* than *OUI*, approximately a 10 point difference. This was interpreted variously, but most felt that it was due to two major factors, one economic and one philosophical. Women and their children are much more dependent on the state than are men, both for social assistance plans and for jobs. They knew what the situation was in Canada, and were less certain of the economic future of an independent Québec. In addition, the PQ had not shown particular sensitivity to women's concerns and issues that had been presented. During the referendum of 1995, the threads of the feminist and nationalist identity were, as ever, intertwined.

The relations between Québécoise feminists and other Pan-Canadian women's groups continue to be strained. The unity with Anglo women was hurt by the Meech Lake debate, and Québécoise see their problematics as different from the rest of Canada.[102] The language problem exacerbates this in that many Québécoises do not speak or read English, and many Anglo women do not function in French. Further, not all Québec feminists are nationalists. There is a group of women, many prominent, who are feminists and federalists, and do not want to see Québec split from Canada. This points out the problem with the term *feminist* when it does not account for one's ideology, language, place of birth, and generation.[103] Québécoise feminists argue for the multiplicity of feminisms that affects any conception of feminist nationalism. No single, unilateral feminism would fit every case.[104]

Conclusion

Since the beginning of Québec's history, French-Canadian nationalism has included the struggle for the maintenance of the French Canadian language and cultural autonomy as a majority within their province. Nationalists have sought to maximize their interests both provincially and federally. When the Meech Lake Accord offered the promise of maintaining cultural identity within the federation, Québecers felt there was a federalist option. When that option was removed, they were pushed toward sovereignty.

Feminists have struggled between the varying levels of contradiction between feminism and nationalism. Women hated to pit their love for their cultural heritage and language against their desire for equality rights. When given the chance, they preferred to walk a tightrope between their needs for individual citizen rights and public roles, and their knowledge of the collective needs of the family and state, as well as the interrelation between the two. This was evidenced in earlier clerico-feminist-nationalism and even in later radical feminism. Despite the pro-family, pro-natalism historically built into the coalitions between Church and provincial state, feminists felt that the province has offered them more opportunities for equal rights than the federal government. Certainly this was the case under the French legal traditions, and during the social changes of the 1970s and 1980s. Feminists became cognizant of the ways in which these contradictions might operate in their lives and sought to work out a compromise or balance between them, just as they had sought compromise with non-francophone Canadian feminists.

The political culture in Québec now accepts women's rights and the active, organized women's groups who influence policy. Many women in Québec feel that they can protect their rights and that the government must listen to them. They rely on themselves and their political power to gain and keep their rights.[105] Despite on-going problems, the relationship to the "National" state of Québec, particularly on Constitutional questions, is a strong one. Women are cognizant that these gains might not have been possible without the ties to nationalism. They are proud that their situation in Québec appears to them to be better than in the rest of Canada, and that this is due, in part, to the intertwining of these social movements.

This intertwining may be demonstrated by two additional events. In the summer of 1995, a "Bread and Roses" march took place, organized by a coalition of over eighty women's groups. After they had marched to Québec City, the Premier used the occasion to announce a significant increase in the provincial minimum wage, one of the major demands of the march. In the winter of 1996, a primary issue on the legislative agenda is pay equity, a promise the Parti Québécois had made and must now address.

In their brief to the Special Joint Committee on the Constitution, the Fédération des femmes du Québec argued that the distinct society is a neutral concept within the context of women's rights.[106] The progress of women for many Québécoises is linked to their concept of the distinct society. The threads of feminism and nationalism are so interwoven that even for federalist feminists or the ambivalent or anarchist feminists, the strands are difficult to separate. Whatever the eventual outcome of the sovereignty issue, the future of Québec feminism and its ties to Canada and the international arena will be very much determined by Québec nationalism of the 1990s and whether Québec remains in the confederation of Canada or creates its own nation-state.

Notes

Both authors acknowledge the Québec government for research grants for fieldwork in Québec and thank Micheline de Sève for comments on an earlier draft.

1. Québec feminism can be discussed in stages: early feminism from the latter nineteenth century until 1907; Catholic reformist feminism, 1907–1960; secular feminism, 1960–1969; radical and socialist feminism after 1969. Danielle Couillard, "Féminisme et nationalisme: histoire d'une ambiguité: L'experience du regroupement des femmes Québécoises (1976–1980)" (master's thesis, University of Montréal, 1987), p. 31. According to Micheline de Sève, with the end

241

of the 1970s came the end of *idéologisme* (interview with L. West, Montréal, 1991). Coalition-building and the rise of feminist nationalism and consensus-building mark the late 1980s into the 1990s.

    2. Michel Bélanger and Jean Campeau, *Report of the Commission on the Political and Constitutional Future of Québec* (Montréal: Commission sur l'avenir politique et constitutionnel du Québec, 1991), p. 15.

    3. Jan Noel, "New France: Les femmes favorisées" in *The Neglected Majority*, ed. Alice Prentice and Susan Mann Trofimenkoff (Toronto: McClelland & Stewart, 1985), p. 30.

    4. Conseil du statut de la femme, "La lente progression des femmes" (Québec: Gouvernement du Québec, 1990).

    5. Clio Collective, *Québec Women: A History* (Toronto: Women's Press, 1987), p. 104.

    6. Paul Linteau, Réné Durocher, and Jean-Claude Robert, *Québec: A History, 1867–1929* (Toronto: James Lorimer, 1983).

    7. There was a brief interlude when the Union Nationale ruled, 1936–1939.

    8. Clio Collective, *Québec Women*, p. 160; Linteau, Durocher, and Robert, *Québec*, p. 189.

    9. Clio Collective, *Québec Women*, p. 187.

    10. Ibid. p. 250.

    11. Linteau, Durocher, and Robert, *Québec*, p. 447.

    12. Susan Trofimenkoff, *Dream of a Nation* (Toronto: Gage, 1983), p. 189.

    13. Linteau, Durocher, and Robert, *Québec*, p. 446.

    14. Diane Lamoureaux, "Nationalism and Feminism in Québec: An Impossible Attraction," in *Feminism and Political Economy*, ed. Heather Jon Maroney and Meg Luxton (Toronto: Methuen, 1987), p. 59.

    15. Trofimenkoff, *Dream of a Nation*, p. 187.

    16. Sylvie Augerot-Arend, "Concilier nationalisme et féminisme: un defi pour le Québec de l'avenir," *L'action nationale* 81 (1991): 56–68.

    17. Trofimenkoff, *Dream of a Nation*, p. 263.

    18. Clio Collective, *Québec Women*, p. 263.

    19. Cardinal Villeneuve's communiqué, March 1, 1940, ibid. p. 265.

    20. Ibid., p. 282.

    21. Ibid., p. 284; Alison Prentice, Paula Bourne, Gail Cuthbert Brandt, Beth Light, Wendy Mitchinson, and Naomi Black, *Canadian Women: A History* (Toronto: Harcourt Brace Jovanovich, 1988), p. 299.

    22. The Union Nationale Party took over from the Liberals in 1944 and ruled until 1959.

    23. Prentice et al., *Canadian Women*, p. 328.

    24. Clio Collective, *Québec Women*, p. 304.

    25. Ibid., p. 330.

26. Hubert Guidon, *Québec Society: Tradition, Modernity and Nationhood* (Toronto: University of Toronto Press, 1988).

27. Dominique Clift, *The declin du nationalisme au Québec* (Montréal: Les Quinze, 1991).

28. Simon Langlois, "Québec Society: Recent Trends and Changes" (paper presented at the Canadian Studies Center, Duke University, November 1989).

29. Louis Balthazar, "French Canadian Civilizations," Association for Canadian Studies in the United States Papers (Provo: Brigham Young University Press, 1989).

30. In 1971 an anglophone earned 64 percent more than a francophone; Torfimenkoff, *Dream of a Nation*, p. 318.

31. Lamoureaux, *Nationalism and Feminism in Québec*, p. 53.

32. Balthazar, "French Canadian Civilization."

33. Denis Moniere, quoted in Couillard, "Féminisme et nationalisme," p. 35.

34. Trofimenkoff, "Féminisme et nationalisme," p. 318.

35. Prentice et al., *Canadian Women*, pp. 321–322.

36. Lamoureux, "Nationalism and Feminism in Québec," p. 56.

37. de Sève, interview with L. West, 1991.

38. Prentice et al., *Canadian Women*.

39. Clio Collective, *Québec Women*, p. 360.

40. Heather Jon Maroney and Meg Luxon, eds., *Feminism and Political Economy*, (Toronto: Methuen, 1988).

41. Claudie Solar, interview with L. West, Concordia University, Montreal, 1991.

42. Lamoureaux, "Nationalism and Feminism in Québec," p. 60.

43. Ibid., p. 66.

44. Ibid., p. 54.

45. Couillard, "Féminisme et nationalisme," p. 48.

46. Clio Collective, *Québec Women*, p. 361.

47. Trofimenkoff, *Dream of a Nation*.

48. Couillard, "Féminisme et nationalisme."

49. Prentice et al., *Candian Women*.

50. Mariangela Di Domenico, interview with L. West, Conseil du statut de la femme, Montréal, 1991.

51. Conseil du statut de la femme, "Pour les Québecoises: égalité et indépendence" (Québec City: Government du Québec," 1978).

52. Lamoureaux, "Nationalism and Feminism in Québec," pp. 60–61.

53. Di Domenico, interview with L. West, 1991.

54. Monique Simard, interview with L. West, Conféderation des syndicats nationaux, Montréal, 1991.

55. Trofimenkoff, *Dream of a Nation*.

56. Linteau, Durocher, and Robert, *Québec*.

57. Sue Findlay, "Feminist Struggles with the Canadian State: 1966–1988," *Resources for Feminist Research/Documentation sur la recherche féministe* 17, no. 3 (1988).

58. Balthazar, "French Canadian Civilization."

59. Lysiane Gagnon, *Vivre avec les hommes* (Montréal; Québec/Amerique, 1983).

60. Lamoureux, "Nationalism and Feminism in Québec."

61. Couillard, "Féminisme et nationalisme," p. 63. They advocated on behalf of an Algerian woman who was drugged and kidnapped by her Algerian family, who disapproved of her marriage and sought to return her to Algeria.

62. Ibid., p. 90.

63. Ibid.

64. Michele Jean, Jacqueline Lamothe, Marie Lavigne, and Jennifer Stoddart, "Nationalism and Feminism in Québec: The 'Yvettes' Phenomenon," in *The Politics of Diversity: Feminism, Marxism, and Nationalism* ed. Roberta Hamilton and Michele Barrett (London: Verso 1986), pp. 322–388.

65. de Sève, interview with L. West, 1991.

66. Penny Kome, *The Taking of Twenty-Eight* (Toronto: Toronto Women's Press, 1983).

67. Roberta Hamilton and Michele Barrett, introduction to Hamilton and Barrett, *The Politics of Diversity*, p. 24.

68. de Sève, interview with L. West, 1991.

69. Jean et al., "Nationalism and Feminism in Quebec," p. 338.

70. Simard, interview with L. West, 1991.

71. de Sève, interview with L. West, 1991.

72. Simard, interview with L. West, 1991.

73. Di Domenico, interview with L. West, 1991.

74. Simard, interview with L. West, 1991.

75. Bélanger and Campeau, *Report of the Commission on the Political and Constitutional Future of Québec*, pp. 31–32.

76. Ibid. p. 36.

77. Barbara Roberts, *Smooth Sailing or Storm Warnings? Canadian and Québec Women's Groups on the Meech Lake Accord* (Ottawa: Canadian Research Institute for the Advancement of Women, 1988).

78. Chaviva Hösek, "Women and the Constitutional Process," in *And No One Cheered* ed. Keith Banting and Richard Simeon, (Toronto: Methuen, 1983).

79. Di Domenico, interview with L. West, 1991.

80. Andrée Levesque, interview with P. LeClerc, 1987.

81. Quoted in Roberts, *Smooth Sailing or Storm Warnings?*, p. 4.

82. Ibid., p. 14.

83. Ibid., p. 17.

84. Ibid., p. 22.

85. Micheline de Sève personal communication with P. LeClerc, 1990.

86. Bélanger and Campeau, *Report of the Commission on the Political and Constitutional Future of Québec*, pp. 4–5.

87. There are many position papers on the Constitution from women's groups. We will list only several here, but see also papers such as the Centre pour femmes immigrants, *Considérations inopportunes sur l'exclusion de la population immigreé des grands débats de la société québecoise* (October 1990); Comite d'action politiques des femmes du parti québecois, *Mémoire à la commission parlementaire élargie sur l'avenir politique et constitutionnel du Québec* (November 1990); Regroupement des femmes de la Côte-Nord, Inc., *Mémoire à la commission parlementaire sur l'avenir politique constitutionnel du Québec* (October 31, 1990); Le conseil des femmes de Montréal, *Mémoire à la commission sur l'avenir politique et constitutionnel du Québec* (November 1990); L'Association des femmes d'affaires du Québec, *Mémoire* (November 2, 1990).

88. Micheline Dumont argued there was ambiguity in the "distinct society" concept. Dumont, "L'expérience historique des femmes dans le présent débat constitutionnel" (text presented to the Constitutional Commission, Montréal, 1990); also, personal communication with P. LeClerc, 1990.

89. Elaine Audet interview with L. West, Montréal, 1991. See also Audet, "Feminisme et question nationale," *L'Aut Journal* 88 (1990).

90. Fédération des femmes du Québec, "Mémoire présente à la commission sur l'avenir politique et constitutionnel du Québec" (Montréal, 1990), p. iii.

91. Simard, interview with L. West, 1991.

92. Comité de condition féminine, "L'independence, manifeste, notre manière d'y voir!" (Montréal: Confédération des Syndicats Nationaux, 1991).

93. Audet, interview with L. West, 1991.

94. Andrée Lévesque personal correspondence with L. West, 1991.

95. Greta Hofmann-Nemiroff personal correspondence with L. West, 1991.

96. See the interesting discussion in Micheline Dumont, "The Women's Movement Then and Now" (Ottawa: Canadian Research Institute for the Advancement of Women, 1990).

97. Augerot-Arend, "Concilier nationalisme et féminisme."

98. Yolande Cohen, "Thoughts on Women and Power," in *From Pressure to Politics*, ed. Angela R. Miles and Geraldine Finn (Montreal: Black Rose Books, 1989), p. 365.

99. Audet, "Féminisme et question nationale"; interview with L. West, 1991.

100. Feminists believed their impact on Québec resulted in a social backlash that was manifested in a massacre of feminists on December 6, 1989. Fourteen women were murdered in Montréal at the École Polytechnique by a man who had a "hit list" of "feminists, who have always ruined my life." See Louise Malette

and Marie Chalouh, eds., *The Montréal Massacre*, trans. Marlene Wildeman (Charlottetown, Prince Edward Island: Gynergy Books, 1991), p. 180. (French edition: Louise Malette and Marie Chalouh, eds., *Polytechnique, 6 décembre* [Montréal: Les Editions du remue-ménage, 1990]). There was some sense that "women went too far and that's why the boy went too far," de Sève, interview with L. West, 1991. Feminists felt that the media presented the murders as the act of a sole madman, but feminists wanted some analysis of the significance of the man's motives and backlash against feminism to be discussed in the media. They believed there was censorship by the mainstream presses, so they published a French-language version of their analysis, and an English version followed that included the text of the murderer's suicide note, which had been withheld from the press for almost a year after the event. Ramifications continued to be felt two years later when a male student who was despondent about the deaths of his friends committed suicide. His parents, distraught over his death, also committed suicide. See Tu Thanh Ha, "Polytechnique Toll Continues to Climb," *Montréal: The Gazette*, July 17, 1991, p. Al.

101. de Sève, interview with L. West, 1991.

102. Micheline Dumont personal communication with P. LeClerc, 1990.

103. Sylvie Augerot-Arend, "Féministes et l'état canadien: tensions théorique et divergencies pratiques," *Resources for Feminist Research/Documentation sur la recherche féminin* 17, no. 3 (1988): 22–25.

104. Lamoureaux, "Nationalism and Feminism in Quebec," p. 64; Andrée Yanacopoulo personal communication with L. West, 1991.

105. Roberts, *Smooth Sailing or Storm Warnings?*.

106. Fédération des femmes du Québec, "Presentation to the Joint Committee of the Senate and the House of Commons on the Constitutional Accord of 1987" (Montréal, 1987).

The Development of
Chicana Feminist Discourse

Alma M. Garcia

Between 1970 and 1980 a Chicana feminist movement developed in the United States that addressed the specific issues that affected Chicanas as women of color. During the 1960s, the Chicano movement, characterized by a politics of protest, came into being,[1] and focused on a wide range of issues: social justice, equality, educational reforms, and political and economic self-determination for Chicano communities in the United States. Various struggles evolved within the Chicano movement: the United Farmworkers' unionization efforts;[2] the New Mexico Land Grant movement;[3] the Colorado-based Crusade for Justice;[4] the Chicano student movement;[5] and the Raza Unida Party.[6]

Chicanas were active in each of these struggles. By the end of the 1960s, Chicanas began to assess the rewards and limits of their participation. The 1970s witnessed the development of Chicana feminists whose activities, organizations, and writings can be analyzed in terms of a feminist movement by women of color in American society. Chicana feminists outlined a cluster of ideas that crystallized into an emergent Chicana feminist debate. In the same way that Chicano males were reinterpreting their historical and contemporary U.S. experience, Chicanas began to investigate the forces shaping their own experiences as women of color.

In the 1960s and 1970s, the American political scene observed far-reaching social protest movements whose political courses often paralleled and at times exerted influence over one another.[7] The development of feminist movements has been explained by the participation of women in larger social movements. Macias, for example, links the early development of the Mexican feminist movement to the participation of women in the Mexican Revolution.[8] Black feminists have traced the development of a Black feminist movement during the 1960s and 1970s to their experiences with sexism in the larger Black movement.[9] Similarly, the origins of Chicana feminism emerged as a result of the Chicano movement's dynamics.

Origins of Chicana Feminism

Rowbotham argues that women may develop a feminist consciousness as a result of their experiences with sexism in revolutionary struggles or mass social movements.[10] Chicana feminists began the search for a "room of their own" by assessing their participation within the Chicano movement. Their feminist consciousness emerged from a struggle for equality with Chicano men and from a reassessment of the role of the family as a means of resistance to oppressive societal conditions.

Historically, as well as during the 1960s and 1970s, the Chicano family represented a source of cultural and political resistance to the various types of discrimination experienced in the American society.[11] At the cultural level, the Chicano movement emphasized the need to safeguard the value of family loyalty. At the political level, the movement used the family as a strategic organizational tool for protest activities.

As women began to question their traditional female roles,[12] dramatic changes in the structure of Chicano families occurred. Thus, a Chicana feminist movement originated from the nationalist Chicano struggle: Rowbotham refers to such a feminist movement as "a colony within a colony."[13] But as the Chicano movement developed during the 1970s, Chicana feminists began to draw up their own political agenda and entered into a dialogue with the movement that explicitly reflected their struggles to secure a room of their own within it.

Defining Feminism for Women of Color

The lack of consensus on the definition of feminism is reflective of the different political ideologies and divergent social-class bases. Chicana feminists shared the task of defining their ideology and movement with white, Black, and Asian American feminists. Like them, Chicana feminists struggled to gain social equality and to end sexist and racist oppression. Like them, Chicana feminists recognized that the nature of social inequality for women of color was multidimensional.[14] And like Black and Asian American feminists, Chicana feminists struggled to gain equal status in the male-dominated nationalist movements and also in the American society. To Chicana feminists, feminism was a movement to end sexist oppression within a broader social protest movement. Again, like Black and Asian American feminists, Chicana feminists understood that their movement needed to go beyond women's rights and include the men of their group, who also faced racial subordination.[15] Chicanas believed that feminism involved more than an analysis of gender because, as women of color, they were affected by both race and class in their everyday lives. Thus, Chicana feminism represented a struggle that was both nationalist and feminist.

Ngan-Ling Chow identifies gender stereotypes of Asian American women and the patriarchal family structure as major sources of women's oppression.[16] Cultural, political, and economic constraints have, according to Ngan-Ling Chow, limited the full development of a feminist consciousness and movement among Asian American women. The cross-pressures resulting from the demands of a nationalist and a feminist struggle led some Asian American women to organize feminist organizations that, however, continued to address broader issues affecting the Asian American community.

Black women were also faced with addressing feminist issues within a nationalist movement. According to Thornton Dill, Black women played a major historical role in Black resistance movements and, in addition, brought a feminist component to these movements.[17] Black women have struggled with Black men in nationalist movements but have also recognized and fought against the sexism in such political movements in the Black community.[18] Although they wrote and spoke as Black feminists, they did not organize separately from Black men.

Among the major ideological questions facing all three groups of feminists were the relationship between feminism and the ideology of cultural nationalism or racial pride; feminism and feminist-baiting within the larger movements; and the relationship between their feminist movements and the white feminist movement.

Chicana Feminism and Cultural Nationalism

During the 1960s and 1970s, Chicana feminists responded to the criticism that Chicano cultural nationalism and feminism were irreconcilable. Cultural nationalism represented a major, but not monolithic, component of the Chicano movement. It emphasized cultural pride, resistance, and survival within an Anglo-dominated nation-state. Thus, cultural nationalism shaped the political direction of the Chicano social protest movement. Sharing ideological roots with Black cultural nationalism, Chicanismo, as Chicano cultural nationalism became known, advocated a movement of cultural renaissance and resistance within Chicano communities throughout the United States. Chicanismo emphasized Mexican cultural pride as a source of political unity and strength capable of mobilizing Chicanos as an oppositional political group within the dominant American political landscape. Thus, Chicanismo provided a framework for the development of a collective ethnic consciousness—the essence of any nationalist ideology—that challenged the ideological hegemony of Anglo America. Moreover, Chicano cultural nationalism situated the sociohistorical experiences of Chicanos within a theoretical model of internal colonialism. Chicano communities were analyzed as ethnic "nations" existing under direct exploitation by the dominant society. "Nationalism, therefore, was to be the common denominator for uniting all Mexican Americans and making possible effective political mobilization."[19]

By the late 1960s Chicano cultural nationalism had successfully united various factions within the Chicano social protest movement. Specifically, Chicanismo became the ideological force behind numerous university-student strikes under the leadership of such student organizations as MEChA. Nevertheless, Chicano cultural nationalism came under dramatic ideological scrutiny:

> The ideology of Chicanismo had settled the internal confusion over identity. But in spite of this tremendous accomplishment Chicanismo could

not even begin to answer the substantive questions concerning the ultimate shape of a political ideology and strategy that could take into account
the diversity of political orientations. . . . There is no question that Chicanismo propelled the movement's politics against racism. But . . . it did
not offer a framework for the concrete analysis of the dominant political
and economic institutions of US society.[20]

Chicana feminists were among those who began to voice ideological disagreements with a Chicano cultural nationalist political framework. They
challenged Chicanismo by formulating an analytical framework which
focused on the interrelationship of race and gender.

In the first issue of the newspaper *Hijas de Cuauhtemoc*, Anna Nieto
Gomez stated that a major issue facing Chicanas active in the Chicano
movement was the need to organize to improve their status as women
within the movement.[21] Francisca Flores, another leading Chicana feminist, stated:

[Chicanas] can no longer remain in a subservient role or as auxiliary forces
in the [Chicano] movement. They must be included in the front line of
communication, leadership and organizational responsibility. . . . The issue
of equality, freedom and self-determination of the Chicana—like the right
of self-determination, equality, and liberation of the Mexican [Chicano]
community—is not negotiable. Anyone opposing the right of women to
organize into their own form of organization has no place in the leadership
of the movement.[21]

Supporting this position, Bernice Rincon argued that a Chicana feminist
movement that sought equality and justice for Chicanas would strengthen
the Chicano movement.[22] Yet in the process, Chicana feminists challenged traditional gender roles because they limited their participation
and acceptance within the Chicano movement.

Nieto Gomez said,

Chicana feminism is in various stages of development. However, in general, Chicana feminism is the recognition that women are oppressed as a
group and are exploited as part of la Raza people. It is a direction to be responsible to identify and act upon the issues and needs of Chicana women.
Chicana feminists are involved in understanding the nature of women's oppression.[23]

One source of ideological disagreement between Chicana feminism and this cultural nationalist ideology was cultural survival. Many Chicana feminists believed that a focus on cultural survival did not acknowledge the need to alter male-female relations within Chicano communities. For example, Chicana feminists criticized the notion of the "ideal Chicana" that glorified Chicanas as strong, long-suffering women who had endured and kept Chicano culture and the family intact. To Chicana feminists, this concept represented an obstacle to the redefinition of gender roles. Nieto Gomez stated:

> Some Chicanas are praised as they emulate the sanctified example set by [the Virgin] Mary. The woman par excellence is mother and wife. She is to love and support her husband and to nurture and teach her children. Thus, may she gain fulfillment as a woman. For a Chicana bent upon fulfillment of her personhood, this restricted perspective of her role as a woman is not only inadequate but crippling.[24]

Chicana feminists were also skeptical about the cultural nationalist interpretation of machismo. Such an interpretation viewed machismo as an ideological tool used by the dominant Anglo society to justify the inequalities experienced by Chicanos. According to this interpretation, the relationship between Chicanos and the larger society was that of an internal colony dominated and exploited by the capitalist economy.[25] Machismo, like other cultural traits, was blamed by Anglos for blocking Chicanos from succeeding in the American society. In reality, the economic structure and colony-like exploitation were to blame.

Some Chicana feminists agreed with this analysis of machismo, asserting that a mutually reinforcing relationship existed between internal colonialism and the development of the myth of machismo. According to Sosa Riddell, machismo was a myth "propagated by subjugators and colonizers, which created damaging stereotypes of Mexican/Chicano males."[26] As a type of social control imposed by the dominant society the myth of machismo distorted gender relations within Chicano communities, creating stereotypes of Chicanas as passive and docile women. As Nieto concluded: "Although the term 'machismo' is correctly denounced by all because it stereotypes the Latin man . . . it does a great disservice to both men and women. Chicano and Chicana alike must be free to seek their own individual fulfillment.[27]

Some Chicana feminists criticized the myth of machismo used by the dominant society to legitimate racial inequality, but others moved beyond this level of analysis to distinguish between the machismo that oppressed both men and women and the sexism in Chicano communities in general, and the Chicano movement in particular, that oppressed Chicana women.[28] According to Vidal, the origins of a Chicana feminist consciousness were prompted by the sexist attitudes and behavior of Chicano males, which constituted a "serious obstacle to women anxious to play a role in the struggle for Chicana liberation."[29]

Furthermore, many Chicana feminists disagreed with the cultural nationalist view that machismo could be a positive value within a Chicano cultural value system. They challenged the notion that machismo was a source of masculine pride for Chicanos and therefore a defense mechanism against the dominant society's racism. Chicana feminists called for changes in the ideologies responsible for distorting relations between women and men. One such change was to modify the cultural nationalist position that looked upon machismo as a source of cultural pride.

Chicana feminists called for a focus on the universal aspects of sexism that shape gender relations in both Anglo and Chicano culture. Although they acknowledged the economic exploitation of all Chicanos, they outlined the double exploitation experienced by Chicanas. Sosa Riddell concluded: "It was when Chicanas began to seek work outside of the family groups that sexism became a key factor of oppression along with racism."[30] Francisca Flores summarized some of the consequences of sexism:

> It is not surprising that more and more Chicanas are forced to go to work in order to supplement the family income. The children are farmed out to a relative to baby-sit with them, and since these women are employed in the lower income jobs, the extra pressure placed on them can become unbearable.[31]

Thus, while the Chicano movement was addressing the issue of racial oppression facing all Chicanos, Chicana feminists argued that it lacked an analysis of sexism. Similarly, Black and Asian American women stressed the interconnectedness of race and gender oppression. The writings of Black feminists criticized a Black cultural nationalist ideology that overlooked the consequences of sexist oppression.[32] Many Asian American women were also critical of the Asian American movement, whose focus on racism ignored the impact of sexism on the daily lives of women. The participation of Asian American women in various community struggles increased their encounters with sexism.[33]

Alma M. Garcia

Chicana Feminism and Feminist Baiting

The systematic analysis by Chicana feminists of the impact of racism and sexism on Chicanas within American society and, above all, within the Chicano movement was often misunderstood as a threat to the political unity of the Chicano movement. But Marta Cotera a leading voice of Chicana feminism pointed out:

> The aggregate cultural values we [Chicanas] share can also work to our benefit if we choose to scrutinize our cultural traditions, isolate the positive attributes and interpret them for the benefit of women. It's unreal that Hispanas have been browbeaten for so long about our so-called conservative (meaning reactionary) culture. It's also unreal that we have let men interpret culture only as those practices and attitudes that determine who does the dishes around the house. We as women also have the right to interpret and define the philosophical and religious traditions beneficial to us within our culture, and which we have inherited as our tradition. To do this, we must become both conversant with our history and philosophical evolution, and analytical about the institutional and behavioral manifestations of the same.[34]

Such Chicana feminists were attacked for developing a "divisive ideology"—a feminist ideology that was frequently viewed as a threat to the Chicano movement as a whole. As Chicana feminists examined their roles as women activists within the Chicano movement, an ideological split developed. One group saw itself as "loyalists" who believed that the Chicano movement did not have to deal with sexual inequities because Chicano men as well as Chicano women experienced racial oppression. According to Nieto Gomez, who was not a loyalist, their belief was that if men oppress women, it is not the men's fault but rather that of the system.[35]

Even if such a problem existed, and they did not believe that it did, the loyalists maintained that such a matter would best be resolved internally, within the Chicano movement. They denounced the formation of a separate Chicana feminist movement on the grounds that it was a politically dangerous strategy, perhaps Anglo-inspired. Such a movement would undermine the unity of the Chicano movement by raising an issue that was not seen as central. Loyalists viewed racism as the most important issue within the Chicano movement. Nieto Gomez quotes one such loyalist:

I am concerned with the direction that the Chicanas are taking in the movement. The words such as liberation, sexism, male chauvinism, etc., were prevalent. The terms mentioned above plus the theme of individualism is a concept of the Anglo society; terms prevalent in the Anglo women's movement. The familia has always been our strength in our culture. But it seems evident . . . that you [Chicana feminists] are not concerned with the familia, but are influenced by the Anglo woman's movement.[36]

Chicana feminists were also accused of undermining the values associated with Chicano culture. Loyalists saw the Chicana feminist movement as an "anti-family, anti-cultural, anti-man and therefore an anti-Chicano movement."[37] Feminism was, above all, believed to be an individualistic search for identity that detracted from the Chicano movement's "real" issues, such as racism. Nieto Gomez quotes a loyalist: "And since when does a Chicana need identity? If you are a real Chicana then no one regardless of the degrees needs to tell you about it. The only ones who need identity are the vendidas, the falsas, and the opportunists."[38]

The ideological conflicts between Chicana feminists and loyalists persisted throughout the 1970s, exacerbated during various Chicana conferences. At times, such confrontations served to increase Chicana feminist activity that challenged the loyalists' attacks, yet these attacks also served to suppress feminist activities.

Chicana feminist lesbians experienced even stronger attacks from those who viewed feminism as a divisive ideology. In a political climate that already viewed feminist ideology with suspicion, lesbianism as a sexual lifestyle and political ideology came under even more attack. Clearly, a cultural nationalist ideology that perpetuated such stereotypical images of Chicanas as "good wives and good mothers" found it difficult to accept a Chicana feminist lesbian movement.

Cherríe Moraga's writings during the 1970s reflect the struggles of Chicana feminist lesbians, who, together with other Chicana feminists, were finding the sexism evident within the Chicano movement intolerable. Just as Chicana feminists analyzed their life circumstances as members of an ethnic minority and as women, Chicana feminist lesbians addressed themselves to the oppression they experienced as lesbians. As Moraga stated:

My lesbianism is the avenue through which I have learned the most about silence and oppression. . . . In this country, lesbianism is a poverty—as is being brown, as is being a woman, as is being just plain poor. The danger

255

lies in ranking the oppressions. The danger lies in failing to acknowledge the specificity of the oppression.[39]

As they organized around feminist struggles, women of color encountered criticism from both male and female cultural nationalists, who often viewed feminism as little more than an "antimale" ideology. Lesbianism was identified as an extreme derivation of feminism. A direct connection was frequently made: feminism and lesbianism are synonymous. Feminists were labeled lesbians, and lesbians, feminists. Attacks against feminists—Chicanas, Blacks, and Asian Americans—derived from the existence of homophobia within each of these communities. As lesbian women of color published their writings, attacks against them increased.[40]

Responses to such attacks varied within and between the feminist movements of women of color. Some groups tried one strategy and later adopted another. Some lesbians pursued a separatist strategy within their own racial and ethnic communities;[41] others attempted to form lesbian coalitions across racial and ethnic lines. Both strategies represented a response to the marginalization of lesbians produced by recurring waves of homophobic sentiments in Chicano, Black, and Asian American communities.[42] A third response consisted of working within the broader nationalist movements in these communities and the feminist movements within them in order to challenge their heterosexual biases and resultant homophobia. Moraga challenged the white feminist movement to examine its racist tendencies; the Chicano movement, its sexist tendencies; and both, their homophobic tendencies. In this way, she argued, movements would begin to respect diversity within their own ranks.[43]

Chicana feminists as well as Chicana feminist lesbians continued to be labeled *vendidas*, or "sellouts." Chicana loyalists continued to view Chicana feminism as associated not only with melting into white society but, more seriously, with dividing the Chicano movement. Similarly, many Chicano males were convinced that Chicana feminism was a divisive ideology incompatible with Chicano cultural nationalism. Nieto Gomez said that "[with] respect to [the] Chicana feminist, their credibility is reduced when they are associated with [feminism] and white women." She added that as a result, Chicana feminists often faced harassment and ostracism within the Chicano movement.[44] Similarly, Cotera stated that Chicanas "are suspected of assimilating into the feminist ideology of an alien [white] culture that actively seeks our cultural domination."[45]

Chicana feminists responded quickly and often vehemently to such charges. Flores answered, in an editorial, that birth control, abortion, and sex education are not merely "white issues." Reacting to the accusation that feminists were responsible for the "betrayal of [Chicano] culture and heritage," Flores said, "Our culture hell"—a phrase that became a dramatic slogan of the Chicana feminist movement.[46]

Chicana feminists' defense throughout the 1970s against those declaring that a feminist movement was divisive for the Chicano movement was to reassess their roles within the Chicano movement and to call for an end to male domination. Their challenges of traditional gender roles represented a means to achieve equality.[47] To increase the participation of and opportunities for women in the Chicano movement, feminists agreed that both Chicanos and Chicanas had to address the issue of gender inequality.[48] Furthermore, Chicana feminists argued that the resistance that they encountered reflected the existence of sexism on the part of Chicano males and the antifeminist attitudes of the Chicana loyalists. Nieto Gomez, in reviewing the experiences of Chicana feminists in the Chicano movement, concluded that Chicanas "involved in discussing and applying the women's question have been ostracized, isolated and ignored." She argued that "in organizations where cultural nationalism is extremely strong, Chicana feminists experience intense harassment and ostracism."[49] Black and Asian American women also faced severe criticism as they pursued feminist issues in their own communities. Indeed, as their participation in collective efforts to end racial oppression increased, so did their confrontations with sexism.[50]

Chicana Feminists and White Feminists

The historical relationship between Chicana feminists and white feminists developed along problematic, if not contentious, lines. A major ideological tension between them involved the analysis by Chicana feminists of their experiences as both women and members of an ethnic community. Although Chicana feminists were critical of the patriarchal tendencies within the Chicano cultural nationalist movement, their feminist writings reveal a constant focus on the nature and consequences of racism on their daily lives, as well as on the role of a modified nationalist response as a form of resistance against the pernicious effects of racism.

Chicana feminists struggled to develop a feminist ideology that would successfully integrate race and gender as analytical tools. Feminism and nationalism were seen as political ideologies that could complement each other and, therefore, provide a more sharply focused view of the structural conditions of inequality experienced by Chicanas in American society. To the extent that Chicana feminists viewed the white feminist movement as incapable of integrating women of color and their nationalist struggles, political coalitions between the two groups appeared impossible. Nevertheless, Chicana feminists engaged in an ideological dialogue with white feminists.

It is difficult to determine the extent to which Chicana feminists sympathized with the white feminist movement. A 1976 study by the University of San Diego of the attitudes of Chicanas regarding the white feminist movement found that the majority of respondents believed that it had affected their lives. In addition, they identified with such key issues as the right to legal abortion on demand and access to low-cost birth control. Nevertheless, "even though the majority of Chicanas . . . could relate to certain issues of the women's movement, for the most part they saw it as being an elitist movement [comprising] white middle-class women who [saw] the oppressor as the males of this country."[51]

Some Chicana feminists considered the possibility of entering into coalitions with white feminists as their attempts to work within the Chicano movement were suppressed. Because white feminists were themselves struggling against sexism, such coalitions were seen as an alternative strategy for Chicana feminists.[52] Almost immediately, however, Chicana feminists recognized potential problems. As Longeaux y Vasquez acknowledged, "Some of our own Chicanas may be attracted to the white woman's liberation movement, but we really don't feel comfortable there. We want to be a Chicana *primero* [first]."[53] For other Chicanas, the demands of white women were "irrelevant to the Chicana movement"[54]

Several issues made coalition-building difficult. First, Chicana feminists criticized what they considered to be a cornerstone of white feminist thought: an emphasis on gender oppression to explain the life circumstances of women. Chicana feminists believed that the white feminist movement overlooked the effects of racial oppression experienced by Chicanas and other women of color. Thus, Del Castillo maintained that the Chicana feminist movement was "different primarily because we are [racially] oppressed people."[55] In addition, Chicana feminists criticized white feminists who believed that a general women's movement would be able to overcome racial differences among women. Chicanas interpreted this as a failure by the white feminist movement to deal with racism. Without the incorporation of an analysis of racial oppression to explain the experiences of Chicanas as well as of other women of color, a coalition with white feminists would be highly unlikely.[56] Longeaux y Vasquez concluded: "We must have a clearer vision of our plight and certainly we cannot blame our men for the oppression of the women."[57]

In the 1970s Chicana feminists reconciled their demands for an end to sexism within the Chicano movement and their rejection of the saliency of gender oppression by separating the two issues. They clearly identified the struggle against sexism in the Chicano movement as a major issue: sexism prevented their full participation.[58] They also argued that sexist behavior and ideology on the part of both Chicano males and Anglos represented the key to understanding women's oppression. However, they remained critical of an analysis of women's experiences that focused exclusively on gender oppression.

Chicana feminists adopted an analysis that began with race as a critical variable in interpreting the experiences of Chicano communities in the United States. They expanded this analysis by identifying gender as a variable interconnected with race in analyzing the specific daily life circumstances of Chicanas in Chicano communities. They did not view women's struggles as secondary to the nationalist movement but argued instead for an analysis of race and gender as multiple sources of oppression.[59] Thus, Chicana feminism went beyond the limits of an exclusively racial theory of oppression that tended to overlook gender and also beyond the limits of a theory of oppression based exclusively on gender that tended to overlook race.

A second factor preventing an alliance between Chicana feminists and white feminists was the middle-class orientation of white feminists. Throughout the 1970s Chicana feminists viewed the white feminist movement as a middle-class movement.[60] In contrast, they viewed the Chicano movement in general as a working-class movement. They repeatedly made reference to the difference, and many began their works with a section disassociating themselves from the "women's liberation movement." Chicana feminists as activists in the broader Chicano movement identified as major struggles the farmworkers' movement, welfare rights, undocumented workers, and prisoners' rights. Such issues were seen as far removed from the demands of the white feminist movement, and Chicana feminists could not get white feminist organizations to deal with them.[61]

White feminist organizations were also accused of being exclusionary, patronizing, or racist in their dealings with Chicanas and other women of color. Cotera states:

> Minority women could fill volumes with examples of put-downs, put-ons, and out-and-out racism shown to them by the leadership in the [white feminist] movement. There are three major problem areas in the minority-majority relationship in the movement: (1) paternalism or materialism, (2) extremely limited opportunities for minority women . . . , (3) outright discrimination against minority women in the movement.[62]

Although Chicana feminists continued to be critical of building coalitions with white feminists toward the end of the seventies, they acknowledged the diversity of ideologies within the white feminist movement. Chicana feminists sympathetic to radical socialist feminism because of its anticapitalist framework wrote of working-class oppression that cut across racial and ethnic lines. Their later writings discussed the possibility of joining with white working-class women, but strategies for forming such political coalitions were not made explicit.[63]

Del Castillo and other Chicana feminists favored coalitions between Chicanas and other women of color while keeping their respective autonomous organizations. Such coalitions would recognize the inherent racial oppression of capitalism rather than universal gender oppression. When Longeaux y Vasquez stated that she was "Chicana *primero*," she was stressing the saliency of race over gender in explaining the oppression experienced by Chicanas. The word *Chicana*, however, simultaneously expresses a woman's race and gender. Not until later in the 1980s would Chicana feminist ideology call for an analysis that stressed the interrelationship of race, class, and gender in explaining the conditions of Chicanas in American society, just as Black and Asian American feminists have done.[64]

Chicana feminists continued to stress the importance of developing autonomous feminist organizations that would address the struggles of Chicanas as members of an ethnic minority and as women. Rather than attempt to overcome the obstacles to coalition-building between Chicana feminists and white feminists, Chicanas called for autonomous feminist organizations for all women of color.[65] Chicana feminists believed that sisterhood was indeed powerful but only to the extent that racial and class differences were understood and, above all, respected. Nieto concludes: "The Chicana must demand that dignity and respect within the women's rights movement which allows her to practice feminism within the context of her own culture. . . . Her approaches to feminism must be drawn from her own world."[66]

Chicana Feminism: An Evolving Future

Chicana feminists, like Black, Asian American, and Native American feminists, experience specific life conditions that are distinct from those of white feminists. Socioeconomic and cultural differences in Chicano communities directly shaped the development of Chicana feminism and the relationship between Chicana feminists and feminists of other racial and ethnic groups, including white feminists. Future dialogue among all feminists will require a shared understanding of the existing differences as well as of the similarities. Like other women of color, Chicana feminists must address issues that specifically affect them as women of color. In addition, Chicana feminists must address issues that have particular impact on Chicano communities, such as poverty, limited opportunities for higher education, high school dropouts, health care, bilingual education, immigration reform, prison reform, welfare, and recently, United States policies in Central America.

At the academic level, an increasing number of Chicana feminists continue to join in a collective effort to carry on the feminist legacy inherited from the 1970s. In June 1982 a group of Chicana academics organized the national feminist organization Mujeres Activas en Letras y Cambio Social (MALCS) in order to build a support network for Chicana professors, undergraduates, and graduate students. The organization's major goal is to fight the race, class, and gender oppression facing Chicanas in institutions of higher education. In addition, MALCS aims to bridge the gap between academic work and the Chicano community.

In 1984 the national conference of the National Association for Chicano Studies (NACS), held in Austin, Texas, adopted the theme "*Voces de la Mujer*" in response to demands from the Chicana Caucus. As a result, for the first time since its founding in 1972, the NACS national conference addressed the issue of women. Compared with past conferences, a large number of Chicanas participated by presenting their research and chairing and moderating panels. A plenary session addressed the gender inequality in higher education and within NACS. And at the business meeting, sexism within NACS was again seriously debated because it continues to be one of the "unsettled issues" of concern to Chicana feminists. A significant outcome of the conference was that its published proceedings that year were the first to be devoted to Chicanas and Mexicanas.[67]

Chicana feminists continue to raise critical issues concerning the nature of the oppression experienced by Chicanas and other women of color. They, like African American, Asian American, and Native American feminists, focus on the consequences of the intersection of race, class, and gender in the daily lives of women in American society. Chicana feminists have adopted a theoretical perspective that emphasizes the simultaneous impact of these critical variables for women of color.[68]

Chicana feminists have emphasized that Chicanas have made few gains in comparison to white men and women, as well as Chicano men, in terms of labor-force participation, income, education levels, rates of poverty, and other socioeconomic status indicators. Over the past forty years, Chicanas have made only small occupational moves from low-pay unskilled jobs to higher-pay skilled and semiprofessional employment. Studies indicate that about 66 percent remain occupationally segregated in such low-paying jobs as sales, clerical, service, and factory work. Further, Chicanas experience major social-structural constraints that limit their upward social mobility.[69] Less than 15 percent of all Chicanas have entered the occupational ranks of professionals, educational administrators, and business managers. In addition, Chicano families had approximately two-thirds of the family income of non-Hispanic families—approximately the same as ten years ago—and about 46 percent of families headed by Chicanas had incomes below the poverty level.

Chicana feminists are also concerned about Chicano schooling; the persistently low levels of educational attainment are deemed to be evidence of the role of race, class, and gender stratification in reinforcing and perpetuating inequalities. Chicanas, as well as all Latinas, have shockingly high dropout rates, with the not surprising consequence that Chicanas are scarce in the halls of academe.[70] According to one of the few studies on Chicanas in higher education, "of all the major population groups, Mexican American females are the poorest and the most underrepresented in higher education."[71]

Despite the limited numbers of Chicana academics, Chicana feminist discourse has developed within the academy as Chicana feminists have entered into specific dialogues with other feminists. Chicanas have criticized feminist scholarship for the exclusionary practices that have resulted from the discipline's limited attention to differences among women relating to race, ethnicity, class, and sexual preference.[72] Interestingly, Chicana feminists are also critical of Chicano studies and ethnic studies scholarship, which have too often lacked a systematic gender analysis.[73] As a result, Chicana feminist discourse is integrating the experiences of Chicanas within these academic disciplines. Chicana feminist scholars advocate restructuring the academy in order to integrate the "new knowledge" about women,[74] in this case, Chicanas. Indeed, Chicana feminist scholarship "came of age" in the 1990s, with publication of a variety of anthologies written by and about Chicanas.[75]

Chicana feminist scholars are revitalizing the fields of Chicano studies, ethnic studies, and women's studies. Indeed, many of them argue that their writings are creating a separate, interdisciplinary field: Chicana studies.

Sociologist Denise Segura reflects on the different approaches found among Chicana feminist scholars:

> There are several types of Chicana scholarship. One type tries to connect research on Chicanas to mainstream frameworks in the respective fields; another type tries to develop an understanding of the status and oppression of Chicanas, using feminist frameworks as points of departure; another type, connected to postmodernist frameworks, tries to get away from all mainstream thought. It begins with Chicanas as a point of departure and builds from there an understanding of their uniqueness as well as their commonalitities with other oppressed peoples in this society.[76]

In their study of Chicana feminism among Chicanas in higher education and Chicana white-collar workers, Pesquera and Segura found that Chicana feminism is not ideologically monolithic. Pesquera and Segura documented the emergence of ideologically divergent strands of Chicana feminism based on the social positioning of specific groups of Chicanas.[77] A future task for Chicana feminist scholars will be to explore further the dynamic interaction of cross-cutting memberships based on class, education, sexual orientation, and other critical variables in order to understand better the continued development of Chicana feminist discourse in the twenty-first century.

Chicana scholars are truly moving in new directions. Chicana feminist writings represent the accumulated maturity of an intellectual tradition rooted in the political activism of the 1960s. Nevertheless, Chicana feminists, like other feminist women of color, continue to join their intellectual discourse with their political activism. Indeed, each informs the other. Pesquera and Segura succinctly characterize the major underlying force of Chicana feminist discourse as a

Chicana critique of cultural, political and economic conditions in the United States. It is influenced by the tradition of advocacy scholarship, which challenges the claims of objectivity and links research to community concerns and social change. It is driven by a passion to place the Chicana, as speaking subject, at the center of intellectual discourse.[78]

The voices of Chicana feminists will continue to resonate as the next century approaches. Their struggles and triumphs will continue to shape the ideological direction of American feminism and future generations of feminists.

Notes

1. Mario Barrera, "The Study of Politics and the Chicano," *Aztlan* 5 (1976): 9–26; Carlos Munoz, Jr., "The Politics of Protest and Liberation: A Case Study of Repression and Cooptation," *Aztlan* 5 (1974): 119–141; Armando Navarro, "The Evolution of Chicano Politics," *Aztlan* 5 (1974): 57–84.

2. John Dunne, *Delano: The Story of the California Grape Strike.* (New York: Straus, 1967); Sam Kushner, *Long Road to Delano* (New York: International, 1975); Eugene Nelson, *Huelga: The First 100 Days* (Delano, CA: Farm Workers Press, 1966).

3. Peter Nabokov, *Tijerina and the Courthouse Raid* (Albuquerque: University of New Mexico Press, 1969).

4. Tony Castro, *Chicano Power* (New York: Saturday Review Press, 1974): Matt Meier and Feliciano Rivera, *The Chicanos* (New York: Hill & Wang, 1972).

5. F. Chris Garcia and Rudolpho O. de la Garza, *The Chicano Political Experience* (North Scituate, MA: Duxbury, 1977).

6. John Shockley, *Chicano Revolt in a Texas Town* (South Bend: University of Notre Dame Press, 1974).

7. Jo Freeman, "On the Origins of Social Movements," in *Social Movements of the Sixties and Seventies,* ed. Jo Freeman (New York: Longman, 1983); Frances Fox Piven and Richard A. Cloward, *Poor People's Movements: Why They Succeed, How They Fail* (New York: Vintage, 1979).

8. Anna Macias, *Against All Odds* (Westport, CT: Greenwood Press, 1982).

9. Angela Davis, "Reflections on Black Women's Role in the Community of Slaves," *Black Scholar* 3 (1971) 3–13; Angela Davis, *Women, Race and Class* (New York: Random House, 1983); Bonnie Thornton Dill, "Race, Class, and Gender: Prospects for an All-Inclusive Sisterhood," *Feminist Studies* 9 (1983): 131–50; bell hooks, *Ain't I a Woman? Black Women and Feminism* (Boston: South End Press, 1981); bell hooks, *Feminist Theory: From Margin to Center* (Boston:

South End Press, 1984); Gloria Joseph and Jill Lewis, *Common Differences: Conflicts in Black and White Feminist Perspectives* (Garden City, NY: Doubleday, 1981); Frances White, "Listening to the Voices of Black Feminism, *Radical America* 18 (1984): 7–25.

10. Sheila Rowbotham, *Women, Resistance and Revolution: A History of Women and Revolution in the Modern World* (New York: Vintage, 1974).

11. Maxine Baca Zinn, "Political Familism: Toward Sex Role Equality in Chicano Families," *Aztlan* 6 (1977): 13–27.

12. Ibid.

13. Rowbotham, *Women, Resistance and Revolution*, p. 206.

14. Lucie Cheng, "Asian American Women and Feminism," *Sojourner* 10 (1984): 11–12; Esther Ngan-Ling Chow, "The Development of Feminist Consciousness Among Asian American Women," *Gender and Society* 1 (1987): 284–299; hooks, *Feminist Theory*.

15. hooks, *Feminist Theory*.

16. Chow, "The Development of Feminist Consciousness."

17. Dill, "Race, Class, and Gender"; Davis, "Reflections on Black Women's Role."

18. hooks, *Feminist Theory*

19. Carlos Munoz, Jr. *Youth, Identity, Power: The Chicano Movement* (New York: Verso, 1989), p. 77.

20. Ibid., p. 90.

21. Anna Nieto Gomez, "Chicanas Identify," *Hijas de Cuahtemoc*, April 1971, p. 9.

21. Francisca Flores, "El Mundo Femenil Mexicana," *Regeneracion* 1, no. 10 (1971): 1.

22. Bernice Rincon, "La Chicana: Her Role in the Past and Her Search for a New Role in the Future," *Regeneracion* 1, no 10 (1971): 15–17.

23. Nieto Gomez, "Chicanas Identify," p. 10.

24. Ibid., p. 4

25. Tomas Almaguer, "Historical Notes on Chicano Oppression," *Aztlan* 5 (1974): 27–56; Mario Barrera, *Race and Class in the Southwest* (Notre Dame: University of Notre Dame Press, 1979).

26. Adaljiza Sosa Riddell, "Chicanas en el Movimiento," *Aztlan* 5 (1974): 159.

27. Nieto Gomez, "Chicanas Identify," p. 4.

28. Henri Chavez, "The Chicanas," *Regeneracion* 1 (1971): 14; Marta Cotera, *The Chicana Feminist* (Austin, TX: Austin Information Systems Development, 1977); Marta Cotera, "Feminism: the Chicana and Anglo Versions: An Historical Analysis," in *Twice a Minority: Mexican American Women*, ed. Margarita Melville (St. Louis, MO: C. V. Mosby, 1980), pp. 217–234; Adelaida Del Castillo, "La Vision Chicana," *La Gente* 8 (1974). p. 8, Evelina Marquez and Margarita Ramirez,

"Women's Task Is to Gain Liberation," in *Essays on La Mujer*, ed. Rosaura Sanchez and Rosa Martinez Cruz (Los Angeles: UCLA Chicano Studies Center, 1977), pp. 188–194; Riddell, "Chicanas en el Movimiento"; Maxine Baca Zinn, "Chicanas: Power and Control in the Domestic Sphere," *De Colores* 2 no. 3, (1975): 19–31.

29. Mirta Vidal, "New Voice of La Raza: Chicanas Speak Out," *International Socialist Review* 32 (1971): 8.

30. Riddell, "Chicanas en el Movimiento," p. 159.

31. Francisca Flores, "Conference of Mexican Women: Un Remolino," *Regeneracion*, no. 1 (1971) 4.

32. Frances Beale, "Slave of a Slave No More: Black Women in Struggle," *Black Scholar* 6 (1975): 2–10; Toni Cade, *The Black Woman* (New York: Signet, 1970); Davis, "Reflections on Black Women's Role"; Joseph and Lewis, *Common Differences*.

33. Chow, "The Development of Feminist Consciousness."

34. Cotero, *The Chicana Feminist*. p. 9.

35. Anna Gomez Nieto, "La Feminista," *Encuentro Remenil* 1 (1973): 34–47, 1t p. 35.

36. Ibid.

37. Ibid.

38. Ibid.

39. Cherrie Moraga, "La Guera," in *This Bridge Called My Back: Writings by Radical Women of Color*, ed. Cherrie Moraga and Gloria Anzaldua (Watertown, MA: Persephone, 1981), p. 28.

40. Ibid.

41. *Common Differences*. White, "Listening to the Voices of Black Feminism."

42. Moraga and Anzaldua, *This Bridge Called My Back*.

43. Moraga, "La Guera."

44. Anna Gomez Nieto, "Sexism in the Movement," *La Gente* 6, no. 4 (1976): 10.

45. Cotera 1977, p. 30.

46. Flores, "Conference of Mexican Women," p. 1

47. Enriqueta Longeaux y Vasquez, "The Woman of La Raza." *El Grito del Norte* (November 1969): 11. Also, Enriqueta Longeaux y Vasquez, "La Chicana: Let's Build a New Life," *El Grito del Norte* 2 (November 1969): 11.

48. Evey Chapa, "Report from the National Women's Political Caucus," *Magazin* 11 (1973): 37–39; Chavez, "The Chicanas"; Del Castillo, "La Vision Chicana"; Cotera, *The Chicana Feminist*; Dorinda Moreno, "The Image of the Chicana and the La Raza Woman," *Caracol* 2 (1979): 14–15.

49. Nieto, "La Feminista," p. 31.

50. Chow, "The Development of Feminist Consciousness," p. 288; hooks, *Ain't I a Woman*; White, "Listening to the Voices of Black Feminism."

51. Yolanda Orozco, "La Chicana and "Women's Liberation,' " *Voz Fronteriza* 6 (January 5, 1976): 12.

52. Rincon, "La Chicana."

53. Enriqueta Longeaux y Vasquez, "Soy Chicana Primero." *El Grito Del Norte* 4 (April 26, 1971) p. 11.

54. Carmen Hernandez, "Carmen Speaks Out," *Papel Chicano*, June 12, 1971, p. 9.

55. Del Castillo, "La Vision Chicana." p. 8.

56. Chapa, "Report from the National Women's Political Caucus"; Cotera, *The Chicana Feminist*; Nieto Gomez, "La Feminista"; Longeaux y Vasquez, "Soy Chicana Primera."

57. Longeaux y Vasquez, "Soy Chicana Primera."

58. Guadalupe Valdes Fallis, "The Liberated Chicana—A Struggle Against Tradition," *Women: A Journal of Liberation* 3 (1974): 20; Gomez.

59. Cotera, *The Chicana Feminist*.

60. Chapa, "Report from the National Women's Political Caucus"; Cotera, *The Chicana Feminist*; Longeaux y Vasquez, "Soy Chicana Primero"; Martinez, "The Chicana"; Nieto, "The Chicana and the Women's Rights Movement"; Orozco, "La Chicana and `Women's Liberation.' :

61. Cotera, *The Chicana Feminist*.

62. Cotera, "Feminism," p. 227.

63. Cotera, *The Chicana Feminist*; Marquez and Ramirez, "Women's Task Is to Gain Liberation."

64. Teresa Cordova et al., *Chicana Voices: Intersection of Class, Race and Gender* (Austin: Center for Mexican American Studies, 1986); Zinn, "Political Familism."

65. Cotera, *The Chicana Feminist*; Sylvia Gonzalez, "Toward a Feminist Pedagogy for Chicana Self-Actualization." *Frontiers* 5 (1980): 48–51; Consuelo Nieto, "Consuelo Nieto on the Women's Movement," *Interracial Books for Children Bulletin* 5, no. 4 (1975).

66. Consuelo Nieto, "The Chicana and the Women's Rights Movement," *La Luz*, September 3, 1974, p. 4.

67. Cordova et al., *Chicana Voices*.

68. Moraga and Anzaldua, *This Bridge Called My Back*; Moraga, "La Guera"; hooks, *Feminist Theory*; Alma Garcia, "Studying Chicanas" in *Chicana Voices* ed. Teresa Cordova et al. (Austin, Texas; Center for Mexican American Studies, 1986); Gloria Anzaldua, *Borderlands/La Frontera: The New Mestiza* (San Francisco: Aunt Lute Press, 1987); Gloria Anzaldua, *Making Face, Making Soul—Haciendo Caras: Creative and Critical Perspectives by Feminists of Color* (San Francisco: Aunt Lute Press, 1990).

69. Denise Segura, "Chicana and Mexican Immigrant Women at Work: The Impact of Class, Race, and Gender on Occupational Mobility," *Gender and Soci-*

ety 3 (1989): 37–52; Mary Romero, *Maid in the U.S.A.* (New York: Routledge, 1992).

70. Christine Marie Sierra, "The University Setting Reinforces Inequality," in Cordova et al., *Chicana Voices*, pp. 5–7; Orozco, "La Chicana and 'Women's Liberation'"; Denise Segura, "Chicanas and Triple Oppression in the Labor Force," in Cordova et al., *Chicana Voices*, pp. 47–65; Denise Segura, "Slipping Through the Cracks: Dilemmas in Chicana Education," in *Building with Our Hands*, ed. Adeala de la Torre and Beatrice Pesquera (Berkeley: University of California Press, 1993).

71. Maria Chacon, *Chicanas in Post-Secondary Education* (Stanford: Stanford University Press, 1982).

72. Maxine Baca Zinn, Lynn Weber Cannon, Elizabeth Higginbotham, and Bonnie Thornton Dill, "The Cost of Exclusionary Practices in Women's Studies," *Signs* 11 (1986): 290–302.

73. Mujeres en Marcha, *Chicanas in the 80s: Unsettled Issues* (Berkeley: Chicano Studies Publication Unit, 1983); Orozco, "La Chicana and 'Women's Liberation' "; Norma Alarcon, "The Theoretical Subject(s) of This Bridge Called My Back and Anglo American Feminism," in *Criticism in the Borderlands: Studies in Chicano Literature, Culture and Ideology*, ed. Hector Calderon and Jose David Saldivar (Durham: Duke University Press, 1991); Alma Garcia, "Chicano Studies and 'La Chicana' Courses: Curriculum Options and Reforms," in *Community Empowerment and Chicano Scholarship: Selected Proceedings of National Association of Chicano Studies, 1992*.

74. Joan Wallach Scott, *Gender and Politics in History* (New York: Columbia University Press, 1988).

75. Adeala de la Torre and Beatrice Pesquera, eds., *Building with Our Hands* (Berkeley: University of California Press, 1993); Tey Diana Rebolledo and Eliana S. Rivero, *Infinite Divisions: An Anthology of Chicana Literature* (Tucson: University of Arizona Press, 1993); Norma Alarcon et al., *Chicana Critical Issues* (Berkeley: Third World Press, 1993).

76. Segura, quoted in *Building With Our Hands* p. 6.

77. Beatriz M. Pesquera and Denise M. Segura, "There Is No Going Back: Chicanas and Feminism," in *Chicana Critical Issues*, ed. Norma Alarcon (Berkeley: Third Woman Press, 1993), pp. 95–115.

78. Ibid., p. 1.

Biographies

Jill Benderly is currently co-director of the STAR Project—Strategies, Training and Advocacy for Reconciliation, a project to provide technical and financial assistance to women's NGOs in the Yugoslav successor states—and lives in Croatia. She is coeditor of *Independent Slovenia: Origins, Movements, Prospects* (St. Martin's Press, 1994.)

Alice Yun Chai, who was born in Korea, is a retired women's studies professor at the University of Hawai'i. She is doing research on Asian immigrants, Asian American women, and Korean women, and advocacy research and advocacy work on "comfort women"/sex slaves drafted by Japan during World War II.

Norma Stoltz Chinchilla received her Ph.D. in sociology and Latin American studies from the University of Wisconsin, Madison, and is currently a women's studies and sociology professor at California State University, Long Beach. She has published articles on women and social movements in Latin America, Marxism and feminism, and political and economic change in Central America.

Alma M. Garcia is Director of the Ethnic Studies Program and a professor of sociology and ethnic studies at Santa Clara University. She has written elsewhere on Chicanas and has been the national president of the National Association for Chicano Studies and Mujeres Activas en Letras y Cambio Social.

Sherna Berger Gluck directs the oral history program and teaches women's studies at California State University, Long Beach. A longtime feminist activist scholar, her most recent book is *An American Feminist in Palestine: The Intifada Years*, (Temple University Press, 1994).

Gisela Kaplan is professor in the Centre for Research in Aboriginal and Multi-cultural Studies, the University of New England, Armidale, Australia. She is the author of *Contemporary Western European Feminism* (New York University Press, 1992), coeditor of *Hannah Arendt, Thinking, Judging, Freedom*, (Allen & Unwin 1989), and *The Meagre Harvest: The Australian Women's Movement 1950–1990* (Allen and Unwin, 1996).

Lynn Kwiatkowski is an assistant professor of anthropology at the University of South Alabama. She has lived and worked in the Philippines since 1984, where she conducted reseach on malnutrition and gender. She got her Ph.D. in anthropology from the University of California, Berkeley.

Patrice LeClerc is a sociology professor at Concordia University in Montreal. She writes about comparative Canada/U.S. social movements, especially women's movements, and comparative health-care policies.

Zengie A. Mangaliso is a sociology professor at Westfield State College, Massachusetts. She is the author of the *South African Mosaic: A Sociological Analysis of Post-Apartheid Conflict* (American University Press, 1994). Zengie resides in Amherst with her husband, Mzamo, and two daughters, Bande and Unati.

Valentine M. Moghadam is director of Women's Studies at Illinois State University and formerly senior researcher at WIDER Institute, Helsinki, Finland, of the United Nations University. She is author of *Modernizing Women* (Lynne Rienner 1993), and editor of *Gender and National Identity* (Zed Books, 1994).

Carmel Roulston is a professor in the School of History, Philosophy and Politics, the University of Ulster, Northern Ireland. She has written articles on the women's movements in Ireland and in Russia.

Haunani-Kay Trask is director and professor in the Center for Hawaiian Studies, University of Hawai'i. She is the author of *Eros and Power: The Promise of Feminist Theory* (University of Pennsylvania Press, 1986), and *From a Native Daughter: Colonialism and Sovereignty in Hawai'i* (Common Courage Press, 1993).

Lois A. West is a professor of sociology and women's studies at Florida International University. She has her Ph.D. in sociology from the University of California, Berkeley, and is the author of *Militant Labor in the Philippines* (Temple University Press, 1996). She resides in Miami with her husband, Jack, and children.

Index